Marriage, domestic life and social change

Marriage, Domestic Life and Social Change is an important tribute to the life and work of Jacqueline Burgoyne, a major figure in family studies in Britain, who died in 1988 aged 43. The book includes an appreciation of her life by the editor and one of her previously unpublished papers on couple relationships.

The other contributions are from friends and colleagues of Jacqueline Burgoyne, all well-known in the field of family studies. Drawing on a wide range of disciplines, including sociology, history, psychology, social work and psychotherapy, they provide a comprehensive review of changes in domestic life in Britain since the Second World War. The subjects explored range from the major demographic trends relating to marriage and the family over the last forty years, through the key themes in family research in the 1980s, to investigations of the inner world of marriage, from psycho-dynamic and sociological perspectives.

An up-to-date and wide-ranging guide to the sociology of the family, *Marriage, Domestic Life and Social Change* will be of interest to specialists and will be invaluable to students of the family, gender and social change.

David Clark is Principal Lecturer in the School of Health and Community Studies, Sheffield City Polytechnic and Senior Research Fellow, Trent Region Palliative and Continuing Care Centre. He was a close friend and colleague of Jacqueline Burgoyne, and was co-author with her of a major study of stepfamilies in Britain, *Making a Go of It* (1984).

KT-377-853

Marriage, domestic life and social change

Writings for Jacqueline Burgoyne (1944–88)

Edited by David Clark

London and New York

First published 1991
by Routledge
11 New Fetter Lane, London EC4P 4EE

Simultaneously published in the USA and Canada
by Routledge
a division of Routledge, Chapman and Hall, Inc.
29 West 35th Street, New York, NY 10001

Laserset by LaserScript Limited, Mitcham, Surrey
Printed and bound in Great Britain by
Biddles Ltd, Guildford and King's Lynn

British Library Cataloguing in Publication Data
Marriage, domestic life and social change: writings for
    Jacqueline Burgoyne 1944–88.
    1. Marriage, history
    I. Clark, David *1953–* II. Burgoyne, Jacqueline *1944–88*
    306.8109

Library of Congress Cataloging in Publication Data
Marriage, domestic life, and social change: writings for
    Jacqueline Burgoyne, 1944–88/edited by David Clark.
    p. cm.
    Includes bibliographical references and index.
    1. Family – Great Britain. 2. Marriage – Great Britain. 3. Great
    Britain – Social conditions – 1945–   4. Burgoyne, Jacqueline L.
    (Jacqueline Lesley), 1944–88   . I. Burgoyne, Jacqueline L.
    (Jacqueline Lesley), 1944–88   . II. Clark, David, 1953–
    HQ614.M37 1991
    306.8'0941 – dc20   90-8824
                                                           CIP

ISBN 0-415-03246-6
      0-415-03247-4 (pbk)

Contents

List of figures and tables   vii
Contributors   ix
Foreword: a researcher's life   xi
David Clark

Part I   Biography and history

Introduction   3

1 Social reconstruction and the emergence of companionate
   marriage, 1945–59   7
   Janet Finch and Penny Summerfield

2 Sex and marriage in the 1960s and 1970s   33
   Martin P.M. Richards and B. Jane Elliott

3 Marriage in the 1980s: a new sense of realism?   55
   Janet Finch and David Morgan

Part II   Demographic trends

Introduction   83

4 Demographic trends in domestic life, 1945–87   85
   B. Jane Elliott

Part III   Private troubles, public issues

Introduction   111

5 Ideologies of marriage and family life   114
   David Morgan

 6 Constituting the marital world: a qualitative perspective   139
   David Clark

 7 Making, breaking and remaking marriage   167
   Christopher Clulow

 8 Interventions in families   188
   Janet Walker

 9 Pretended family relationships   214
   Jeffrey Weeks

10 Afterword: does the ring make any difference? Couples and the
   private face of a public relationship in post-war Britain   235
   Jacqueline Burgoyne

   Publications by Jacqueline Burgoyne   257

   Name index   259

   Subject index   264

Figures and tables

Figures

4.1 General first-marriage rates (per 1,000 population aged 16 and over), England and Wales, 1941–87   86

4.2a Male, nubile first-marriage rates (per 1,000 population)   87

4.2b Female, nubile first-marriage rates (per 1,000 population)   88

4.3 Petitions filed each year (000s) and divorce rates per 1,000 married population, England and Wales, 1941–87   91

4.4 Remarriage and divorce rates, England and Wales, 1941–87   95

4.5 Age-specific fertility rates (total births per 1,000 women in each age group), England and Wales, 1941–87   97

4.6 Illegitimate births and the illegitimacy ratio in England and Wales, 1941–87   100

4.7 Outcome of conceptions outside marriage for women of all ages, England and Wales   101

Tables

4.1 Social class and socioeconomic differentials in divorce   94

4.2 Marriage and remarriage, a typology, England and Wales, 1987 and (1950)   94

4.3 Fertility rates by cohort and age group   98

4.4 Women's economic activity, 1951–81   102

4.5 Women's economic activity by age of youngest child   102

4.6 The distribution of household types in 1961 and 1987   104

Contributors

David Clark is Principal Lecturer in the School of Health and Community Studies, Sheffield City Polytechnic and Senior Research Fellow at the Trent Region Palliative and Continuing Care Centre. His research interests include sociological aspects of family life, health and illness and terminal care.

Christopher Clulow is Chair of the Tavistock Institute of Marital Studies, where he has worked since 1974 as a psychoanalytic marital therapist, teacher and researcher. He is also Chair of the Commission on Marriage and Interpersonal Relations of the International Union of Family Organisations and serves on the editorial advisory boards of the *Journal of Sexual and Marital Therapy* and the *Journal of Social Work Practice*.

B. Jane Elliott graduated from King's College, Cambridge, in 1987 with a degree in Mathematics and Social Psychology. She is currently a member of the Child Care and Development Group, University of Cambridge. Her research is on the consequences of divorce for adults and children and involves secondary multi-variate analysis of the Health and Lifestyle Survey and the National Child Development Survey.

Janet Finch is Professor of Social Relations, Lancaster University. Her main research interests are in the sociology of the family and family policy, with a particular focus on gender. She has recently been involved in major ESRC-funded research projects on kin relationships.

David Morgan is Senior Lecturer in the Department of Sociology, Manchester University. His main interest is the study of the family and gender. He has been an active member of the British Sociological Association and is currently sharing with Liz Stanley the editorship of the association's journal, *Sociology*.

Martin P.M. Richards is Reader in Human Development, University of Cambridge. He heads the Child Care and Development Group which carries out research on parents, children and family life. After a first degree in zoology he moved to developmental psychology by way of research on animal behaviour.

Penny Summerfield is Senior Lecturer in the Social History of Education and Director of the Centre for Women's Studies, Lancaster University. Her current work includes a book on gender, class and schooling 1850–1950 and an ESRC-funded project on gender, training and employment, 1939–50.

Janet Walker is Director of the Family and Community Dispute Research Centre and Senior Lecturer in Social Policy, University of Newcastle-upon-Tyne. She is a practising mediator and family therapist, a training consultant and member of journal editorial boards in Britain and the USA. In 1985 she was Co-director of the Conciliation Project Unit and is now undertaking follow-up research on various aspects of divorce and mediation as well as new work on domestic violence.

Jeffrey Weeks is the author of numerous articles and several books on the history and social organisation of sexuality. He has held academic posts at the London School of Economics and at the Universities of Essex, Kent and Southampton, and has worked in academic administration in London. During 1989–90 he was Simon Senior Fellow at the University of Manchester, and is currently Professor of Social Relations and head of research and consultancy in the Department of Economics and Social Science, Bristol Polytechnic.

Foreword
A researcher's life

David Clark

Jacqueline Burgoyne died of ovarian cancer at the beginning of 1988; she was 43 years old. For the past year Jackie (as everyone knew her) had been living with her diagnosis in a manner which tells us a great deal about her life and personality. During months of chemotherapy she had continued with her regular programme of exercise and heightened her commitment to healthy eating. She appeared fit and well and was adopting a positive and highly characteristic attitude to overcoming cancer. In particular she had been writing about her illness, both in her regular monthly column in *The Times Higher Educational Supplement*, and more privately in the chapters of a never-to-be finished book, exploring her life and her illness. Jackie was a sociologist of extraordinary commitment and saw in most of her experiences some opportunity to link the everyday world of friends, family and relationships with the concerns of the social researcher and teacher. For that reason this book, written in her honour, straddles a boundary between the 'private' and the 'public' in which she had become deeply absorbed.

I first met Jackie in 1977 when I was interviewed for a research post to work with her on a study of stepfamilies. The project was one which began with a series of ill-defined hunches which were slowly formulated into a clear set of research questions. This was the way Jackie loved to work. She was the first person I ever met who practised what C. Wright Mills preached about 'intellectual craftsmanship' (though she wouldn't have liked the gendered terminology). Jackie kept a journal in which she noted down random thoughts, ideas to be followed up and insights from her reading; she taught me to do the same and I have subsequently encouraged others in the practice. Her preference was for traditional hard-backed, lined writing books but in the early days economy dictated the use of out-of-date desk diaries, bought cheaply and in bulk at stationers' sales. She wrote copiously and these volumes provide a fascinating map of her intellectual journeyings.

The late 1970s was a crucial period in Jackie's career. Born in Worcester on 10 September 1944 and educated in Bristol, she became an undergraduate in Sheffield in 1963, taking a degree in sociology. She then went to Bath to qualify as a teacher, before returning to the city which was to become her permanent home. She worked at first with Peter Mann on a study of books and reading and then briefly as a schoolteacher. In 1971 she became a lecturer at the Sheffield City College of Education, which a few years later became a part of Sheffield City Polytechnic. It was in the new environment of the Polytechnic that her research plans began to take shape, but her interests were not without other biographical determinants. Writing in the summer of 1987, she described this clearly in her unfinished manuscript:

> Up until about five years ago I would have vehemently denied the possibility of there being any connection between my own experience of family life and my longstanding intellectual and research interest in the subject. I trained as a social scientist in an era when they really did try to make us into scientists of the white-coated variety. We were expected to view the occupants of the social world we studied with complete detachment and it would have been quite improper to admit to choosing to investigate an issue or problem because you had a particular interest in it. Ten years ago when a piece of research which I had been doing on stepfamilies was widely discussed in the popular press, several journalists included the information that I had been a stepchild myself. I did not think then, nor do I now, that this had any particular bearing on the decisions which led up to doing this piece of work but I recognise now that my intense and abiding curiosity about the way people inhabit their home and domestic lives has grown, albeit unconsciously, out of my search for a family of my own childhood and adolescence. Whether, equally unconsciously, I may have believed that the investigation of other people's family lives would give me the key I needed to come to terms with complicated feelings I have about my own relatives, I am not sure.

The research on stepfamilies was surrounded by many of the hallmarks and difficulties of sociological studies of marriage and domestic life. There were snags in getting access to a sample; dilemmas and sensitivities surrounding the subject matter; questions of ethics and confidentiality; problems in making sense of the data and in writing it up for a wider audience. But at the centre of things, Jackie was consumed by a delight in getting on with the job in hand; the 'sociological imagination' was working its spell and inspired by it we set about producing a carefully documented study, which still remains the only major sociological work on stepfamilies in Britain.

Our principal focus was on the stepfamilies which are created when divorced parents marry again. Most of the literature on stepfamilies at that time was psychiatric and psychological, mainly written by clinicians who had worked with stepfamilies in a therapeutic context. Our concern was to conduct a study of families which had not, at least by definition of the method of their selection for the study, had encounters with the social work and psychotherapeutic agencies. Adopting the popular sociological mantle of the day, we saw our task as one of letting the husbands and wives in our study 'tell their story', prompted only by low-key, open-ended questioning, which would allow *them* to set the agenda for our research interviews, within the broad context of the life-history method we adopted. The results of this approach were lengthy transcriptions of interviews in which we found two common threads.

First, these personal accounts of intimate life proved to be heavily coloured by encounters with the public world 'outside'. So that, for example, we saw how apparently 'private' experiences of marriage break-up, divorce and remarriage carried a significant public script, in the form of encounters with solicitors, the courts, welfare and probation officers, with teachers and employers, with doctors and with social workers. This meant that accounts of the making and breaking of relationships intermingled with issues about money, jobs, housing and health. Our understanding of relationships and dynamics *within* step-families therefore could only be developed by taking into consideration a wide range of *external* factors. Second, we saw how the expectations and experiences surrounding second marriages are shaped and moulded to a considerable degree by legacies of the past, both material and emotional. This would mean that couples who saw remarriage as a 'fresh start', an opportunity to 'put the past behind' were often frustrated, as intrusions from earlier marriage continued to affect their day-to-day lives. This could mean problems over issues to do with custody of children, or difficulties arising out of the non-custodial parents' access visits, or arguments about maintenance payments. But it could also show up in the difficulties of beginning a new marriage in the 'former' matrimonial home, in continuing ambivalent feelings about a previous partner or the reason for the divorce, in anxieties about having made a 'better' choice the second time around. The Sheffield study of remarriage therefore pointed up a number of theoretical and methodological issues central to an improved sociological understanding of family and domestic life in British society. It was these issues which constituted the main agenda for Jackie's subsequent intellectual interests and which constantly brought her back to a number of key themes: public/private, structure/process, outer/inner, biography/history. These themes are variously touched on and explored in the chapters of this book.

Others quickly became interested in this work and were drawn by Jackie's engaging personality, her wit, irreverence and remarkable ability to translate the preoccupations of sociology into questions of wider relevance. Although she could tire of the media's attentions (I remember a hot summer's afternoon when she accused an enquiring local journalist of 'manufacturing the news' about stepmothers for the sake of something to write), Jackie was also drawn to broadcasting. Over the next few years she made several appearances on television, but in particular was fond of radio, going on to act as consultant to a major BBC Radio Four series on divorce and children and to make regular contributions to other programmes. At the same time, those concerned with family and domestic life at a professional level, particularly as doctors, social workers and counsellors, also wanted to hear about Jackie's ideas. She became much in demand to speak at professional conferences and seminars, where she was as at home debunking bishops as listening attentively to a questioner's own thinly disguised personal concerns expressed through some hypothetical instance of marriage break-up or divorce. She was an enemy of pomposity of any kind and I well remember her causing amused uproar at the Eugenics Society when following a speaker who had referred continuously and with no sense of irony to Kalahari 'bushmen-women', Jackie began her talk by saying she hoped no 'bushmen-persons' had been listening! She was a friend to a number of voluntary organisations and became a member of the National Marriage Guidance Council's Research Advisory Board in the early 1980s, a position from which she was able to promote an interest in practitioner research and to offer critical support through individual contacts and her participation in the organisation's research seminars. More locally, within Sheffield, she was active in the formation of a family conciliation service, in which she worked both as Chair and as conciliator, equally willing to fund-raise or deal with the face-to-face realities of a couple in the process of ending their marriage.

All of this activity was underpinned by an assiduous attention to the development of a sociological understanding of marriage and domestic life. Although she struggled with a number of contradictory feelings towards her feminism, it developed with her methodological and theoretical understanding to provide a rigorous framework for making sense of what goes on within marriages and families. She had an enormous commitment to sociology as a profession and was an active member of the British Sociological Association. In particular she had great energy for supporting and encouraging the work of others, especially in helping colleagues at the early stages of a research idea. She could push people forward, often through conveying an unwavering sense that what they wanted to do was both important and possible. There are many who benefited from Jackie's support in this way and who continue to miss it.

Her later work in particular was concerned with issues of gender and social change within families across the life course. She found intellectual inspiration from a variety of sources: from C. Wright Mills and Peter Berger; from Jessie Bernard and Ann Oakley; and also the classic British community studies of the 1950s. Later she became greatly interested in counselling and psychotherapy, recognising the importance of psychodynamic as well as sociological explanations of marital and family relationships. Neither was this idle dabbling in other disciplines; she was among the first to begin to raise questions about the interrelationships between the research and therapeutic enterprises and is sadly missed from the interesting debates which are now beginning to develop on this topic. It was characteristic of Jackie's approach to her work and of her sheer determination to carry on with it that within the final few months of her life she should be invited onto both the editorial board of the journal *Sociology* and the Economic and Social Research Council's Human Development Group. Her last ever speaking engagement, in October 1987, was at the AGM of the National Marriage Guidance Council, an occasion which many present remember as one of her finest talks, though few were aware that she was too ill to stand to deliver it.

Following the completion of the Sheffield study in the early 1980s, Jackie went into a period of prodigious activity. Whilst she and I collaborated on a public-attitude survey about family life, she also wrote a self-help book for divorcing parents, drawing on her own research materials; the book was widely praised and has subsequently been published in Spanish. Later she worked with Martin Richards and Sir Roger Ormrod on a book about divorce which brought together the perspectives of sociology, psychology and the law. She also became interested in the relationship between the family and economic life. As mass recession in the steel industry wreaked its toll in Sheffield, she supervised Nick Forster's thesis on unemployment and family life. She also obtained funding from the ESRC for a study of cohabitation, carried out with Paul Wild; a previously unpublished paper from the cohabitation study appears in this collection. Later she conducted research with Polytechnic colleagues Peter Ashworth and John Stoddart on management education. More and more she became engaged by the process of writing; when she finally abandoned her beloved Parker 51 fountain pen in favour of a word processor, the output soared. She successfully encouraged *New Society* to run a series on contemporary family and became one of the founding editors of Polity Press's *Family Life* series. At the time of her death she was negotiating a secondment to BP to work on the issue of women managers in the oil industry and was also working on a project concerned with the needs of children with cancer and their parents.

All of this work illuminated and inspired her teaching. Although she was the kind of lecturer who would always carefully prepare a set of notes for a class, never trusting her own ability to order the material from memory, in practice she could draw on a fabulous array of anecdotes and illustrations, many of them involving herself, and to my eternal bemusement, most of them apparently true. Students liked her teaching and also benefited from her care; a significant number of Jackie's nights or weekends would be broken by her willingness to help, counsel or advise in situations of personal difficulty. Research and teaching, the public and the private, were constantly intertwined in Jackie's view of things and she would on occasion take the consequences of this at some cost to herself.

I am not going to attempt here critically to assess the importance of Jackie Burgoyne's work, though I hope that someone more distant from it may in due course take on such a task. A full list of her publications appears at the back of this book and it will serve as a guide to further reading. The last chapter in the book, an afterword, is a piece which Jackie had drafted in the mid-1980s, though it was never published. To newcomers, it serves as an excellent introduction to her style and also as a warm reminder of it for those of us more familiar with her writings. Here she is on her favourite territory, skilfully reviewing a wide range of themes relating to social changes in marriage and partnership in Britain since the Second World War, and then going on to present some new data from her cohabitation study in which broader historical change is articulated at an individual, human level. This for me is indicative of her major achievements: history and biography, the public and the private, linked and juxtaposed in a thoroughly sociological manner.

The idea for this collection has an interesting history. Shortly after Jackie's death a number of friends and colleagues suggested some lasting form of memorial. The Jacqueline Burgoyne memorial collection was established in the library at Sheffield City Polytechnic and the Polytechnic also went on to initiate a series of annual memorial lectures. A *festschrift* also seemed a possibility, with a number of people eager to contribute; but how to structure such a book? Whilst mulling over this question I was asked to take on a speaking engagement that Jackie was to have undertaken in the Summer of 1988. It was the fortieth anniversary celebrations of the Tavistock Institute of Marital Studies, whose organisers suggested the topic of *marriage and social change*. I prepared for the lecture by reviewing a range of material on marriage in Britain in the period since the end of the Second World War and was struck by the fact that the period was almost exactly co-terminous with Jackie's life. The period seemed to be character-ised by certain more-or-less distinct phases: post-war reconstruction up to the end of the 1950s; followed by a great deal of apparent, if not real change in marriage and family life during the 1960s and 1970s; capped in the 1980s by a decade in which social realism became the dominant theme. Cutting across all of this were important issues affecting the whole period: demo-graphic changes, particularly in relation to marriage, cohabitation, divorce and remarriage; shifting ideological debates about gender, sexuality and sexual divisions; advances in psychological and psychodynamic theories and the development of a wide range of statutory and non-statutory inter-ventions in family life; and all this matched by new ways in which social researchers were framing and carrying out research into marriage and domestic life. It soon became apparent that the structure for the lecture was also the outline for a book in three parts, which might appeal not only to specialists, but also to student readers.

I want therefore to express my thanks here to Chris Rojek and others at Routledge for encouraging me to go ahead with this project. In particular, though, I am indebted to all the contributors who, as friends and colleagues of Jackie, have produced such an eloquent tribute to her life and work; the range of disciplines they represent reflects Jackie's wide-ranging interests – sociology and history, psychology and psychotherapy, social policy and social work. The proceeds of the book will be donated to the Gynaecology Cancer Research Fund, which is supporting a programme of enquiry at the London Hospital, concerned with the development of screening procedures for the early detection of ovarian cancer. From the earliest stages, working on the idea of the book has mirrored some of the well-known processes of grief; there has been numbness, anger, sadness and now with time, some sense of accommodation. For me it has been both a very personal and a very public form of tribute. I feel sure that it is Jackie's sort of book and for that reason it is appropriate and fitting that she has the last word in it.

Part I

Biography and history

Introduction

In this first part of the book the contributors take as their theme some of the changing aspects of marriage and domestic life in Britain since the end of the Second World War. Their intention, however, is not to produce a detailed family history of the period. The authors have been selective and in so doing have produced an original set of arguments which largely revolve around the predominant characteristics of marriage in the post-war period. At the centre of these chapters are the debates about companionate marriage, notions of marriage as partnership and the extent to which there is any evidence over time of greater equality between men and women in marriage. These are explored on a number of dimensions, ranging from the prescriptions of social policy to the more private territories of sexual and intimate relationships. In all cases, however, the authors place a strong emphasis on understanding both the public and the private dimensions of marriage and domestic life and in particular the interactions between them.

Janet Finch and Penny Summerfield offer a critical exploration of the relationship between ideas about companionate marriage and the processes of post-war social and economic reconstruction, showing how a combination of factors served to place new pressures on women. They describe the interconnections between anxieties about the falling birth rate and the call for mothers to renounce full-time paid employment and remain inside the home as carers of children, making this their unique contribution to the marital 'team'. At the same time these 'thoroughly maternal wives' were also expected to contribute to an enthusiastic and fulfilling sexual life within marriage. Sociologists of the period add some detail to this picture, though studies of marriage in the 1950s generally reveal a rather optimistic and cosy picture of domestic harmony. Nevertheless, there were some counterpoints to this, in public anxieties about rebellious youth and juvenile crime, which were attributed in part to a breakdown in family life. These anxieties were crystallised in a Royal Commission which took the view that couples were taking marriage 'less seriously' than before. Only those

writers who were able to locate anxieties about marriage in the wider
context of historical change were able to provide an analysis which
explained some of the external pressures on domestic life and suggested the
implications for social policy. Crucial to this debate was an appreciation of
the importance of falling family size, the concentration of childbearing
within the early years of marriage, increased life expectancy, the rising
proportion of married women in the population and the falling average age
at marriage. Such trends could combine to foster a set of expectations about
marriage, as a fulfilling partnership in which the needs of husbands and
wives were given increasing prominence. These were expectations that
might easily be disappointed. Finch and Summerfield conclude that post-
war ideologies of marriage were often at variance with lived experience,
and that the benefits of the companionate model were far more in evidence
for men than for women.

Moving on to the 1960s and 1970s, Martin Richards and B. Jane Elliott
take as their theme the place of sexuality within marriage. They, too, draw
upon debates about companionate marriage and explore some of the
assumptions which construct the 1960s as a period of major change in
sexual attitudes and behaviour. Richards and Elliott choose an intriguing
data set: letters and advice appearing on the problem pages of *Woman's
Own* magazine. They show how during these years replies to letters shift
from an emphasis on didactic advice to the mutual sharing and discussion
of problems between husbands and wives. Survey evidence from the 1950s
and 1960s points to an increasing emphasis on the quality of sexual
relationships within marriage. Problem-page advice reflects this and
reveals an increasing openness and frankness about sexual matters, which
is linked to the notion that sex within marriage is a crucial form of intimacy
and sharing. Sex *before* marriage also gains growing acceptance during
these years and is seen as more and more inevitable, indeed normative. This
is not the case with *extramarital* sex, however. Although some dispensers
of popular advice, such as the writers of marriage manuals, do advocate the
notion of sexually 'open' marriage, survey evidence still suggests that
sexual relationships outside of marriage are widely disapproved. Likewise,
problem-page advice is unlikely to condone such behaviour, which is
generally regarded as a 'threat' to marriage. As Richards and Elliott point
out though, such attitudes, which if anything are becoming more rather than
less strongly held, are widely at variance with behaviour. Although beset
with a variety of methodological problems, research evidence suggests that
sexual relationships outside marriage are now probably the experience of
the majority. Despite this intriguing paradox, these authors point out that
recent sociological studies of marriage have almost universally ignored the
issue of extramarital sexual relationships.

It is the growing range of research-based writing on marriage and domestic life which is the main concern of Janet Finch and David Morgan in their chapter on the 1980s. Their theme is *realism* and the extent to which it may serve as a useful organising principle, particularly in relation to some of the more optimistic accounts of family life which have been produced in earlier decades. In part this is due to the extent to which 'the family' came onto the political agenda in the 1980s, but the most important influence on a new and more realistic approach to understanding marriage and domestic life in the 1980s, was the growth of feminist analysis. Finch and Morgan show how a number of studies tend to support the idea that domestic life in the 1980s was characterised as much by continuity as by change, in both aspirations and lived experience; and this work continued to place a strong emphasis on the importance and centrality of marriage within our culture. However, another body of work gets behind some of this in drawing attention to some of the material aspects of marriage, including the economics of the household, not least in a period characterised by high levels of unemployment. Debates on gender came to the fore in these years and research from the period drew attention to continuing inequalities within marriage and family life across a range of dimensions, from employment outside the home, through domestic labour, to the care of children. Despite a good deal of rhetoric in these years, there appeared to be little evidence for any major shifts in male attitudes and behaviour; and as the authors cryptically put it, there were 'few sightings' of the 'new man'. Indeed, male violence within the home became more visible through a number of research studies which argued that domestic violence should be regarded as a normative aspect of patriarchy, rather than a product of individual pathology. In highlighting the darker dimensions of marriage and domestic life, research in the 1980s might be seen to contain a new realism. For Finch and Morgan this underlines the fact that such research cannot stand alone as detached and disinterested scholarly activity and must be seen in the context of wider political and policy debates about the nature of change in domestic life. The evidence they present suggests that sociology and feminism are currently well placed to further these debates.

All three chapters in this part of the book share certain themes in common. In particular, they are concerned with the relationships between biography and history and the ways in which the experiences of intimate life might be shaped by wider social forces. All of the authors raise important questions about research methodology and the problems which face those who seek to carry out research on marriage and domestic life. We are given examples of a number of approaches, from the interpretation of policy documents and a variety of documentary materials, through to evidence produced both in large surveys and small-scale studies using qualitative methods. This enormous spread of approaches has contributed to the range and depth of our understanding over the period 1945–89. Perhaps the most exciting conceptual breakthrough however, with the potential to influence a variety of methods, has been the growth of interest in a life-course analysis, as explained by Finch and Morgan. In recognising the interconnections between personal and social time, between individuals and generations, such an approach sets an exciting framework for further development.

1 Social reconstruction and the emergence of companionate marriage, 1945–59

Janet Finch and Penny Summerfield

The purpose of this chapter is to explore the development of marriage and family life in the period of post-war social reconstruction and up to the end of the 1950s. We have chosen to focus principally on the emerging concept of *companionate marriage* which, in our view, is the most distinctive feature of domestic life during this period.

Central to the aims of the post-war social reconstruction was the desire to consolidate family life after the disruptive effects of war and to build a future in which marriage and the home would be the foundations of a better life. Partly this required the kind of economic and environmental reconstruction which would provide a physical and material environment conducive to stable family life – most obviously the rebuilding of houses destroyed by war and 'slum clearance' programmes which would reshape decaying urban areas. The prominence of this aspect of post-war reconstruction is evidenced by a Gallup Poll produced at the time of the 1945 election, which showed that 40 per cent of voters saw housing as the major issue of the election campaign (Thane 1982: 260).

In much of the official and semi-official literature of the period, this physical reconstruction of living conditions was seen as providing the backdrop for the consolidation of stable family life, based upon the type of relationship between marriage partners which itself was suited to the post-war world. Although the phrase 'companionate marriage' had been employed as early as the 1920s, it is in the post-war period that it appears more widely, being used to summarise a set of ideas about marriage which ranged from the notion that there should be greater companionship between partners whose roles essentially were different, through the idea of marriage as 'teamwork', to the concept of marriages based on 'sharing' implying the breakdown of clearly demarcated roles. 'Partnership' and 'equality' in marriage clearly can mean very different things and both can be traced in the literature of this period. The prominence of these ideas about companionate marriage in the 1950s marks one of the key shifts from the idea of marriage as an institution to marriage as a relationship (discussed by Morgan in Chapter 5).

In the first two parts of this chapter we discuss the advent of an ideology of companionate marriage, drawing on bodies of literature concerning the birth rate and motherhood, women's sexuality and girls' education and women's employment, in order to explore the different meanings contained within it and their inconsistencies and limitations. Such ideological constructions influenced perceptions of the lived reality of marriage in this period. Sociologists interested in the question of how marriage was developing were not free from them, and indeed contributed to them. In the third part of the chapter we therefore use contemporary empirical sociological studies not as an 'uncontaminated' account of reality, but as a source which gives some sense of the interplay between ideological constructions and lived experience. Further, sociological writing on marriage in the 1950s was very well known, and influenced thinking about British society and social policy well beyond the confines of academic scholarship.

In spite of the optimistic tone in which companionate marriage was discussed in both 'official' sources and sociological writing, there were underlying anxieties about whether it would in fact live up to the expectations of the optimists, or whether it might prove to be incompatible with marital stability. Such fears were voiced in particular in discussions of divorce and also of juvenile delinquency. The fourth part of the chapter reviews the warnings sounded in the period about the dangers of the companionate style for the future of marriage.

We finish by listening briefly to some dissenting voices among those thinking and writing about marriage in this period, from a minority which subscribed neither to the optimism of the protagonists of companionate marriage nor the pessimism of those who doubted its viability. This enables us to draw together our discussion by considering the question which no sociologist then posed: was the companionate marriage in a woman's interests, or did the benefits accrue mainly to the male?

THE BIRTH RATE, MOTHERHOOD AND MODELS OF MARRIAGE

We begin by considering an issue which was of prime importance to public discussions of family life at the end of the Second World War – the birth rate and the overall shape of the British population. Pre-war and wartime anxiety about the falling birth rate of the 1930s which reached a record low in 1940, gave rise to intense discussion about the possibility that the population would fall below replacement level. This preoccupation peaked in the years 1945–47. Public discussion which surrounded it had obvious implications for ideas about motherhood in the immediate post-war period, but also contained a number of implications for models of marriage appropriate to a situation where women were to be encouraged officially to produce children.

The main clearing house for 'pronatalist' ideas concerning ways in which the birth rate might be raised was the Royal Commission on Population (RCP), which reported in 1949. Its policy recommendations embraced larger family allowances (introduced in 1945) starting with the first rather than the second child in a family; 'family services' for 'mothers of young children', including a glittering array of assistance from home helps and 'sitters in', to rest homes for mothers, nurseries, nursery schools and children's playgrounds; and health care based on the new National Health Service to provide the normally healthy married woman, rather than just those medically at risk, with advice on all aspects of reproduction, as well as treatment where necessary. Finally, the housing shortage was felt to be one of 'the main deterrents of parenthood' and a programme was urged of building more and larger houses and modernising old ones in the context of a rent- and rate-rebate system linked to family size (Royal Commission on Population [RCP] 1949: paras 658–79). To summarise, post-war British pronatalism was concerned with improving the material conditions of motherhood in order to promote it as a function.

Motherhood, it was assumed, would take place within marriage. 'Unmarried mothers' were by the early 1950s depicted in psychosociological literature as 'pathologically disturbed' (Riley 1983: 196). Yet in spite of the importance of marriage as a site for the developments advocated, it was given relatively scant attention in post-war pronatalism. In so far as marriage was discussed overtly there were contradictory elements in the way in which it was conceptualised. The recommendations of the RCP reflected the view that the cause of raising the birth rate had been impeded by 'the movement for equality of the sexes' originating in the nineteenth century, in two ways. First, as more women were drawn into paid work a potential conflict was created with the demands of motherhood. One might expect the Commission to have brought forward proposals to ease this situation but it did not. The second effect of greater equality between the sexes, in the Commission's view, was to weaken the traditional dominance of the husband and to give more emphasis to 'the wife's role as companion to her husband as well as a producer of children'. On one level it was difficult to disapprove of this tendency towards companionate marriage especially in so far as it had raised women's status. On the other hand, in the process of becoming 'more considerate' to their wives, husbands had shown themselves increasingly reluctant to put them through the hardship and danger of 'unrestricted childbearing', with the unfortunate effect – from the

Commission's point of view – of contributing to the fall in family size to an average of just over two children (RCP 1949: para. 103). In this sense, companionate marriage itself was potentially a threat to the birth rate, even if in other respects it was to be welcomed. Many of the RCP's policy recommendations were intended to reconcile what was seen as a 'modern' marital style based on a small number of children, with the three- or four-child family regarded by the Commission as essential in the national interest.

Evidence given to the RCP reflects similar contradictions, although some of it welcomes the advent of companionate marriage rather more enthusiastically than the official Report. Particularly groups on the left, such as the Fabian Society, put greater emphasis on the role of the wife as a companion to her husband, and also paid more attention to the issue of working wives. Though their views were not incorporated in the Report, they are indicative of left-wing thinking which influenced the sociological approaches we shall be reviewing later in this chapter. The Fabians saw the 'new marriage' of the post-war world as 'teamwork' between husband and wife, in contrast to the separatism of marriages a generation earlier which was seen as leading to 'sex antagonism'. In 'comradely' marriages the individual interests of wives were to be subsumed within those of the family group, in an analogous way to that in which 'citizens' of either sex were expected to put the interests of the community before their own in the wider society. The Fabian prescription for motherhood endeavoured to reconcile the interests of the family and the community. For the sake of the family, mothers should not combine motherhood with paid work when their children were young, but in the interests of society, wives 'must realise they should give part-time service to the community when the children are older'. Part-time paid work generally was mentioned, and more specifically 'teaching and welfare work' (Fabian Society, quoted by Riley 1983: 176).

All this was seen as belonging in the context of marriage as teamwork, but no thought was given in these sources to how the 'team' was to be constructed, in the sense of the roles of its members, their degree of equality, and the issue of leadership. In other words, no-one questioned the sexual division of labour: power in the home and shifting its balance were not on the agenda. The implication of this ideology of marriage was that wives were to add to conventional subservience to an admittedly 'more considerate' but still bread-winning husband, a responsibility to be his 'companion', to produce and rear more children and to engage in paid work in response to social needs if and when they could do so without ill effects on either husband or children.

Only a minority of those involved in pronatalist debates voiced qualms about the possibilities of achieving genuinely companionate marriage in which wives would be persuaded to have more children, without doing something about income sharing between husbands and wives. They included the Labour MP Edith Summerskill, Edward Hulton, the editor of *Picture Post*, and two wartime feminist organisations – the Six Point Group and the Women's Publicity Planning Association – formed respectively in 1941 and 1943 to protest against the conscription of women without commitment to equal pay and to support a parliamentary bill removing all sex-based discrepancies from British legislation (Riley 1983: 174–5, 179). They advocated legislating to give wives a proportion of their husbands' incomes. It is in the writings of these groups that one finds some hints that companionate marriage might not be wholly in women's interests. But while social policy might intrude in all sorts of ways on the mother, intervention into the 'private' relations between husbands and wives was not considered appropriate in 'orthodox' circles.

Ironically, almost by the time the RCP report was available, fears about the declining birth rate had subsided in the post-war baby boom. At this point the specifically pronatalist political agenda receded, but concern with the conditions of motherhood consolidated in the 1950s around the issue of material deprivation. If anything, these ideas are even more difficult to reconcile with the concept of companionate marriage – or at the very least they imply a version in which there is a clear division of roles between husband and wife.

The view that maternal care in infancy was crucial for the physical development of the child had long roots stretching back to the late nineteenth century. The medical profession had easily grafted on to such views the idea that emotional development also depended upon it. The Ministry of Health used the authoritative pronouncements of its Medical Officers of Health about the physical and emotional harm day nurseries would do to children to limit the supply of wartime nurseries set up to free mothers for war work in the Second World War (Summerfield 1984). In 1952 the publication of John Bowlby's *Maternal Care and Mental Health* gave further psychological credence to such views which were popularised in the 1940s and 1950s above all by D.W. Winnicott, through radio broadcasts and in the press. He depicted the marital home as a private, emotional world in which mother and child were bound to each other and in which the mother had control and found freedom to fulfil herself. In Winnicott's view it was natural and inevitable that she would want such an existence, to the exclusion of any alternatives (Winnicott: 1957).

Such a view of motherhood represents a narrowing of some aspects of pronatalism. No longer were women being told that they ought to have opportunities to pursue 'outside interests', even if only in order to do their social duty and preserve their marriages. Children were expected to be their consuming passion, and childrearing and paid work were seen as mutually exclusive. Bowlby argued that maternal deprivation caused by any sort of absence, including mothers working, led to delinquency and psychosis in their children. Winnicott also warned of the perils awaiting the 'latch key child'. The tendency to see successful childrearing in terms of constant mothering rendered the father relatively unimportant. Where did the emphasis on the mother leave marriage as a team? The 1950s fixation on the mother rather than the parent contributed to the construction of the companionate marriage as a form in which men and women had markedly different roles in spite of an appearance of greater togetherness than in earlier marital styles.

IMAGES OF COMPANIONATE MARRIAGE IN OTHER LITERATURE OF THE PERIOD

We have paid particular attention to the issue of childbearing, and especially to the Royal Commission on Population, because of the report's official status and its key importance in distilling ideas about family life in the immediate post-war years. However, various other bodies of official and semi-official literature of the 1940s and 1950s can be used to trace the development of ideas about companionate marriage. We shall look briefly in this section at three of these: writing on women's sexuality, on girls' education and on married women's employment.

Women's sexuality

An emphasis on sexuality was an important dimension of marriage during this period and of course this fits with the emerging notion that marriage should be seen as a relationship, not simply as an institution. Marital stability was increasingly seen as dependent on both contraception and sexual pleasure in the 1940s and 1950s. Pronatalist literature acknowledged the widespread use of contraception, and though some of the contributors (e.g. Hubback 1947; Mass Observation 1945) would have liked to restrict access to it in order to encourage in people 'a more courageous and robust faith in life among those who do not want more children owing to a defeatist attitude' (Hubback quoted by Riley 1983: 160), the Royal Commission on Population advocated its wider availability. It argued that it was necessary for the better spacing of children, but more fundamentally it was felt that birth control was now 'generally accepted' and the clock could not be turned back. Even the Anglican church had (after giving Marie Stopes hell for two decades) come round. 'Christians are generally agreed upon the need for responsible family planning' wrote the Church of England Moral

Welfare Council in 1957 (quoted by Birmingham Feminist History Group 1979: 58).

Such sources considered the use of birth control as a palliative for poor health or a way for couples to raise their standard of living, and not as a means by which, as of right, a woman could control her fertility, nor as the path to greater sexual freedom. However, the literature on sexuality was growing, bringing with it the message that married couples had a duty to give each other sexual pleasure, and that this was increasingly important for a successful marriage. Indeed it has been argued that in the United States the concept of 'companionate marriage' was based on 'a new domestic ideal of "mom" as sexy housewife' (Ferguson 1989: 115). Kinsey *et al.*, in *Sexual Behavior in the Human Female* published in Britain in 1953, asserted that women could and did enjoy sex. And during the 1950s numerous public bodies including the church and the Marriage Guidance Council agreed that pleasurable marital sex was important, increasing the burden on women to give, as well as receive and express, pleasure.

There was, however, anxiety in some quarters that pleasurable sex was not stopping at the marriage bed and that the emphasis on it would in fact undermine the stability of marriage. Rowntree and Lavers, authors of *English Life and Leisure* published in 1951, believed that the new emphasis on 'eroticism' in the media and the open availability of contraceptives were encouraging indulgence in 'illicit sexual relations'. Their analysis of what they saw as a rising (though unquantifiable) tide of immorality was based on the view that many aspects of post-war Britain were leading to the submergence of spiritual life in 'selfishness and hedonism'. As far as marriage and the family were concerned, such indulgence had a destabilising effect both in so far as it led to illegitimate births, abortions and venereal disease, and through the deceit within the family which it encouraged. A strong streak of puritanism ran through their work. Illicit (i.e extramarital) sex was seen as an 'obsessional activity, the desire for which grows with indulgence . . . to the satisfaction of which are sacrificed energy, time, money and thought that should have been harnessed to constructive purposes' (Rowntree and Lavers 1951: 214). Not only the viability of marriage but that of Britain as 'a great and vigorous nation' depended on the checking of 'sexual excesses' (ibid: 215).

Such views put a further burden on companionate marriage, of which we are building a cumulative picture. Such marriage was to be between considerate, breadwinning husbands and comradely but thoroughly maternal wives surrounded by numerous children. The wives were told by some sources that they should maintain 'outside interests' and even that they had a duty to do paid work if they could fit it around their primary domestic role. But other sources frowned on anything lessening their ties to children, particularly paid work, warning that if they did such work they would irreparably damage the mental health of their 'latch key children'. At the same time husbands and wives were told that the stability of their marriages, the viability of marriage as an institution and even the future of the country, depended on regular marital sex which they should enjoy to the exclusion of sexual indulgence outside marriage.

The education of girls

To add a further level of complexity to the picture which we are building, when we look at literature of this period concerned with the education of girls, it appears that there is an almost complete withdrawal from the idea of companionate marriage, even in its most conservative versions. Indeed much educational prescription of the 1940s and 1950s contradicted the ideology of marriage as teamwork. None of the commentators thought it necessary for boys to learn about their responsibilities as future husbands and fathers, nor to develop any special skills they might require, beyond those associated with acquiring sufficient education to get a steady job of an appropriate sort given their individual mix of ability and social status. This would enable them to fulfil what was expected of them as men, and by implication becoming a breadwinner was an aspect of this (see Board of Education 1943; Newsom 1948; Central Advisory Council for Education 1959). Educational prescription for girls, on the other hand, heavily emphasised their future roles as wives and mothers. Domestic science, argued the Norwood Report (Board of Education 1943), was valuable because young girls were all 'potential makers of homes'. John Newsom in 1948 disagreed that girls should be taught domestic skills before they left school, as most would do by the age of 15, because they would forget them by the time they married. However, as adults they should attend continuation classes in domestic science in County Colleges, for the benefit of their husbands' digestions (Newsom 1948: 127) and the stability of their marriages. But though domestic skills were not to be taught to schoolgirls, Newsom wanted to give their education a thoroughly domestic orientation, preparing them for what he saw as their true destination as wives and mothers and reflecting what he saw as the interests of all but a tiny minority of 'academic' girls. In his scheme all subjects would be linked together by their applicability to the home (Newsom 1948: Chapter 6).

Newsom's book *The Education of Girls* was not an official report, but its tone was echoed in the Crowther report (Central Advisory Council for Education 1959), which emphasised the preoccupation of the majority of girls with domesticity and also personal relationships, and recommended that their schooling should reflect these alleged interests. Both Newsom and Crowther acknowledged the long-standing pattern of girls engaging in paid work between school and marriage, but dismissed such work as inherently less important than the sort of paid work done by boys and men. It was seen as inevitably un- or semi-skilled with a low training component, since it was widely recognised as a mere stopgap before a young woman commenced her true 'career', that of a wife and mother. Even informal education within, for example, the Youth Service and the Girl Guides, was designed to promote a girl's 'social maturity and technical competence at her job as home-maker' (Ministry of Education 1960). Girl Guides could acquire strings of badges indicating their proficiency as cooks, child carers, seamstresses, knitters and nurses, crowned, once they had enough, by the 'Little House' emblem of domestic proficiency.

The emphasis within prescriptive literature on the education of girls in and for domesticity inevitably produced a one-sided view of whom within marriage was primarily responsible for the home. At the same time, no-one recommended that either girls or boys should think about the difficulties of meeting the demands that the new ideal of the companionate marriage might make, especially given the reality of a rising proportion of wives engaging in paid work during the 1950s. Such literature deepens one's scepticism about the concept of the companionate marriage used at this time. It increasingly appears to have given no more than a gloss to the conventional division of labour and distribution of economic power between husband and wife, while imposing new demands on women to be more comradely wives, more devoted mothers of more children, more satisfying and satisfied sexual partners and more professional homemakers.

Married women's employment

Logically one might expect that more equal marriages should mean that both women and men have similar opportunities to engage in all aspects of public and private life, including employment. However, this was not the dominant theme of the period. Reference has already been made to the ways in which the relationship between women's employment and marriage was depicted in pronatalist and educational literature. As we have seen, within orthodox opinion, as represented by the Royal Commission on Population, the paid employment of wives was not compatible with producing larger families. However, in the view of some commentators it might be necessary to permit some women to pursue careers alongside motherhood, lest they abandon the latter altogether, and according to others, wives of older children might be required to engage in paid employment for the general good of society. Psychological and educational literature, on the other hand, regarded paid work as something which would cease on marriage/ motherhood as far as the majority of women were concerned.

However, simultaneously in the 1940s married women were being urged to return to paid work to fill gaps in the labour force created by the labour shortage in particular areas and types of work. Teaching was one of these. In 1949 the Ministry of Education issued a document urging married women to return to teaching, arguing that schools would gain from their maternal qualities although it said nothing about the impact of such a dual role on marriage (Ministry of Education 1949: 5). In relation to manual work, the official literature similarly emphasised the benefits to production of the employment of married women (e.g. the application of 'household pride', the steadiness and sense of responsibility older married women brought to the work compared with flightier young single women).

As far as managing the double burden was concerned, part-time work, introduced on a large scale during the war to recruit women who were otherwise exempt from mobilisation, was seen as the answer (Summerfield 1984: Chapter 6). Part-time work would enable married women to perform all their essential wifely and maternal tasks without threatening the stability of their marriages or detracting from their productivity at work. Employers might have to allow 'latitude . . . for the performance of home duties' mainly in terms of the arrangement of hours and leave (Smith 1961: 22) but no change in the nature of marriage was required. The economic benefits of their work were small, so part-time women workers could be seen un-threateningly as supplementing a family income earned principally by the husband. A survey in 1948 showed that these were the values that women themselves espoused. Women workers were reported as saying that 'women should go out to work only if they could carry out their duties to their homes and families' (Thomas 1948: 3). The repetition of such views in another survey undertaken in the late 1950s suggests that the higher post-war female participation rates had not altered the basic belief that home and family came first in a woman's life. In this survey, married women workers were presented as wanting to earn as much as possible 'to raise the standard of living of the family as a whole' rather than for themselves (Smith 1961: 20). A wife's earnings would thus not signi-ficantly enlarge her own independence, though they would enable a couple to spend on the new 'family' consumables of the fifties, such as processed foods, synthetic clothing, vacuum cleaners, fridges and washing machines, to the production of which the new married women workers were them-selves contributing.

The literature on women's employment did not prescribe the most appro-priate marital style to go with it, yet it implied marriages in which husbands would tolerate wives working, and thus husbands who were not committed to the bourgeois ideology of the man as sole breadwinner (Thomas 1948: 19). It was an implication which fitted comfortably with the concept of companionate marriage without upsetting the conventional distribution of economic and other power within marriage. At the same time it imposed another strain on women. In addition to the demands that a wife should be more comradely, more motherly, more sensuous and a better homemaker, was added the expectation that she should be a part-time wage earner.

Thus, in exploring the concept of companionate marriage which developed during the 1940s and 1950s, a rather contradictory picture emerges. The idea of companionate marriage was being officially encouraged whilst at the same time there were anxieties that – if pushed too far – it could undermine other features of family life which were seen as central to its stability: the position of the man as main breadwinner, the incentive to produce and rear children, the attachment to one lifelong sexual partner. We have highlighted particularly the implications of these ideas about companionate marriage for women. Superficially they appear to be in women's interests but we have argued that, by producing quite contradictory pressures, they actually placed strains upon women especially by pushing them towards a type of marriage which made extra demands without necessarily providing extra rewards.

We have constructed this argument on the basis of official and semi-official literature, but how far does our case match up to the social reality of what was happening in women's lives during the 1940s and 1950s? To pursue that question, we turn now to a different kind of literature from this period.

MARRIAGE AND FAMILY IN SOCIOLOGICAL WRITING

In the fifteen years following the end of the Second World War, the young but expanding discipline of sociology took marriage and family life as one of its key topics. We are fortunate in having a number of contemporary empirical studies for this period, and they form the basis of our discussion here. What do these studies tell us about domestic life in general and marriage in particular? Do they document a noticeable change towards the companionate model? If so, what were its implications for women and men?

The picture of marriage which emerges from these different sources is in some ways puzzlingly diverse. From the windows of the Institute of Community Studies, the modern husbands of working-class Bethnal Green could be seen pushing the pram or playing with their children in the park – activities which, according to the researchers, their fathers and grandfathers would have found shocking. In advanced middle-class Woodford, husbands would go so far as to make a commitment to wash the dishes every night and do the hoovering on Saturday mornings. Meanwhile, in the Yorkshire mining town of Ashton, they were still throwing their dinners on the back of the fire if the wife had failed to select the right menu (Dennis *et al.* 1956; Young and Willmott 1957; Willmott and Young 1960). Some showed the signs of 'partnership' much more obviously than others. Were the researchers documenting differences in marriage customs in different localities, or different social classes, or different occupational groups? Were some people simply quicker than others to latch onto the idea of companionate marriage?

We shall explore these questions initially by drawing upon the 1950s' sociological literature and then, in the following section, consider different kinds of data which shed light on the image of post-war marriage which emerges from these studies. We have selected three prominent themes which emerge from this literature, which can be summarised in three words: optimism, cosiness, anxiety.

Optimism: the security of family life in a welfare state

We have already indicated that economic, social and environmental reconstruction formed the essential backdrop to the more qualitative changes to family life upon which we are focusing. The building of decent houses, new towns and the establishment of a welfare state which took care of its citizens 'from cradle to grave' were the soil upon which, *inter alia*, family life could flourish.

The sociological studies of the period reflect a spirit of optimism about the beneficial consequences of the newly established welfare state: the basic economic pressures were being taken off an increasing number of people; living standards were rising, bringing with them the prospect of a more secure and more satisfying family life. This tone of optimism is clearly in evidence in the influential Bethnal Green studies of working-class family life (Young and Willmott 1957; Willmott and Young 1960; and see discussion in Fletcher 1962). The authors of these studies argued that the conditions of the household had changed dramatically by comparison with those described in earlier generations of studies on the working classes in London, done by Mayhew, Booth and Rowntree. Key changes were: improved housing conditions and less sharing of houses; shorter working hours and higher wages for men in a situation of full employment; smaller family size, easing the pressure on household budgets; increased life expectancy and improved medical care, making it less likely that one or more parent would die whilst their children were young (Young and Willmott 1957: 17–27).

The general tone of optimism is evident in the Bethnal Green studies and elsewhere, but it is not universal. For example, in a study done in London in 1949–51, Spinley compared the family life of young people in two contrasting social groups, one selected from 'one of the worst slums in London' and the other a group of public school boys (Spinley 1953). The living conditions which he describes do not seem to show much sign of significant post-war improvements. Moving outside London, in another study done at around the same time as the Bethnal Green research, Dennis and colleagues were discussing the conditions of family life in a Yorkshire mining community which they named Ashton. Although certainly not subject to overcrowding and poor housing conditions of the type described by Spinley, the men and women of Ashton did not seem to have much money to spare and many of them still needed to worry about the male breadwinner missing even one day's work (Dennis *et al.* 1956: 185–6).

If we go beyond specific studies of family life, some other sociologists were not entirely convinced of the efficacy of the welfare state. Although in a political sense poverty was 'rediscovered' in the 1960s, this was possible in part because some sociologists, especially Peter Townsend, who was publishing on poverty in the 1950s, were not seduced by the benefits of the social reconstruction, and the more obvious signs of the 'affluent society', into believing that the noble aim of eradicating poverty had actually been achieved (Townsend 1954: Coates and Silburn 1971).

Although the message of optimism comes across strongly in some writing, the evidence of sociological studies is actually rather mixed on the issue of whether the material conditions of family life really had improved, or what proportions of the population benefited from this. It is difficult to discern how many people during this period really were enjoying the kind of material conditions which were thought to be conducive to a more companionate style of marriage.

Cosiness: the nuclear family and companionate marriage

A major theme in this literature is that the 'new' family life was much more home-centred in various senses. Houses had become more pleasant places and people now had more money with which to make them comfortable; relationships within the wider kin group were becoming less significant and the nuclear family household was of enhanced importance; men as well as women were more likely to centre their lives on the home in a significant way. The image of the new family life is therefore essentially one of cosiness, in which people live in tight little units, rather inward-looking, interacting very much more with each other than with others outside the household, harmonious for the most part. This picks up on a dominant theme in American sociology of this period (Parsons and Bales 1956) although often the British studies do not refer to the American literature explicitly.

A more companionate style of marriage was seen as an integral part of this package. Many of the sociologists of this period seemed wholly convinced that they were indeed observing its rapid spread. There was a general sense that the creation of this type of family life was a natural consequence of the social and economic changes of the post-war world. This view is expressed most explicitly by Josephine Klein (1965) who, although her work was published after the period which we are considering, was writing sympathetically about studies published in the 1950s and trying to draw out their common themes. She attributes the development of companionate marriage, and the consequent reduced attachment to kin, explicitly to growing prosperity:

> In the traditional communities . . . when financial stress intensifies, the rift between husband and wife must deepen. The man will work more overtime, and so be in the house less than before. The woman will rely more on her kin, hence be involved with her spouse less than before. The poorer the family is, the more restricted their lives will become, and the less man and wife will have to share emotionally and socially. Conversely . . . where the stress is lifting, one tends to find more affectionate relations between members, or at least more interaction which expresses and demonstrates such affection, more consultation between members and a less authoritarian structure.
>
> (Klein 1965: 291)

Authors of the period saw the changing status of women as an integral part of the nèw family life, although whether a consequence or a cause is not always clear. For the most part, writers presented the changed position of women as a matter of uncontentious progress, both inside and outside the family. A particularly explicit example of this can be found at the end of the first chapter of *Family and Kinship in East London*, where Young and Willmott have no difficulty in concluding that 'man and wife are now partners':

> (There is) a new kind of companionship, reflecting the rise in status of the young wife and children which is one of the great transformations of our time. There is now a new approach to equality between the sexes and, though each has its peculiar role, its boundaries are no longer so rigidly defined, nor performed without consultation . . . man and wife are partners.
>
> (Young and Willmott 1957: 30)

This partnership model of marriage apparently reached its full flowering in places like middle-class Woodford where, despite the fact that many travelled into London to work, men as well as women had become strongly oriented to the home and the nuclear family:

> Most Woodford men are emphatically not absentee husbands. They hurry back from their offices and factories, arriving between 6 and 7, to spend the evening at home, and they are there for two full days at weekends. It is their work, especially if rather tedious, which takes second place in their thoughts. They are as devoted as their wives to the house they share.
>
> (Willmott and Young 1960: 21)

Meanwhile one wonders what the miners' wives of Ashton would have made of being told that the era of the companionate marriage, based on equality between the partners, had arrived. The picture of the marriage relationship which emerges from this study is very different: the man's centre of activity lay firmly outside the home; the house was the woman's domain; a clearly bounded division of labour, between the male bread-winner and the female homemaker, was evident at every turn. Dennis and colleagues are very clear on this point. Although men might grow vege-tables in an allotment or do some household repairs, none of these activities are of the type which would 'demand co-operation or encourage the growth of companionship between husband and wife' (Dennis *et al.* 1956: 183). Marriage in Ashton had a clearly understood contractual basis, expressed most concretely at the point where the husband handed over part of his wages to his wife:

> The husband's duty to his family goes little further than delivering part of his wage each Friday. Here the duties and responsibilities of his partner begin. It is for him to earn the money and for her to administer it wisely. In actual fact this means that the wife takes virtually all the responsibility for the household and the family.
>
> (Dennis *et al.* 1956: 196)

These arrangements are a particularly clear example of what feminists later were to argue about marriage: that essentially, from women's point of view, it is a labour contract (Delphy 1984). This is very far removed from cosy companionship.

Varieties of experience in marriages

How do we account for this apparent variation in the experience of mar-riage in the 1950s? This was an issue which interested sociologists working in the period, and they came up with a range of possible answers, of which we will mention four. First, social-class differences: it was suggested that middle-class marriages were inherently more companionate. This was an obvious possible explanation although it was difficult to get it to fit the empirical evidence, since the Bethnal Green research on working-class couples so confidently portrayed the younger ones as having already slotted into the companionate mode. Second, and as a variation on a similar theme, the authors of the Ashton study were inclined to explain the distinctiveness of the marriage relationship in their research in specific occupational terms. The distinctive features of the mining industry (long days in an all-male environment, physically demanding work, an occupationally homogeneous community) were conducive to a particular type of family organisation, they argued.

A third line of argument was quite simply that contemporary studies were documenting social change, which took place at a variable rate in different localities. The implication was that everyone would catch up sooner or later. This view is implicit throughout Young and Willmott's work and of course it is very much in tune with the general tone of optimism about social reconstruction. They were to elaborate it most fully in a book published in 1973, where they suggested that this progressive form of family life had slowly percolated down the class structure from the middle class to different levels of the working class. The onward march of progress was inevitable.

Fourth, the work of Elizabeth Bott (1957) – in many ways the most interesting and sophisticated sociological study of family life in this period – suggested that different types of marriage relationship were the product of a wider set of relationships in which individuals are involved, rather than of their personal or social characteristics. Bott's carefully documented study of twenty couples shows that the nature of a couple's relationships with their wider kin network is closely linked to the type of relationship which they have with each other. Couples whose networks of relationships were close-knit needed to rely less on each other for practical and emotional support, and therefore were likely to develop a marriage in which each has their own sphere and tasks. Where the network of a couple was rather loose-knit, they needed to rely on each other more and therefore were likely to develop a more co-operative conjugal relationship. This line of argument represents a rather more subtle, complex and less deterministic way of explaining variations in the incidence of companionate marriage than do the others. It is also consistent with the findings of other studies, in that close-knit networks were more likely to be found in certain localities than in others.

But in the end, it seems difficult to judge on the basis of these studies just how far the fifteen years following the Second World War was a period in which the cosy nuclear family, with companionate marriage as its corner-stone, became a widespread reality. Looking at these studies from a dis-tance of three or four decades, we have a niggling worry about the way in which all the authors take for granted the desirability of this family model. One is bound to wonder how far the fact that they were enthusiastically seeking this phenomenon influenced the evidence which they found.

These sociological studies are also somewhat restricted in scope, in the sense that there must have been other variations on domestic life which simply were not covered. An obvious example is that none of the socio-logical studies of the family published in this period sets out to encompass black as well as white families, yet this was a period in which migration from the New Commonwealth was firmly established. Sociologists of the family seem barely to have noticed its potential significance. The first British sociological study in a non-white area was actually conducted in the late 1950s, but it concentrates more on employment than on family relationships and in any case was not published until some years later (Patterson 1963). When one adds this to the lack of attention paid to gender issues in these studies of family life, the evidence starts to look very partial. It was only after the impact of second-wave feminism that sociologists began to question what the cosy nuclear family might mean for women.

ANXIETIES ABOUT COMPANIONATE MARRIAGE

The theme of optimism and cosiness has its counterpoint in the sociological literature. This is a sense of anxiety that perhaps things have gone too far, or not in the right direction, or that they are getting a bit out of hand. These anxieties also are reflected in some official literature of the period. In this section we will look at evidence from both types of source, as a way of exploring some key contradictions about the concept of companionate marriage and also highlighting some themes which were to become pro-minent in debates about marriages in the following three decades.

The sense of anxiety in sociological literature

In the sociological literature, a source where this sense of anxiety is made explicit is Fletcher's book on *Marriage and Family in Britain*, which was published in 1962 but which drew all its evidence from 1950s sociological studies. This book was written explicitly to counter views, expressed in public debate, that the quality of family life was actually deteriorating rather than improving and that its decline was responsible for the growth of other social evils. Much of this anxiety was focused upon two issues: divorce and juvenile delinquency. In a way, each was seen as a consequence of greater post-war prosperity, of the easing of the conditions of family life, and of the trend towards a more isolated nuclear family. Fletcher sets out the parameters of these issues very clearly in his introduction:

> What effects have industrial and urban changes, the increase in material wealth, the increased provision of education, the new independence of women, the new affluence and freedom of teenagers, and other aspects of modern society had upon the nature and stability of the family? Are these changes such that we can welcome and encourage them? Or are they to be feared and opposed? Do they constitute a deterioration or an improvement of moral standards and family relationships? Is the family really to blame for all the ills modern society is said to suffer – crime, delinquency, irresponsibility, hooliganism – as many moralists would have us believe? Or are such charges false, unjustified and harmful?
>
> (Fletcher 1962: 12)

Fletcher's own answer to this is essentially twofold: things are not as bad as they seem when the facts are examined and placed in historical perspective; the changes which people worry about are really signs of social and economic progress, and therefore basically to be welcomed. Whether or not his work was convincing as an intervention in public debate need not concern us here. But the very fact that he felt the need to write this kind of book picked up on the underlying anxiety in many of the sources which we are reviewing in the 1950s.

Concern with the stability of marriage as a lifelong relationship seems to have been quite widely shared. Bott, for example, felt the need to point out that – in her estimation – the different types of conjugal relationships which she had identified were an equally stable basis for marriage and that in principle people could be happy in either contrasting arrangement (Bott 1957: 217–18). Young and Willmott present the conditions of working-class life in the post-war period as inherently *more* stable as a basis for marriage than arrangements in earlier generations, but at the same time there is a clear concern that marriage breakdown be avoided wherever possible (Young and Willmott 1957: 22).

Much of the apparent anxiety about juvenile delinquency was focused on the image of the slum and the social organisation associated with it. In the slum, lawlessness of both minor and major kinds was encouraged by a family life which was impoverished in every sense. In the area which Spinley studied in the late 1940s, he linked high levels of delinquency explicitly with childrearing practices such as unplanned children, so-called broken homes, and mothers going out to work, as well as to material poverty (Spinley 1953: 131–2). The same kinds of anxieties were reflected, perhaps less overtly, in other studies of the period, even in the very different social setting of Ashton (Dennis *et al.* 1956). The slum, as it had been known before the war, was supposed to be disappearing, and with it the undesirable patterns of behaviour which it promoted. But it looked as if increased prosperity was having the effect of increasing rather than decreasing a tendency to irresponsible and lawless behaviour among the young and 'the family' in general – women in particular – looked conveniently available to be blamed.

These issues are addressed explicitly in Fyvel's book *The Insecure Offenders*, given the subtitle 'Rebellious Youth in the Welfare State'. It was published in 1961 and reflects very much the concerns of the period which we are discussing, in particular the idea that affluence has created its own problems. Young people are seen here as the *victims* of the welfare state, expressed most graphically in Teddy Boy culture:

> For some years, each Saturday and Sunday towards dusk, I used to witness a curious procession. From my distant window I could see small, dark figures of boys and half-grown youths, all of them wearing the identical Teddy Boy suits at that time in fashion. All of them, as if drawn by a magnet, made off in the same direction towards the main streets beyond the big railway stations . . . aesthetically a God-awful wilderness, but to the boys obviously representing life with a capital L.
>
> (Fyvel 1961: 10)

The most visible sign that something was changing was the rising rates of juvenile crime and Fyvel reflects a common theme when he argues that the weakening of family life must be seen as a major cause of this. Increased rates of women's employment certainly play a prominent part in his analysis, although he, in company with other writers, is keen not to condemn this out of hand. However, 'everything has its price' and this trend has contributed to a 'new social atmosphere . . . whereby "home" for many boys and girls becomes less important in their lives and the rules of the irresponsible gang therefore become more important' (Fyvel 1961: 129). Men are part of the problem too. Changes in the types of jobs which men do, in the employment of women, and in the greater capacity of teenagers to earn good wages all have 'diminished the status of the working-class father as head of the family' thus reducing men's capacity to exercise authority over their teenage children (ibid: 130). One cannot help noticing that men are seen as the unwitting parties to the weakening of family life, whereas women are treated – at least in part – as active initiators of these changes through their desire to be in the labour market. In reflecting a sense of

anxiety about these features of family life, most of the sociological literature seemed inclined to put up a spirited defence of a post-war family as a
success story. In that sense, optimism was the more dominant theme, but, at
the same time, there was an underlying uncertainty about what had really
been created, a sense perhaps that there was more to the 'new' family than
was meeting the sociological eye.

Anxieties about companionate marriage: the Royal Commission on Marriage and Divorce

The subtext of anxiety about marriage in sociological writing was mirrored
in the post-war discussion of divorce which led to the setting up in 1951 of
the Royal Commission on Marriage and Divorce (RCMD) which reported
in 1955. Indeed the public debate generated by its publication was one
major reason why sociologists felt the need to defend contemporary marriage and family life. The concern of the Commission focused on 'the large
number of marriages which each year are ending in the divorce court'
(Royal Commission on Marriage and Divorce 1956: 39). The proportion of
marriages terminated by divorce had risen from 1.6 per cent in 1937 to 7.1
per cent in 1950. It had sunk slightly from this high point, to 6.7 per cent in
1954, but had not returned to the pre-war level (RCMD 1956: 369).

The Commission was concerned to discover the causes of the higher
divorce rate. Two factors made divorce more widely available. Changes in
the law in 1937 made cruelty, insanity and desertion grounds for divorce for
the first time (in addition to adultery). And the Legal Aid and Advice Act
of 1949 provided help with the costs of divorce for those who could not
previously have afforded it. The Commission considered that to some
extent the post-war pattern was entirely understandable. Wartime pressures
on marriage, notably 'over hasty' marriages and wartime separations, had
led to a natural increase after the war. And there had been a sharp rise in
1952 because a 'backlog' of cases could now be brought under legal aid.
But it was felt that the effects of war should have worked themselves out by
the 1950s and that 1952 should have been an exceptional year which would
not be repeated. Instead, the higher rate of divorce seemed to have become
a permanent phenomenon. The Report stated: 'Weighing all the evidence
before us, we are satisfied that marriages are now breaking up which in the
past would have held together' (RCMD 1956: para. 42).

Why was this so? The 'complexities of modern life', the housing shortage and the falling average age of marriage were cited. But the Commission
was most concerned about the 'greater demands' now made of marriage.
Like the Royal Commission on Population (RCP), it presented modern
marriage based on greater equality between the sexes in a favourable light,

as a natural outcome of historical changes, particularly the emancipation of women: 'Women are no longer content to endure the treatment which in past times their inferior position obliged them to suffer. They expect of marriage that it shall be an equal partnership; and rightly so' (RCMD 1956: para. 45). But just as the RCP feared that this kind of marriage was in some ways dysfunctional, since it had inevitably led to smaller families, so the RCMD feared that it gave rise to all kinds of pressures which threatened the viability of marriage itself. Though desirable, the companionate marriage was, in short, a high-risk venture:

> the working out of this ideal exposes marriage to new strains. Some husbands find it difficult to accept the changed position of women; some wives do not appreciate that their new rights do not release them from the obligations arising out of marriage itself and, indeed, bring in their train certain new responsibilities.
>
> (RCMD 1956: para. 45)

Just what these rights and responsibilities were, the Commission did not spell out, but it sounds as if its members meant by 'responsibilities' the conventional 'duties' of wives and mothers, which still needed to be performed even if a woman had a right to greater freedom to pursue the 'outside interests' stressed by the RCP and the paid work for which she was in demand in the labour market. The Report asserted that the contemporary emphasis on sexual satisfaction had weakened restraints on extramarital sex and that the 'community' was more inclined to 'acquiesce' in divorce especially in view of the growing tendency for public figures to resort to it.

Taken together, all these factors were leading couples to 'take the duties and responsibilities of marriage less seriously than formerly' even though companionate marriage made greater demands, such that 'more not less should be put into it' (RCMD 1956: para. 47). The paternalistic recommendations of the Commission suggest an underlying lack of confidence in companionate marriage. The proposed solution for the rising tide of marriage failures was 'education in the widest sense' which could be achieved 'by specific instruction before marriage, and by providing facilities for guidance after marriage and for conciliation if breakdown threatens' (RCMD 1956: para. 51). In a statement confusingly cast in the male gender (but presumably intended to embrace women as well as men in the universal 'he'), the Commission recommended that moral and social sanctions should be re-implanted. The ultimate remedy lay: 'in fostering in the individual the will to do his duty by the community; in strengthening his resolution to make marriage a union for life; in inculcating a proper sense of his responsibility towards his children' (RCMD 1956: para. 51). As to the question of the availability of divorce, the Commission was evidently not united. On the one hand it stated the belief that making divorce more difficult to obtain would not stop marriages breaking down. But on the other hand it ended the first section of the Report with a dire warning. The tendency 'to resort too readily and too lightly to divorce' might lead to the abandonment of 'the conception of marriage as a life-long union of one man with one woman' (RCMD 1956: para. 54). If that happened some of those on the Commission believed it would be better to abolish divorce altogether.

DISSENTING VOICES: TITMUSS AND GORER

The tone of the Report of the Royal Commission on Marriage and Divorce was both moralistic and in places hysterical, implying that the general optimism about companionate marriage was fundamentally misplaced. Meanwhile, most sociologists were inclined to put up a spirited defence of post-war changes, whilst demonstrating similar anxieties. There are other writers, however, who enable us to get a different perspective upon the reality of marriage in the 1940s and 1950s by taking a longer view and by writing in a way which does not betray an obvious investment in demonstrating that contemporary marriage was 'good' or 'bad'. The two writers whom we find helpful in this respect are R.M. Titmuss and Geoffrey Gorer.

R.M. Titmuss struck a note which challenged many of the assumptions of the RCMD. He saw plenty of problems in post-war marriage, but no grounds for serious anxiety. His analysis is so valuable because it was based on an understanding of the demographic changes which had taken place over the previous fifty years. This enables him to contextualise contemporary changes in a longer view. He identified five important factors: the fall in family size, the concentration of childbearing in the early years of marriage, the increasing life expectancy of women, the rising proportion of married women in the female population and the falling average age of marriage. The RCMD stated that 'matrimony . . . is not so secure as it was a hundred or even fifty years ago' (RCMD 1956: para. 70, xii), but Titmuss argued that there was evidence that marriage had never been so popular. More marriage at an earlier average age had been accompanied by an increase in the years of married life experienced by married couples, since declining death rates meant people were married for longer. Moreover, in 1955 three-quarters of those who divorced also remarried (Titmuss 1958: 100). And smaller and more concentrated families meant that couples had more years of married life without children to care for.

Titmuss noted that the ideology of marriage had changed profoundly since Victorian times: 'the idea of companionship in marriage is being substituted for the more sharply defined roles and codes of behaviour set by the Victorian patriarchal system' (Titmuss 1958: 98). In common with others reviewed above, he did not look into the implications of such a style for marital relations. Nor did he present his view of what companionate marriage might mean in practice. But he did state that the ideal created higher expectations which might not always be met, particularly in view of the demographic changes which meant that more people were 'exposed to the hazards of married life and childrearing' for longer (Titmuss 1958: 100). He focused on the particular problems confronting married women as a result of these changes. By the age of 40, a 1950s wife had typically completed her mothering role, but had 35 to 40 years of life ahead of her, and more opportunities both for spending money and for leisure than ever before. The tendency for older married women to engage in paid work was one response, but it was accompanied by two sorts of problems, the difficulty for such women to gain training or enter pensionable occupations, and the conflicts they encountered about their roles as 'mothers, wives and wage-earners' (Titmuss 1958: 102).

Taking all the social changes together, Titmuss regarded a higher marital failure rate as unsurprising (Titmuss 1958: 98). But he felt that those companionate marriages which did survive represented a higher level of marital achievement than hitherto. Rather than fearing change and moralising about re-education in marital responsibilities as the RCMD had done, he pointed to the need for social policies which would support women in their new roles.

The other writer who represents something of a dissenting voice – though in a very different way from Titmuss – is Geoffrey Gorer. We draw here upon his survey published as *Exploring English Character* in 1955, which attempts to document the lived reality of people's lives and which contains some revealing evidence about the marital aspirations and achievements of both sexes in Britain in the 1950s. It sheds interesting light on the gendered nature of companionate marriage.

The ideology of companionate marriage might lead one to expect that men would have valued wives sharing their interests, but this was referred to by only 8 per cent of Gorer's sample. Top of the male list of 'qualities admired in spouses' was 'good housekeeper' (29 per cent) (Gorer 1955: 125–6). The RCMD's opinions might lead one to expect wives to value husbands who gave them freedom. But wives seemed to hanker after a companionate style defined according to their own interests, based on more involvement on the part of husbands in their wives' 'responsibilities'. The qualities most commonly valued by wives were 'understanding' (33 per cent), 'thoughtfulness' (28 per cent) and 'sense of humour' (21 per cent). As far as spouses' failings were concerned, men mentioned 'nagging, scolding, fault finding' most frequently (29 per cent), and women mentioned 'selfishness' (56 per cent) (Gorer 1955: 128–9). What did they mean by that? It was the 'domestic deficiencies' of men that most annoyed women, 'laziness, untidiness and meanness with money' (Gorer 1955: 129).

The volume of female complaints about men's domestic shortcomings, and male complaints about 'nagging' coupled with men's stress on wives' qualities as housekeepers, suggest two things. First, expectations were frequently not fulfilled. Second, while women were increasingly keen on marriage which might be defined as companionate from a wife's point of view, implying an understanding husband who involved himself in domestic tasks and shared his income with her, relatively few men were interested in such a marriage, and many resented the pressure their wives put them under to achieve it.

What one gets from both Gorer and Titmuss (though in very different ways) is a realism about the nature of the changes which actually were occurring in the 1950s and a sense of what it is sensible to expect of marriages, given prevailing social and economic conditions.

CONCLUSION

The ideology of marriage which has been drawn from the various bodies of literature examined in this chapter did not have at its core a concept of marriage as an 'equal partnership'. The literatures of pronatalism and motherhood, sexuality, education and employment did not in fact subscribe to such an ideal, even though the marital norm running through it was of companionate marriage, sometimes described as 'teamwork'. As we have seen, the cumulative picture that can be derived from such literature is of modern marriages which were far from symmetrical. Husbands were expected to be more considerate and might now tolerate their wives doing paid, part-time work outside the home, but they were still to be principal breadwinners. Otherwise very little was said about their role in marriage. The new expectations were heaped on wives, who were to be more comradely, and might be permitted to have outside interests, but were also to be better mothers of larger families, better sexual partners and better homemakers. They were only to take on paid work if they could do so without either making their children psychotic or neurotic, or detracting from their domestic duties. Sociological studies tended to reflect the same expectations, whilst giving very positive support to ideas about partnership in marriage and mostly portraying contemporary family life as a success story.

The reality of the lived experience of marriage in the 1940s and 1950s remains somewhat elusive although – as Titmuss pointed out – marriage had never been so popular in statistical terms as it was in the post-war period. The image of marriage as an equal partnership may well have been very attractive, but the evidence which we have discussed suggests quite strongly that, in reality, it imposed particular pressures upon women. Picking up on the limits in Gorer's research, we suggest that there was a profound dissonance between the post-war ideology of companionate marriage in which the benefits were all on the husband's side, and the lived experience in which wives were striving, evidently not successfully, for a companionate marriage which worked to their advantage.

ACKNOWLEDGEMENTS

We should like to thank Susan White for her enthusiastic typing and David Morgan and Oliver Fulton for their critical comments.

REFERENCES

Birmingham Feminist History Group (1979) 'Feminism as Femininity in the Nineteen-Fifties?' *Feminist Review* 3.
Board of Education (1943) *Curriculum and Examinations in Secondary Schools* (Norwood Report), London: HMSO.
Bott, E. (1957) *Family and Social Network*, London: Tavistock.
Bowlby, J. (1952) *Maternal Care and Mental Health*, Geneva: World Health Organization.
Central Advisory Council for Education (1959) *15 to 18* (Crowther Report), London: HMSO.
Coates, K. and Silburn, R. (1971) *Poverty: The Forgotten Englishmen*, Harmondsworth: Penguin.
Delphy, C. (1984) *Close to Home*, London: Hutchinson.
Dennis, N., Henriques, F. and Slaughter, C. (1956) *Coal is our Life*, London: Tavistock.
Ferguson, A. (1989) *Blood at the Root: Motherhood, Sexuality and Male Dominance*, London: Pandora.
Fletcher, R. (1962) *Marriage and the Family in Britain*, Harmondsworth: Penguin.
Fyvel, T. (1961) *The Insecure Offenders*, London: Chatto & Windus (reprinted by Penguin in 1963).
Gorer, G. (1955) *Exploring English Character*, London: Cresset Press.
Hubback, E. (1947) *The Population of Britain*, London: Allen & Unwin.
Kinsey, A.C., Pomeroy, W.B., Martin, C.E. and Gebhard, P.H. (1953) *Sexual Behavior in the Human Female*, Philadelphia: Saunders.
Klein, J. (1965) *Samples from English Cultures*, vol. II, London: Routledge & Kegan Paul.
Mass Observation (1945) *Britain and Her Birthrate*, London: Advertising Services Guild.
Ministry of Education (1949) *Report of a Working Party on the Supply of Women Teachers*, London: HMSO.
—— (1960) *The Youth Service in England and Wales* (Albermarle Report), London: HMSO.
Newsom, J. (1948) *The Education of Girls*, London: Faber & Faber.

Parsons, T. and Bales, R. (1956) *Family: Socialisation and Interaction Process*, London: Routledge & Kegan Paul.

Patterson, S. (1963) *Dark Strangers: A Sociological Study of the Absorption of a Recent West Indian Migrant Group in Brixton, South London*, Bloomington: Indiana University Press.

Riley, D. (1983) *War in the Nursery. Theories of the Child and Mother*, London: Virago.

Rowntree, B.S. and Lavers, G.R. (1951) *English Life and Leisure*, London: Longman.

Royal Commission on Marriage and Divorce (RCMD) (1956) *Report*, Cmd. 9678, London: HMSO.

Royal Commission on Population (RCP) (1949) *Report*, Cmd. 7695, London: HMSO.

Smith, J.H. (1961) 'Managers and Married Women Workers', *British Journal of Sociology* 12: 12–22.

Spinley, B. (1953) *The Deprived and the Privileged*, London: Routledge & Kegan Paul.

Summerfield, P. (1984) *Women Workers in the Second World War. Production and Patriarchy in Conflict*, London: Croom Helm.

Thomas, G. (1948) *Women and Industry. An Inquiry into the Problem of Recruiting Women to Industry Carried Out for the Ministry of Labour and National Service, the Social Survey*, London: Central Office of Information.

Titmuss, R.M. (1958) *Essays on the Welfare State*, London: Unwin.

Townsend, P. (1954) 'Measuring poverty', *British Journal of Sociology* 5: 130–7.

Thane, P. (1982) *The Foundations of the Welfare State*, London: Longman.

Winnicott, D.W. (1957) *The Child and His Family: First Relationships*, London: Tavistock.

Willmott, P. and Young, M. (1960) *Family and Class in a London Suburb*, London: Routledge & Kegan Paul.

Young, M. and Willmott, P. (1957) *Family and Kinship in East London*, London: Routledge & Kegan Paul (reprinted by Penguin 1962).

—— (1973) *The Symmetrical Family*, London: Routledge & Kegan Paul.

2 Sex and marriage in the 1960s and 1970s[1]

Martin P.M. Richards and B. Jane Elliott

Whether it is seen positively or negatively, there is a widespread view that the 1960s was a period of rapid change, if not a revolution, in attitudes and behaviour related to sex and marriage. It is the purpose of this chapter to discuss some of the evidence on which such a view might be founded. Our conclusion is not a straightforward one because, though there has certainly been change, it is very hard to pin down because of the lack of evidence. We have few studies to go on and there are questions about their validity. Sex and marriage, though important in the lives of most of us, are the epitome of what we hold to be private. As Christopher Lasch (1977) has remarked, 'most studies of the family tell us everything except the things we most want to know.' Considerable problems await anyone who tries to find out what they want to know about some aspects of our domestic lives. Methodological questions will form part of our discussion and, amongst other things, we will suggest that there have been important changes in the relationship of the researcher and the researched which not only affect the validity of studies, but show interesting parallels with the relationship between married partners. As well as drawing on surveys of married people, we will be using evidence from the discussions of the agony aunt of one well-known women's magazine.

Many features of post-war marriage in Britain can be seen in the family life that evolved for middle-class households during the economic changes and religious revivals of the late eighteenth and early nineteenth centuries (Davidoff and Hall 1987). Central to family life of that period was the notion of domesticity and the separation of the world of home, women and children from that of paid work, labour and employment. By the early decades of the twentieth century, the ideal of the companionate marriage became more strongly expressed (Braby, n.d.; Lindsey and Evans 1928). This stressed friendship and a shared domestic and emotional life for husband and wife. As we saw in Chapter 1, the notion of a companionate marriage is a complex one requiring careful analysis (see also Harris 1983).

Here we will be concentrating on aspects that concern a couple's sexual relationships: within the marriage, before and outside it. Our focus is a narrow one; we will not be concerned with the broader economic, legal, social and ideological aspects of the period. Important changes occurred on all these fronts which are discussed in Weeks' (1981) account of 'The Permissive Moment'.

STUDIES OF MARRIAGE AND SEXUAL DIVISIONS

Through the 1960s and 1970s the slow march towards the more companionate marriage continued. The values of closeness, an intense emotional relationship and shared lives were increasingly strongly found in investigations of marriage, especially middle-class marriage. Much of this work took its theme from Bott's (1957) distinction between the segregated conjugal roles (more typical of working-class marriage) and the joint roles (more characteristic of middle-class couples). The notion of joint roles where couples have less segregation of their activities in the home and tend to share interests and social life and spend much of their leisure time together embodies much of the idea of the companionate marriage. A number of studies through the post-war period suggest that features of the companionate marriage were becoming more widespread and could be found increasingly in working-class samples (Young and Willmott 1957; Rosser and Harris 1965; Goldthorpe *et al.* 1968), though as Finch and Summerfield show in the previous chapter, this argument is not without its problems. For some, this movement towards more companionate marriage was seen as an, albeit incomplete, movement towards equality in marriage. However, as Harris (1983) points out, and as the more recent studies illustrate (Pahl and Pahl 1971; Edgell 1980; Komtar 1989; Thompson and Walker 1989), it is crucial to make some conceptual distinctions here. The division of labour, between employment and home, has shifted little and contemporary married life consists of variations around the traditional themes of men out at work and women continuing to take the major share of child care and domestic responsibilities. Men may be more engaged in domestic activities so that marital roles may have become more similar but these must be distinguished carefully from the sexual division of labour. Despite (or including) the examples of dual career marriages (e.g. Rapoport and Rapoport 1971, 1976), the sexual division of labour produces inequality in marriage which is usually legitimated by gender ideologies. So within marriage the subordinate position of women may be interpreted as an adaptation to the demands made by the occupational activity of the man who remains the major breadwinner. So at the same time as great emphasis was being placed on the domestic closeness of the couple, their shared conjugal life and time spent together, studies like the Pahls' of managers and their wives show that the very strong orientation towards the work of the husbands and the acceptance of this by their wives forces a division of roles in the home. The wives could either attempt to participate in the husband's work life in order to maintain closeness, retreat into a segregated complementary domestic role or seek an independent role outside the family. So, at least if we accept Harris's (1983) reasoned interpretation of these studies, the position in the 1960s and 1970s is one of deep tensions. Marriages might start with strongly held attitudes about a shared domestic life and closeness and these attitudes may be relatively easily sustained in the early, generally childless, years when both are employed outside the home. But as work demands grow on the husband and the wife is increasingly likely to be at home and preoccupied by child care, the role segregation becomes more marked.

These values are well illustrated by Gorer's (1971) survey, conducted in 1969, which showed that 'comradeship, doing things together' was held to be the most important thing respondents think make for a happy marriage, followed by 'give-and-take, consideration' and 'discussing things, understanding'; while 'neglect, bad communication, spouse going out' was the factor held most likely to wreck a marriage. Comradeship was much lower on the list in Gorer's previous survey (1955).

COMPANIONATE MARRIAGE IN THE PROBLEM PAGES

The letters and advice on 'Mary Grant's' problem page in *Woman's Own* magazine show a similar shift during the 1960s and 1970s towards emphasising the importance for married couples of talking things over and sharing and understanding each other's feelings, a trend mirrored in the sociological world by the work of the phenomenologists who analysed marriage as a socially constructed, shared reality in which mutual conversation is central (Berger and Kellner 1970). Although letters are edited to be brief, and contain only the outline of the problem rather than a detailed description of a marital relationship, the advice that readers are offered, and the issues which they identify to be problems, can often give us an insight into some of the changes in the values and expectations held about marriage during the 1960s and 1970s.

In the 1970s there is a marked emphasis on talking things through and understanding each other's motivations and behaviour, which is largely absent in the 1960s advice. For example, in 1964 a woman who had been married for three years and had a baby wrote to Mary Grant complaining that her husband refused to give her any housekeeping money, which caused rows. The reader ended the letter by asking how she would stand if she left her husband. The printed reply advised her to refer to an older person and ask them to point out to her husband how important it was for him to give her money. Mary Grant also commented: 'how sad it is that you've reached the stage of wanting to leave each other over a problem that should never be a background for a clash of wills between husband and wife'. This contrasts with the response to a letter which appeared on Mary Grant's problem page in May 1975:

> My husband has been fined for having sex with a girl of 15. He actually had an affair with her lasting for 6 months and believed her to be 18. After 22 years of married happiness it's all beyond my understanding. Would I be right to leave him?

Answer

> It might be the right answer to this crisis and it might not. You can't possibly know without trying to understand why he was unfaithful to you.
>
> Don't try to worry it all out in your head: talk about it with him and work out whether you really would be happier apart, not whether it is right or wrong in my book or anyone else's.

Although it may be argued that this second letter presents a very different problem, and it is this that elicits the rather different type of advice, we would suggest that this example exhibits a clear change in the approach to solving marital difficulties. It is interesting that in response to the first letter the reader is not advised to confront her husband directly but rather to appeal to an outside authority figure to sort out the problem, and altogether the tone of the advice is very authoritarian and prescriptive. As a direct contrast the reply given in the 1970s explicitly refuses to make a judgement about what is 'right or wrong' but encourages the couple to reach their own decision by tackling the problem and discussing a solution together. This new emphasis on the importance of communication in marriage is perfectly illustrated by a 'Mary Grant Special' entitled 'How to talk it over with your husband' which appeared on 12 July 1975. The article was introduced by a short paragraph in bold type:

> What do you suppose is the biggest marriage problem of all? No, it's not money, sex, nagging, in-laws, violence or infidelity. It's not being able to talk over any of these things with the person you love and live with.

The article continued by saying:

Marriage is changing. These days it's more about needs and feelings than about the rules, rights and duties of being a husband and wife. This means that we expect a great deal more from the partnership in emotional terms.

Thus communication and sharing are not only new solutions to the difficulties partners experience in their marital relationship, but lack of communication and insensitivity to the other's needs and feelings can in turn be seen as the new marital problems. A further letter published in June 1975 has no parallel in the 1960s:

We've been married four years and have a daughter aged two. I love my husband but I can't get through to him at a deep level – he just won't let me get that close. I feel secure, he's a good man and I don't want to hurt him. But I need a deeper relationship: this is not enough for a lifetime. Should I break away now so that I'm free to meet someone to really love?

Mary Grant replied:

Seems to me you are looking for an ideal kind of love and I'm afraid it's very rare. It isn't a quick magic thing, either – it can take almost a lifetime to build. So if a deeper relationship is possible for you, it is in your marriage, waiting to be developed over the years ahead.

This ideal of a 'deep' marital relationship was not only to be based on husband and wife talking and discussing their problems, however. The 1960s and 1970s were a period when sexual communication between partners was also thought to be of great importance.

SEX IN MARRIAGE

A strong theme in most of the advice books and other sources of the 1960s onwards is that sex is part of marriage where openness, sharing (including the mutual orgasm) and closeness have a particular value (see also Cancian and Gordon 1988). Gorer's evidence is generally in line with at least a small shift in this general direction. Between 1955 and 1969 the number of men and women who said that 'sexual love' was important in marriage increased. And there was a decline in stereotyped views about sexuality. But perhaps the most interesting difference between the two surveys was in the questions that Gorer asked. Gorer states that in 1950 he was not allowed to ask a question about female orgasm because the editor thought that it might cause unnecessary offence or would be too embarrassing for the young women coding the questionnaires. In pilot work for the second survey he found that the word 'orgasm' was not recognised by 'quite a number' of respondents so in the end he asked 'when a man and woman are making love, do you think that women have a real physical climax to the act of love-making in the same way as men?' To this 77 per cent of the men and 59 per cent of the women said yes. The inclusion of this question in the later survey is important evidence of a change in the climate of what can be discussed and referred to in research.

A parallel shift in the way that sexual matters were discussed can be traced in the letters of the *Woman's Own* problem page. Sexual problems in marriage form a recurrent theme which readers ask for advice about throughout the 1950s, 1960s and 1970s. In 1955 the avoidance of the word sex, and the variety of euphemisms which are used to replace it is striking. Phrases such as 'the intimate side of married life' and 'married in name only' are used by the authors of the letters, while the most explicit references to sexual intercourse term it 'love-making'. In her replies Mary Grant shows a similar reticence about referring directly to sexual intercourse. She uses phrases like 'an important part of marriage', 'physical love' and 'intimate love-making'. By 1965 the vocabulary used had changed dramatically. A 30-year-old woman who said she was a virgin but had experienced petting before she got married one year previously, wrote: 'I'm very depressed about the physical side as, although I enjoy the preliminaries, actual intercourse means nothing to me.' Mary Grant replies in similarly explicit terms: 'It sounds as if through petting experiences, you've got so used to stopping short of intercourse that this inhibition has carried through to marriage' (17 April 1965). As we might expect, this open use of language when discussing sex continues throughout the 1960s and 1970s.

The increasing importance attached to sexual intercourse as a method of communication between husband and wife can perhaps best be illustrated by comparing two letters expressing essentially the same sexual problem, and the advice they received in 1955 and 1980. In 1955 a woman who had been married for fourteen years wrote:

> The intimate side of marriage does not appeal to me at all and I rarely allow him to make love to me.

Mary Grant replied:

> Your husband has a legitimate grievance. However good you are in other ways you are failing in part of your duty towards him.

This rather unsympathetic response and the notion that sex is a duty that a married woman should perform without enjoying it contrasts with the reply given to a woman who wrote in 1980 explaining that after twelve years of marriage she had never been able to relax enough to have sexual intercourse and asking about the possibilities of artificial insemination. Mary Grant replied:

> It would be a tragedy if you chased after these methods of conception . . . you and your husband need sexual intercourse as an expression of your whole selves and of your love for each other.

An emphasis on the emotional importance of sex can also be found in articles in the *Family Doctor* publication *Getting Married*, which was produced annually as an advice booklet for young couples. Each yearly issue typically contained an article on the sexual side of married life. During the 1960s, a substantial part of this article was devoted to explaining the basic anatomical facts about sexual intercourse, information was offered about contraception and practical hints were also given such as keeping a box of tissues by the side of the bed. In the early 1970s, these articles began to put far more emphasis on the emotional/spiritual aspects of sexuality as opposed to the purely physical side. For example, in a 1971 article entitled *And So To Bed* the author, Dr Mary Mason Jones, makes statements such as:

> This (sexual) urge is not only physical, but in marriage is bound up with feelings of affection for and tenderness towards his wife. An erection is after all proof positive of his warm feelings towards her.

It is interesting here that it is specifically sex *within* marriage which is imbued with an emotional content, and also that the author goes so far as to attribute what is usually acknowledged as a purely physiological response to sexual arousal, namely an erection, to 'warm feelings'. The author returns to the theme of the emotional value of sex again, at the end of the article – this time in relation to the man's physiological wellbeing:

> Many a husband feels particularly vulnerable after the birth of a child, and a wife, by responding warmly to her husband's lovemaking, will reassure him of his pride of place in her affections.

SEX BEFORE MARRIAGE

There is a broadly consistent pattern through all the research in Britain and in the USA which shows that successive post-war generations are more likely to have sex before marriage, are more likely to have sex before marriage with partners other than the one they eventually marry, and are more likely to regard premarital sex positively. In Gorer's 1969 sample, 26 per cent of the men and 63 per cent of the women said they were virgins at their marriage and 20 per cent of men and 25 per cent of women married their only premarital partner. Twenty-seven per cent of the men and 49 per cent of the women were against sexual experience before marriage for a young man and 43 per cent of the men and 68 per cent of the women in the case of a woman, again emphasising a continuing double standard. Reporting premarital sexual experience and seeing it in positive terms was much more common amongst informants born after the Second World War. Equally this was a topic – both for attitudes and reported experience – where there was a good deal of change from the situation twenty years earlier. But interestingly enough, those aged under 24 in 1950 and between 35 and 45 in 1969 hardly modified their attitudes at all, suggesting that change is confined to the younger members of each generation.

As we have said, Gorer's results are part of a general pattern which is seen in other data and which can be traced back at least to the turn of the century. Chesser (1956) in his sample of English women, found a steady rise in numbers reporting premarital sex with decade of birth – 19 per cent pre-1904, 36 per cent 1904–14, 39 per cent 1914–24, 43 per cent 1924–34. A similar trend, but with higher figures, is reported by Kinsey *et al.* (1953) from the USA. American data demonstrated a continuing rise in these figures throughout the 1960s and 1970s (Ball and Coughey 1980) and a corresponding increase in positive attitudes towards premarital sex. Gallup surveys in 1969 reported 32 per cent of Americans approved of premarital sex, compared with 52 per cent in 1973. In 1979 a survey of 15–16-year-old Americans found 12 per cent thought a boy and 17 per cent a girl should be a virgin at marriage (Hass 1979; see also Thornton 1989). In England 75 per cent of women marrying between 1971 and 1975 reported they had sex before marriage (Dunnell 1976).

The change in attitudes towards premarital sex as expressed in the pages of *Woman's Own* can be easily traced by looking at the stream of letters from young single people who want to go on holiday with their boyfriend/ girlfriend, but whose parents forbid it. In 1955 a woman in her early twenties writes because she has been 'courting a very nice man for over a year' and he wants her to take a holiday with him and meet his family; the problem is that this man's mother is dead and so the household is entirely male. The author of the letter writes: 'My mother thinks it would be improper if I were to sleep in the house unchaperoned.' Mary Grant makes the practical suggestion that she could ask her fiancé to arrange for another woman to be there, and in response to the mother's concern writes: 'She knows that even in these modern days, such a situation is likely to cause speculation' (19 May 1955). It is interesting that in this case the presence of other male relatives in the same house is viewed as not sufficient to protect the good name of the author of the letter, and also that she herself displays no desire for anything but a completely chaste relationship. Only five years later (9 April 1960) a very different letter on the same subject was published:

> My boyfriend and I hope to become engaged on my 19th birthday this summer. We want to go away together for our holiday, but my mother says it is contrary to all she was ever taught. What do you think? Both my boyfriend and I have very strong principles and she does not doubt that we can be trusted.

This 18-year-old gets a much more permissive response:

> Your mother finds it difficult to realize how much times have changed since she was your age: when she was a girl it would have been unthinkable for a young couple to go away alone together. But times have changed and it is becoming more and more common for engaged couples to spend a holiday together. Is it possible for you to go with a party? Then your mother would probably be quite happy about the holiday.

Although at first reading this letter and its response appear to be dramatically more permissive than the 1955 letter, it should be noted that the letter implies that the writer has no intention of sleeping with her fiancé, and the reply appears to only sanction engaged couples spending a holiday together. In 1970 an even younger girl (she is nearly 17) writes with the same problem and receives substantially the same answer, i.e. reach a compromise with your parents by going with friends. The interesting point to note about the advice that was given in 1970 is that it started with the sentence: 'This isn't really a matter of sense or universal rules, but of how each individual family feels about this.' This is a clear illustration of how advice changed from being prescriptive to discussing the problem in a way that would enable 'the client' to decide upon a solution for him or herself. It is not until 1975 that such a letter received an answer which unequivocally sanctions premarital intercourse. Mary Grant writes: 'There's no reason at all why you shouldn't go if you and your boyfriend want to' (26 April 1975), and goes on to advise that they should not make unrealistic promises of chastity but should make sure that they take precautions. Thus in the space of twenty years we can trace a clear progression from when sleeping in a house with a man you were courting, without another woman on the premises was seen as wrong, to premarital sex being seen as virtually inevitable. But we should remember even at the end of the decade that for many, sex continues to be related to an eventual marriage. In Mansfield and

Collard's (1988) study of London couples marrying in the later 1970s, while half the newly-weds reported starting a sexual relationship with the eventual spouse before 'committing' themselves, a third began at or after the decision to marry or get engaged.

While there are undoubtedly variations according to religion, community, geography and ethnic background, it seems a reasonable conclusion to say that sex before marriage is now a norm. Though the increase began a lot earlier, it seems likely that it was during the 1960s and 1970s that it became acceptable to the majority and was established as a norm, at least for those who regarded their relationship as a 'committed' one. Doubtless the existence of reliable contraception in the form of the pill and abortion from the 1970s onwards played a part in making these trends more acceptable. The issue of commitment is clearly important to some as Mansfield and Collard's study showed; indeed it is interesting to note that a number of couples in this study tried to mislead the researchers in early interviews by claiming the beginning of their sexual relationship post-dated a definite commitment to marriage when this was not in fact the case (Mansfield and Collard 1988).

EXTRAMARITAL SEX

If the changes in attitudes and sexual behaviour before marriage were to be represented as part of a general liberalisation of sexual attitudes, we might expect to find parallel trends in attitudes towards sex outside marriage. Indeed, while it is not difficult to find marriage manuals which advocate 'open' marriage of one kind or another (e.g. O'Neill and O'Neill 1972), there is little evidence of rising rates of extramarital sex, according to surveys from the USA (Macklin 1987; Hite 1987; Blumstein & Schwartz 1983) or the few fragments we have from Britain (Gorer 1971; Lawson 1988). But in contrast to the evidence of a slow rise in incidence, surveys of attitudes show a very different pattern. Samples of Americans through the 1960s, 1970s and 1980s show that the vast majority disapprove of all extramarital sex (Macklin 1987). Recent British data is equally clear and consistent on the matter (Gorer 1971; Jowell *et al.* 1988).

In Gorer's (1971) survey he makes a clear distinction between 'Fidelity and casual adultery' (Chapter 7) and 'Serious adultery, separation and divorce' (Chapter 8). It is interesting to note that while the questions about serious adultery 'If a wife/husband finds her husband/his wife having an affair with another woman/man, what should she/he do?' were also asked twenty years earlier in *Exploring English Character* (Gorer 1955), the question about casual adultery 'Now that the pill provides absolute safety, do you think faithfulness is or is not as important as ever in a marriage?'

was not asked in the earlier survey. However, although the asking of this question about casual adultery may in itself be seen as an indication of a change in the relationship between sex, love and marriage, the answers to the question demonstrate the high premium that people still attached to fidelity in 1970. Eighty-four per cent of men said, yes, faithfulness is as important as ever in a marriage and 7 per cent said, yes, emphatically, while among women 82 per cent said, yes, and 10 per cent said, yes, emphatically. This question unfortunately has several different issues compounded within it; Gorer is asking his respondents about the effect of the pill on morality and the importance of faithfulness in comparison to its importance some time in the past. In answer to the more straightforward questions 'Do you think that when you get married a husband/wife should be faithful for the rest of his/her married life?' about 90 per cent of both women and men said yes, whether the question was about husbands' fidelity, or wives' fidelity. Later surveys show this percentage rising further (Jowell *et al.* 1987). American data seems to follow similar trends but there are changes in the wording of questions over time which complicate interpretations (Thornton 1989).

In contrast to the letters on premarital sex, it is interesting to note the lack of letters on the *Woman's Own* problem page during the 1960s or 1970s in which readers ask Mary Grant to condone their own extramarital relationships. Letters about infidelity may be broadly categorised into three different types. First, letters from wives who are being unfaithful and want advice as to whether to leave their husbands; second, letters from wives who have had an extramarital relationship and cannot decide whether or not to tell their husbands; and third, letters from wives whose husbands are being unfaithful and who do not know what to do about it. In other words, the letters about infidelity convey a belief that extramarital relationships threaten marriage. The content of these letters changes very little over the 1960s and 1970s, although the tone of the advice on this subject in the 1960s is rather more prescriptive and unsympathetic than in the 1970s. For example, in 1965 a woman wrote saying: 'My husband fell in love with another woman and was cold with me for several weeks.' She goes on to explain that although she has forgiven him: 'I just can't forget the hurt of those few weeks.' In the printed reply, Mary Grant writes: 'Just as your husband pulled himself together for the sake of your marriage, it's your turn to do the same.' Five years later (3 May 1970) the problem page contained a letter with essentially an identical story:

> I have been married for three years and my husband has just confessed that he has been unfaithful to me. He says he realizes his mistake and asks me to forgive him. Do you think I should?

The advice printed after this letter is more analytical and less judgemental, encouraging the woman to make her own decision as to what to do:

There really is no 'should' or 'should not' about this – clearly you can only forgive him if you truly understand why he did this . . . since husbands and wives are human and do make mistakes, this under-standing is called for many times in a marriage if it is to be a really happy one.

Although the tone of this advice is not heavily moralistic it is interesting to note that infidelity is clearly seen as a 'mistake', and even if such behaviour may be understood and forgiven, it is certainly not encouraged or tolerated.

Indeed, there is some evidence to suggest that infidelity (particularly on the part of the husband) was more likely to be tolerated and seen as less of a threat to marriage in the 1950s and early 1960s than in the 1970s. In 1963 (6 April) a woman who describes herself as having been happily married for some years wrote: 'Now my husband says he is in love with his secretary.' Mary Grant says: 'I think your husband is under the spell of an infatuation which will pass in time and all you can do is wait patiently until it does.' Similarly, in 1955, a woman in her mid-fifties who writes explain-ing that she has found out that her husband has been unfaithful for some time and asks: 'Is it best to keep quiet or not?' is told: 'Men of this age often feel a compulsion to have a fling before age finally engulfs them', and is advised not to confront him because the affair will probably die a natural death.

Two points seem very significant about this advice on extramarital sex. While the phenomenon seems relatively common and probably increas-ingly so, attitudes towards it seem to have become more negative. The pattern is quite unlike that for sex before marriage where negative attitudes and sanctions have relaxed as the practice has become more general. The contrast between these two patterns certainly suggests that there is no simple process of sexual liberalisation whether we see that as a long, slow change or more sudden 'revolution' in the 1960s and 1970s. We will return later to the question of the explanation we might offer for the contrasting pattern of premarital and extramarital sex.

CHANGING AGENDAS AND RESEARCH

The advice literature and, more generally, discussions of sexuality and relationships in the media became much more open and uninhibited through the 1960s and 1970s. Discussions reflect a greater variety of sexual activities, a plurality of desires and practices, and generally suggest that provided neither you nor your partner are married to anyone else, more or less anything goes. The discussion has moved far beyond the physiological and anatomical concerns of the advice books of the 1950s and is now much more concerned with feelings and the idea that the seat of sexuality is the head rather than the genitals. This shift is well illustrated by recent books about sexual fantasies (e.g. Friday 1974, 1980). It seems a reasonable assumption that as marriage has become more companionate, the emphasis on closeness, shared experience and communication has meant that couples have talked more about sex, among other things, and that the wide availability of a great variety of writing about sexuality has stimulated these conversations and has provided a wider agenda and vocabulary for them. From this it seems also reasonable to assume that couples have a better knowledge of each other's sexual desires and feelings than they did a generation ago. Both are also more likely to come to their marriage (or other sexual relationships) with more experience of other partners and so with a better appreciation of the variety of needs, feelings and possibilities. One of the many factors that have doubtless driven this process forward in the post-war years has been the research on sex. Kinsey was probably of crucial importance, despite the way his research was firmly rooted in the physiological tradition. His surveys were taken as evidence that activities like masturbation or premarital 'coitus' were extremely common, much commoner than was generally considered, as reactions to his publications demonstrated. The 'English Kinsey', the survey by Chesser (1956) and his collaborators, had rather less impact partly because Kinsey had already stolen the thunder and partly because Chesser avoided most of the more unconventional areas of sexuality.

As well as seeing the research as part of a process that widens sexual horizons, it is also a product of those wider horizons in at least two senses. The first is the extent to which researchers feel able to formulate and use questions about particular aspects of sexuality. An example of this we pointed out earlier is Gorer's avoidance of questions about orgasm in his first survey. Researchers, just like participants in sexual activities, may feel that there are topics they are not able to mention. A striking example here is extramarital relations: at least according to the published reports, none of the recent studies of marriage in Britain have asked anything at all about other sexual relations despite their theoretical concerns with commitment and exclusiveness.

The second sense in which we may consider the effects of general openness or otherwise about sexuality, concerns the relationship between researcher and subject and the extent to which subjects are prepared to reveal something to their questioners. How do we know they are telling the truth?

So far in our discussion, we have taken the figures provided by the various research surveys at their face value. However, there are many questions about the validity of their results and the representativeness of their samples. Some studies, such as Gorer's (1955, 1971), attempt to sample a defined population (in this case defined by the electoral roll) but encounter a significant refusal rate – often 20 per cent or more. Others distribute questionnaires to a particular population and analyse what comes back; for instance, Chesser distributed questionnaires via sympathetic GPs but, as in most studies of this kind, a target population was not defined so it is not possible to calculate a response rate or indeed to be definite about the population that the respondents are drawn from. Other techniques include the 'snowball' approach employed by Kinsey. Again, these techniques make the definition of any target population impossible but by comparing the demographic make-up of the sample with the population at large some kind of comparison may be made and statistical adjustment is possible. But all the techniques that have been employed leave major uncertainties about representativeness. With surveys like Gorer's we cannot know how far those who refused to take part may have been similar to those who did, or with Kinsey, how typical his rather middle-class volunteers may have been. Most commentators have assumed that there are likely to be significant differences but it is anyone's guess how distorted the figures may be.

Turning to the relationship between researcher and subject: how far can we be sure that the researcher has obtained an accurate account from the subject? Most researchers make the reasonable assumption that subjects may minimise their accounts of socially disapproved activities and most take what steps they can to reduce such distortion by the obvious means – asking questions using terminology that they believe is familiar to the respondent, ensuring confidentiality, attempting to build good 'rapport' and so on. Is it possible to judge how successful such techniques are? It is important to attempt to establish the validity of findings in order to establish the case we have been putting forward. If it is true that over the decades since the last war there has been a decrease in the general disapproval of premarital sex, the increasing figures for its incidence which studies report may simply represent an increasing confidence and honesty among respondents who have gradually felt able to reveal more to researchers. So the increase might be non-existent, simply an artifact of a changing relationship between researcher and researched. Like couples, a more companionate relationship between researcher and researched may have allowed a greater confiding of all but the great taboo of extramarital relationships.

Many of the studies we have quoted provide internal evidence of underreporting of some activities. Kinsey, for example, provides a long discussion of the validity and reliability of his results.[2] One of his tactics to try to establish credibility was to re-interview subjects some two to three years after the initial interview. A comparison of the two interviews shows differences, especially in the reported frequencies of activities. But most differences in the reported incidence of activities are in the direction of higher rates being described at the second interview – a sign of growing confidence among subjects perhaps. Some of Kinsey's figures are very difficult to account for except by assuming they were a product of the taboos of the time. For example, very low figures for sexual abuse – low by comparison with more recent surveys – and near complete absence of reports of abuse within the family seem much more likely to be the result of what respondents felt able to discuss than a radical change in frequency and nature of sexual abuse. Also we might suggest that many of the patterns of social-class difference that Kinsey and subsequent researchers report may say more about the shared culture of researcher and middle-class informants than variation in sexual activities.

CONCLUSIONS

While it is often believed that during the 1960s there was a 'sexual revolution' which marked a sudden change in marital and sexual behaviour and attitudes, the evidence we have presented suggests that rather there has been a slow shift throughout the post-war decades which represents a continuation of trends that can be traced back well into the last century. But as we have also tried to show, our knowledge of these matters is very limited. The available surveys suffer from a number of methodological difficulties and it is often hard to know to what extent they may chart changes in what people do rather than shifts in what they are prepared to discuss with researchers.

Marriage has become more companionate and close. Heterosexual couples, especially in the middle classes, put a high premium on shared values, the ability to communicate with one another and a minimum of role separation. Whether or not such values are fulfilled in practice, is of course another matter. There is abundant evidence that women, especially, are likely to seek closeness and shared understanding and their high expectations are not always met.

Attitudes towards sexual relationships before marriage appear to have changed steadily throughout the post-war years so that now there is a general expectation that most men and women will have had sexual relationships before they marry and for a growing minority of people marriage will be preceded by cohabitation (e.g. Christensen and Gregg 1970; Macklin 1987; Haskey and Kiernan 1989). Given the very wide acceptance of sex before marriage, it seems likely that the survey data on this topic is now relatively accurate – the behaviour carries little or no stigma, indeed may be seen in positive terms, and most people are willing to tell researchers what they have done or at least most of it. But when we turn to some other aspects of sexuality, the picture is very different, indicating the complexity of the changes and the inadequacy of any simple notion of sexual revolution or general liberalisation – a point made in an earlier discussion by Weeks (1981).

All but a very small minority of married people express negative attitudes towards extramarital sexual relationships (e.g. Blumstein & Schwartz 1983; Jowell *et al.* 1987, 1988). There is little sign that such attitudes are becoming less widely held; if anything the reverse is true.

Our argument is that the strength of such attitudes has grown with the notion of companionate marriage. Or as others would put it, as love becomes more central in marriage, marriage becomes more exclusive (Douglas and Atwell 1988). But here there would appear to be a very wide gap between attitudes and behaviour. We need to be cautious about the accuracy of available survey evidence, as the strong negative attitudes are likely to lead to under-reporting. But we feel it is reasonable to suggest that in recent decades sexual relationships outside marriage are now the experience of the majority (see Blumstein and Schwartz 1983; Macklin 1987), so that we have a direct conflict between a behavioural norm of relationships outside marriage and a near universal disapproval of such behaviour – a conflict well exemplified by the comments of some individual informants in several surveys. Seventy per cent of the women in Hite's (1988) survey who had been married for more than five years said they have had or were having other relationships even though in almost all cases they 'believe in' monogamy. 'Strange, I believe in monogamy, but I am not monogamous.' Before discussing some of the consequences of this situation, we need to examine some of the reasons for it in a little more depth.

In a society where most people already have had sexual relationships before they begin one with the person they will marry, there is clearly a need to mark off the marriage relationship as being special, and to demonstrate commitment to it. In part, this may be achieved by the marriage itself, especially in a society where cohabitation carries very little stigma and may have financial and other advantages. Though cohabitation is becoming more frequent, for the great majority of those who have never married, it remains a prelude to marriage (though this may be rather different for the separated and divorced). Not only do most couples marry but a majority of them have a 'proper' religious wedding. The figures are far in excess of those who regularly attend church, indeed there must be a significant number of people for whom their own wedding must be one of the very few church services they have attended. Even when a marriage is not marked by a church wedding, it will usually be a very important social occasion for family and friends (Leonard 1980). Spending on wedding receptions and associated celebrations is growing and has produced a whole industry to provide the necessary goods and services.

In more emotional and personal terms, the commitment to the marriage is evidenced by the expressed love, the shared social life and leisure time and promise of sexual exclusivity. Askham (1984), developing notions put forward by Berger and Kellner (1970), has described marriage in terms of a balancing act between stability maintenance and identity upholding in which the needs of the former mean avoiding friendships and relationships that could threaten the marriage (see also Gerstel 1988). Despite all the discussions of sexually open marriage, all but a very small minority of couples in the United States and probably Britain too, commit themselves to a sexually monogamous marriage. In Mansfield and Collard's recent (1988) study of marriage in London, half the sample had sex together before they committed themselves to marriage and a further one-third said they began their sexual relationship at the time of commitment. This moment of commitment which the authors refer to as a 'passive engagement' signified the beginning of a moratorium on sexual activity with people other than their partner. This commitment not only serves to give meaning to the marriage, but guards against the increased threat that other relationships pose to a companionate marriage. As couples share more, emotionally and in every other way, the prospect of sharing any of the aspects of this with others outside the marriage becomes more difficult and threatening. There is the added threat that an extramarital relationship might also be a companionate one. Very significantly, among the minority of American couples who have described sexually open marriages there are often conditions that reduce the chances of the outside relationship becoming a close one – that the extramarital partner live a certain distance away, that the relationship should be terminated if love is involved, or that neither spouse should sleep with another partner on more than a single occasion. In short, the agreements try to ensure that the outside relationship is a 'purely' sexual one (Smith and Smith 1973).

As the idea of the companionate marriage has grown, the nature of typical extramarital partners has changed, at least for men. In the highly role-segregated, Victorian, middle-class marriage, men were likely to find their partners among women who were at some social distance to them (Richards 1987). Prostitution has declined as marriages became more companionate. By the end of the Second World War, while social distance might still play a part – boss and secretary, doctor and nurse – increasingly extramarital partners are likely to be the husband or wife next door. Not only can such affairs have all the companionate features of a marriage, but potentially they can become one, given ready access to divorce.

Given the possible threat to marital stability, the commitment to monogamy and the general social disapproval, why do married partners have other sexual relationships? Here the available research is not very helpful, as perhaps we might expect given the negative attitudes. Participants' explanations range widely: falling in love, a response to a bad marriage, a response to a good marriage, anger at spouse, curiosity, self-discovery, personal growth, lust and a need to boost self-confidence (see, for example, Hite 1988). While researchers have gradually given up explanations that deal entirely in terms of marital pathology (but see Strean 1980), few alternatives have been proposed. Attempts to differentiate in social and demographic terms between spouses who have or have not had other sexual relationships have largely failed (Macklin 1987). A rather different proposal is that there might be an incompatibility between marital equality and sexual satisfaction. Veroff and Feld (1971) argued that egalitarianism in companionate marriages might threaten a man's feeling of power and since they assume that male sexuality and power are closely linked, sexual adequacy may be impaired. But as Bernard (1972) points out, the evidence linking egalitarianism with sexual adequacy is weak. And of course there is also a need to make the further assumption that the response to sexual inadequacy that might arise in this way would be to seek sexual relationships elsewhere.

The fact that most spouses will have a variety of sexual experiences with a variety of partners before marriage seems likely to increase the chances that they may come to seek a similar variety after marriage. Correlations have been reported between numbers of partners reported before and after marriage (e.g. Kinsey *et al.* 1953). The growing emphasis on the need for an active, close and varied sexual relationship within marriage may have led some spouses to become less accepting of a slow decline into a domestic friendship over the years of marriage and more inclined to seek new and exciting sexual relationships elsewhere.

But, for whatever reason, most spouses probably have other sexual relationships and, typically, they do not tell their spouse about it. As Blumstein and Schwartz (1983) put it, 'marriage makes couples more deceptive': here they were comparing married members of their sample with the single or cohabiting ones. The commitment to monogamy that marriage brings in a sharing companionate marriage leads to deception. As Hite's (1988) data suggests, the deception usually succeeds and most spouses neither know nor suspect what their partners have been up to. In this perhaps we find another parallel between the communication between spouses and between researcher and researched. As we have pointed out on p. 45, most recent research on marriage has ignored the issue of extramarital relationships. Similarly, this seems an issue that most spouses seem to wish to ignore in respect of their partners. Often, it seems, suspicions are not followed up. Spouses maintain the shared fiction of the monogamous marriage by not asking. Marital therapists seem also to take a similar position and may not pursue issues of third-party relationships unless these are brought up by the couple themselves. Some therapists may also share the commitment to openness and insist that any information that a spouse tells them in an individual session must be told to the marital partner.

One issue we have not commented on is that of gender. Are extramarital relationships as frequent for women as men? Here again we must be very cautious with the evidence, as double standards are as likely to apply in the reporting of behaviour as in its occurrence. The general view, at least among North American researchers, is that in recent decades rates for women have risen to approach those of men (Macklin 1987; Blumstein and Schwartz 1983). Such a trend seems not unlikely as ideas about equality in marriage are likely to apply outside it and will be aided by more material factors such as the greater opportunities afforded by employment outside the home and the availability of abortion and effective contraception. However, it is also likely that earlier research, such as that of Kinsey, not only underestimated the incidence of extramarital sexual relationships for both spouses but also exaggerated the difference in rates for men and women.

We still have very few studies of extramarital relationships (but see Lawson 1988; Strean 1980). The advent of the human immuno-deficiency virus (HIV) has exposed our ignorance here. To build an adequate model of the way the virus may spread through a community and how that spread may be best countered we need to have much better information about how the largest and probably most sexually active part of the heterosexual community behaves – in fact, information to match that which is becoming available for many communities of gay men. In Britain in 1989 a large-scale survey was piloted but was refused funding by the Prime Minister who was reported as saying that such research was an unnecessary invasion of privacy. Presumably her fear was that it might reveal a little too much about the ways in which Britain is not guided by 'Victorian values'. Perhaps closer attention to methodological issues might have convinced the Prime Minister that her fears may have been misplaced. If the argument of this chapter is at all correct, the powerful negative attitude towards extramarital sexual relationships is likely to ensure that such activities would be considerably under-reported by respondents. Thus it may prove very difficult to build up an adequate model of patterns of sexual relationships.

Such negative attitudes are much less strong among gay men and this coupled with their much higher perceived need to have accurate information to contain the spread of HIV infection means that the accuracy of surveys in that community is likely to be much higher than surveys involving the married heterosexual community.

What we reach then, is a view of marriage as containing a basic contradiction: a strong commitment to an exclusive and sharing relationship with a high value placed on communication, trust and openness, but at the same time, for many spouses, involvement in other relationships which necessitate deception. This leads us to question the idea that marriage has been transformed from an institution into a relationship. Marriage relationships are seen to be very different from other kinds of sexual relationship and this is a distinction which participants wish to maintain and to mark even more sharply than in the past. Certainly ideas about the nature of the marriage have changed and the ideals of the relationship between spouses have been transformed by the movement towards companionate marriage. This has given marriage a new precariousness which is reflected in the divorce rate which has grown in parallel with the development of the notion of companionate marriage (Phillips 1989). But, at least if we take the view of the social constructionists like Berger and Kellner (1970), it makes little theoretical sense to polarise the idea of marriage as either institution or relationship. Marriage is a social institution in which spouses build a relationship of a very particular kind. There are clearly defined social understandings about marriage. As Berger and Kellner (1970) argue, it is one of the few rites of passage that are still meaningful to most members of society, with the socially legitimated themes of 'romantic love, sexual fulfilment, self-discovery and self-realisation through love and sexuality with the nuclear family as the site for these processes'.

NOTES

1   We would like to thank Jill Brown and Sally Roberts for their help in the preparation of this chapter and members of the Child Care and Development Group for much helpful discussion. The first author would also like to thank the songwriters, musicians and singers of Music City for sustaining him while working on the chapter and for their stimulating and often original commentary on love, marriage and divorce.

2   Kinsey obviously felt much troubled by the fact that his accounts of sexual activity were 'second' hand. Colleagues later reported (Pomeroy 1967) that he had turned to direct observation towards the end of his career. But it is unclear whether he, like Masters and Johnson (1966), ever came to understand that the nature of private acts is transformed when they are performed in public.

REFERENCES

Askham, J. (1984) *Identity and Stability in Marriage*, Cambridge: Cambridge University Press.

Ball, R.R. and Coughey, K. (1980) 'Premarital sexual experience among college females 1958, 1968 and 1978', *Family Relations* 2 (9): 353–7.

Berger, P. and Kellner, H. (1970) 'Marriage and the construction of reality', in H.P. Dreitzel (ed.) *Patterns of Communicative Behavior*, Recent Sociology, no. 2, New York: Macmillan.

Bernard, J. (1972) *The Future of Marriage*, Harmondsworth: Penguin Books.

Blumstein, P. and Schwartz, P. (1983) *American Couples: Money, Work, Sex*, New York: McGraw-Hill.

Bott, E. (1957) *Family and Social Network*, London: Tavistock.

Braby, M.C. (n.d.) *Modern Marriage and How to Bear It*, London: T. Werner Laurie.

Cancian, F.M. and Gordon, S.L. (1988) 'Changing emotion norms in marriage: love and anger in U.S. women's magazines since 1900', *Gender and Society* 2: 308–42.

Chesser, E. (1956) *The Sexual, Marital and Family Relationships of the English Woman*, London: Hutchinson.

Christensen, H.T. and Gregg, C.F. (1970) 'Changing sex norms in America and Scandinavia', *Journal of Marriage and the Family* 32: 616–27.

Davidoff, L. and Hall, C. (1987) *Family Fortunes, Men and Women of the English Middle Class 1780–1850*, London: Hutchinson.

Douglas, J.D. and Atwell, F.C. (1988) *Love, Intimacy and Sex*, Newbury Park, Calif.: Sage.

Dunnell, K. (1976) *Family Formation*, London: HMSO.

Edgell, S.R. (1980) *Middle Class Couples*, London: Allen & Unwin.

Friday, N. (1974) *My Secret Garden*, New York: Pocket Books.

—— (1980) *Men in Love, New York: Delacorte*.

Gerstel, N. (1988) 'Divorce, gender and social integration', *Gender and Society* 2: 343–67.

Goldthorpe, J.H., Lockwood, D., Beckhoffer, F. and Platt, J. (1968) *The Affluent Worker: Industrial Attitudes and Behaviour*, Cambridge: Cambridge University Press.

Gorer, G. (1955) *Exploring English Character*, London: Cresset Press.

—— (1971) *Sex and Marriage in England Today*, London: Nelson.

Harris, C.C. (1983) *The Family and Industrial Society*, London: Allen & Unwin.

Haskey, J. and Kiernan, K. (1989) 'Cohabitation in Great Britain – characteristics and estimated numbers of cohabiting partners', *Population Trends*, no. 58, London: HMSO.

Hass, A. (1979) *Teenage Sexuality*, New York: Macmillan.

Hite, S. (1988) *Women and Love*, London: Penguin Books.

Jowell, R., Witherspoon, S. and Brook, L. (1987) *British Social Attitudes – the 4th report*, SCPR, Aldershot: Gower.

—— (1988) *British Social Attitudes – the 5th report*, SCPR, Gower:Aldershot.

Kinsey, A.C., Pomeroy, W.B., Martin, C.E. and Gebhard, P.H. (1953) *Sexual Behavior in the Human Female*, Philadelphia: Saunders.

Komtar, A. (1989) 'Hidden power in marriage', *Gender and Society* 3: 187–216.

Lasch, C. (1977) *Haven in a Heartless World, The Family Besieged*, New York: Basic Books.

Lawson, A. (1988) *Adultery, An Analysis of Love and Betrayal*, New York: Basic Books.

Leonard, D. (1980) *Sex and Generation: A Study of Courtship and Weddings*, London: Tavistock.

Lindsey, B.B. and Evans, W. (1928) *The Companionate Marriage*, London: Brentano's Ltd.

Macklin, E. (1987) 'Nontraditional family forms', in M. Sussman and S.K. Steinmetz (eds) *Handbook of Marriage and the Family*, New York: Plenum.

Mansfield, P. and Collard, J. (1988) *The Beginning of the Rest of Your Life? A Portrait of Newly-Wed Marriage*, London: Macmillan.

Masters, W.H. and Johnson, V.E. (1966) *The Human Sexual Response*, Boston: Little, Brown.

O'Neill, N. and O'Neill, G. (1972) *Open Marriage*, New York: Avon Books.

Pahl, J.M. and Pahl, R.E. (1971) *Managers and Their Wives*, London: Allen Lane; Penguin Books.

Phillips, R. (1989) *Putting Asunder – A History of Divorce in Western Society*, Cambridge: Cambridge University Press.

Pomeroy, W.B. (1967) 'The Masters-Johnson Report and the Kinsey Tradition', in R. Brecher and E. Brecher (eds) *An Analysis of Human Sexual Response*, London: Andre Deutsch.

Rapoport, R. and Rapoport, R.N. (1971) *Dual Career Families*, London: Robertson.

—— (1976) *Dual Career Families Re-examined*, London: Robertson.

Richards, M.P.M. (1987) 'Fatherhood, marriage and sexuality: some speculations on the English middle-class family', in C. Lewis and M. O'Brien (eds) *Reassessing Fatherhood: New Observations on Fathers and the Modern Family*, London: Sage.

Rosser, K.C. and Harris, C.C. (1965) *The Family and Social Change*, London: Routledge & Kegan Paul.

Smith, L.G. and Smith, J.R. (1973) 'Co-marital sex: the incorporation of extra-marital sex into the marriage relationship', in J. Zubin and J. Money (eds) *Contemporary Sexual Behavior: Critical Issues in the 1970s*, Baltimore: Johns Hopkins University Press.

Strean, H.S. (1980) *The Extramarital Affair*, New York: The Free Press.

Thompson, L. and Walker, A.J. (1989) 'Gender in families: women and men in marriage, work, and parenthood', *Journal of Marriage and the Family* 51: 845–71.

Thornton, A. (1989) 'Changing attitudes toward family issues in the United States', *Journal of Marriage and the Family* 51: 873–93.

Veroff, J. and Feld, S. (1971) *Marriage and Work in America*, New York: Van Nostrand-Reinhold.

Weeks, J. (1981) *Sex, Politics and Society. The Regulation of Sexuality since 1800*, London: Longman.

Young, M. and Wilmott, P. (1957) *Family and Kinship in East London*, London: Routledge & Kegan Paul (reprinted by Penguin 1962).

Zubin, J. and Money, J. (eds) (1973) *Contemporary Sexual Behavior: Critical Issues in the 1970s*, Baltimore: Johns Hopkins University Press.

3 Marriage in the 1980s
A new sense of realism?

Janet Finch and David Morgan

In turning to the third and most recent 'period' of this review of marriage and domestic life, we have chosen the concept of realism as our central theme. We shall explore the idea that domestic life in the 1980s was characterised by realism, and explore various dimensions of what that means. Inevitably, such a concept has to be handled in a fairly complex way if it is to make analytical sense. However, at its simplest, the theme of realism offers a sharp contrast with the previous two decades, as they are discussed in Richards and Elliott's chapter (Chapter 2, this volume), where the emphasis was on a new sense of openness about the possibilities for domestic relationships, backed up by a greater degree of sexual permissiveness. A sense of change in domestic relationships is also apparent in the 1940s and 1950s (see Finch and Summerfield, Chapter 1, this volume) although in a more muted form. By contrast, in the 1980s we see more of a sense of 'back to fundamentals'.

Of course we are not suggesting that there was a dramatic reversal around 1979/80 in the way people organised their lives, or even in the way in which most of us thought about marriage and other relationships. We are keenly aware of the essential artificiality of an approach which sees particular 'decades' characterised by specific social norms or ways of living. At the same time it is evident that, at least by the late 1980s, the terms of public discussion about family life were *not* predominantly concerned with ideas such as openness, choice, permissiveness or 'doing your own thing'. The demographic evidence (see Elliott, Chapter 4, this volume) shows that the institution of marriage had remained just as popular. For the majority of the population it had *not* apparently been replaced by other forms of relationship, based on informal rather than legal arrangements, as might perhaps have been expected if some of the ideas of the 1960s and 1970s had really taken root.

At the political level, the new emphasis upon the importance of marriage and family life was very apparent from the point at which a Conservative government was elected in 1979, and to some extent before this date. The new emphasis was embodied in some of the social-policy measures introduced in this decade, for example, in the field of social security (Smart 1987). We are not going to discuss this in detail, as the impact of the New-Right thinking on the family has been treated extensively elsewhere (see, for example, Fitzgerald 1983; David 1986). However, we do see this new political emphasis as reflecting one dimension of a new 'realism'. The view is articulated that there had been a lot of talk about permissiveness and rejecting conventional marriage, but that in reality the great majority of people had never really wavered from an adherence to conventional values and practices. This is expressed forcibly in the work of Anderson and Dawson (1986) who argued that the 'normal' family was 'popular but unrepresented'. By this they meant that, while active lobbying had put the needs, demands or life styles of single-parent families, gay couples, cohabitees or feminists to the front of public debate, the silent majority was continuing with the difficult business of living everyday family lives.

Thus in the 1980s the family was on the political agenda in a way which would not quite have been true of the earlier periods considered in this volume. Values associated with family life were highlighted as matters of public concern, but also the experience of family living was subject to a certain degree of public scrutiny. In this context, social researchers were also active in studying different dimensions of the domestic arena. In our discussion, we shall begin with their work and try to tease out some of the key themes which emerged from research in the 1980s, and then consider the question of how far the emphasis of research reflected the reality of marriage and domestic life during this period. In the course of this discussion, we fill out our key concept of 'realism', and show that it has a number of different dimensions as a way of characterising this decade.

'NO CHANGE': ADHERENCE TO CONVENTIONAL FAMILY VALUES?

We begin by examining that aspect of 'realism' raised by the New Right: the idea that most people have continued to adhere strongly to rather conventional values about marriage and the family and have tried to express them in their own lives. There is in fact a good deal of research evidence which would support this view, though it must be said that none of the studies to which we refer is written from a New-Right standpoint, or engages directly with the politics of this debate. It is also worth noting that these studies are mostly small-scale and locally based – a characteristic of much research on the family during this period.

None the less a number of quite disparate sociological studies published in the 1980s do contain evidence which points to continuities with the past, rather than to dramatic changes. Indeed, Jacqueline Burgoyne herself, in an article about family and domestic life in the post-war period published not long before she died, emphasised the importance of seeing the continuities. She took some popular assertions about the changing nature of family life – that men are no longer the main breadwinners and women the home-makers, that men commonly take a full share in domestic work and child care, that divorce and remarriage are undermining the stability of the 'normal' family – and subjected them to scrutiny informed by research data. She concluded that there was considerable potential for: 'disjunctures between assertions about the changing character of family life and the continuities in both beliefs and practice suggested by the available research-based data' (Burgoyne 1987:86).

In looking at the research evidence about marriage specifically in the 1980s, one theme which does emerge is that most people continued to hold in high regard the concept of a 'successful marriage' and were prepared to put considerable efforts into trying to achieve one. This message comes through clearly in various research studies on marriage which are actually very different in orientation and substantive focus. The way in which people apparently were thinking about successful marriages does indeed come through as rather conventional – certainly far removed from the openness and permissiveness which apparently characterised the preceding decade.

We shall refer briefly to five studies which, in very different ways, highlight the continuing importance of achieving a successful marriage. First, Janet Askham's (1984) meticulous and detailed study of twenty couples is concerned with the interiors of marriages and the way that they are managed. She portrays marriage as a balancing act in which both partners strive to retain their own identity and individuality yet, because this potentially pulls them apart, at the same time try to consolidate stability in their relationship. 'Successful' marriages are ones in which couples have managed to achieve a workable compromise between these two forces at work in their relationship and – as her study shows – both women and men put considerable emotional and practical effort into trying to achieve and sustain such compromises.

A common-sense way of expressing this key theme in Askham's work is that marriages need to be 'worked at' and that people mostly regard them as being worth working at. That message is also apparent in our second example, Mansfield and Collard's (1988) study of sixty-five newly-wed couples. These couples commonly held marriage in very high regard and they, especially the women, had strong expectations of the satisfactions which could be derived from it. For these couples, marriage is a relationship with a capital R, where they expect to find the ultimate intimacy, support and personal satisfaction.

The continuing high aspirations for marriage also come through in three other studies, in which the research focus is on marriages under stress. Brannen and Collard (1982), in a study of the way in which people seek help when they perceive their marriages to be in trouble, found that the areas in marriage most likely to be perceived as problematic were sexual compatibility on the one hand, and communication or demonstrativeness between the partners on the other. This underlines the high expectations which people apparently had of what marriage would offer them, and a consequent tendency to see the marriage as 'failing' if it was not providing these things. Burgoyne and Clark's (1984) work on stepfamilies makes a similar point in a different way. It documents the aspirations of people in second marriages to create the kind of close and fulfilling partnership which they perceived as constituting a good marriage, but which they had not quite pulled off the first time round. Even Lawson's research on adultery – a topic where one might expect respondents to reflect a rather low opinion of the married state – demonstrates that still it seems 'marriage is the safe place, adultery the dangerous one' (Lawson 1988: 310).

Thus sociological research on marriage in the 1980s placed a strong emphasis upon the centrality of marriage to most people's definition of a good life, including young people, and an image of the 'good marriage' which probably would have been quite easily recognised by their parents, if possibly not by their grandparents. To that extent the 'realism' of the New Right is justified. Yet alongside this emphasis on striving for a good marriage, research – including all the research cited in this section – has other stories to tell. Such research has opened up perspectives upon marriage and domestic life which force us to view it from a different angle and to make a different assessment of its meaning and significance. It betrays a 'realism' in some very different senses.

The following sections explore these other themes coming out of research in the 1980s, grouping them under four headings. Each has the effect of problematising the straightforward view of marriage and domestic life, as reflected in the work of the New Right and elsewhere, which sees them straightforwardly as providing life's ultimate satisfaction.

THE MATERIAL OF MARRIAGE

Much of the earlier work on marriage prior to and during the 1980s, therefore, laid considerable emphasis on the relational aspects. By 'relational' we mean an understanding of marriage that stresses the overriding importance of the interpersonal dynamics between the partners, the patterns

of communication between them and their sexualities. These understandings are not simply on the part of professionals with an interest in
family matters: they are also shared, as Mansfield and Collard's (1988)
study demonstrates, by many partners themselves. However, professional
understandings are also significant: a variety of influences may be seen as
having contributed to this understanding including the development of
marital, family and sexual therapies and sociological constructions of marriage as being 'egalitarian' or 'symmetrical'. The idea of marriage as *the*
Relationship implies at least some measure of equality between the partners. Berger and Kellner's theoretical exploration of the marital conversation proved to be widely influential during this period (Berger & Kellner
1964). Official recognition of this understanding of marriage came in a
Home Office sponsored working party's report on marriage guidance
(Working Party on Marriage Guidance 1979) which, while it recognised the
economic costs of divorce for both individuals and the nation as a whole,
gave particular endorsement to the perception of marriage in interpersonal
and relational terms.

Part of the so-called 'realism' of the 1980s might be a growing recognition on the part of social scientists of the economic dimension of marriage
and domestic life. In part, this recognition was prompted by the highlighting of particular economic problems associated with, for example,
teenage marriage, single-parent families and unemployment. Further, the
continuing and growing influence of feminist social research drew attention
to the economic significance of the unpaid labour performed by women
within the household. Marxisms and feminisms converged, combined and
sometimes contradicted in their analysis of domestic labour but what
remained was a recognition of the significance of this activity in terms of
effort, time and, in the broadest sense, economic value. Finally, such
debates also contributed to a growing focus on the household as an economic unit and a reconceptualisation and reformulation of the traditional
home/work divide. Best known here, perhaps, was the influence of Ray
Pahl (Pahl 1984) and ESRC-sponsored research into local labour markets
and economic life (Roberts *et al.* 1985). While such debates and approaches
did not replace understandings of domestic life in relational terms, they
certainly posed questions about the interconnections between the emotional
and the economic and constituted a major strand in the sociology of
marriage and the family in the Britain of the 1980s.

The growing focus on the economic dimensions of family living had a
variety of different but overlapping strands, many of them directly inspired
by the feminist critique of social scientific research and assumptions. Some
of the more specific contributions of feminism focusing upon the gendered
character of marriage and domestic life will be dealt with in the next

section; here we shall concentrate on the economic aspects while realising that, in practice, the two cannot be readily separated.

In the first place we may note a deepening sense of the complex and varied ways in which a wife was 'married to the job' (Finch 1983). By 1980 it was certainly no novelty to argue for the inadequacy of the 'male breadwinner' model (a model which stressed a clear sexual division of labour between men and women within the home) or the accompanying political demands in terms of the 'family wage' (e.g. Land 1980). Similarly, the incorporation of this model into functionalist and some Marxist theorising about the family in capitalist or industrial society had also been subjected to some severe criticism by this date. It was argued that there were strong affinities between the former which stressed the functional fit between the sexual division of labour and industrial society, and the latter which stressed how domestic labour contributed to the reproduction of capitalist social relations. Both were found defective. What remained to be explored were the various ways in which a wife was influenced by her husband's work even where she had no formal employment status of her own. This was not simply a matter of the husband's income; the occupational status of the husband often provided spatial and temporal parameters limiting the wife's spheres of activity. One obvious example here would be the various ways in which the geographical career moves on the part of the husband clearly had consequences for the other family members. Further, there were more direct ways in which the wife was incorporated into her husband's work reflected in the phenomenon of 'two for the price of one' that characterised some professionals (most notably, the clergy) and self-employed businessmen. Thus, in a variety of ways, the wife's 'role' in the household was rarely limited to the emotional or the 'expressive'; it had economic significance even where she did not directly earn a wage or a salary.

In the second place, there was a growing focus on the household, reflected in the variety of discussions and presentations of research that took place in the 'Resources within Household' group that met in London during the 1980s (Brannen and Wilson 1987). A variety of research considered the amount and kind of resources which all household members contributed to the household (and not simply the money income of the main breadwinner) and the ways in which these were managed and distributed. The aim was to open up the 'black box' of the household, to go beyond simply seeing the household as an undifferentiated unit in a wider social or economic system, and to explore the gendered economic processes that took place within that unit. Thus Jan Pahl argues for the importance of looking at the ways in which money was managed within the household (Pahl 1989). She discovered considerable variety and complexity in the ways in which earnings were managed within the household and the varying consequences of these patterns for decision making. Nevertheless, her study seemed to argue for continuities as well as for changes in the structures of economic power within the household. Another area which came to receive the attention of researchers was to do with the preparation and consumption of food within the home. Patterns of food consumption were also found to be influenced by considerations of gender (and age) and it may well be argued that in the preparation and distribution of food within the household we have a major illustration of the meeting of the economic and the emotional (Charles and Kerr 1988).

An area which has yet to be explored more comprehensively in this analysis of the economic significance of the household is the actual physical location of the home itself. In speaking about the home we are conventionally referring to both a physical location and a nexus of emotional interconnections. In the case of the former we are dealing with property relations which point to links between the household and the wider economic system (whether through the state or the private housing market or both) as well as to propertied relationships between the household members themselves. The nature and significance of these intrahousehold propertied relationships becomes apparent at times of marital break-up or divorce (Maclean 1987).

One specific area focusing upon the economic significance of the household has been to do with the impact of unemployment. Clearly there was no novelty in pointing out that male unemployment had consequences for other household members, both emotionally as well as economically. The classic unemployment studies of the 1930s demonstrated these multiple consequences of unemployment and their counterparts of the 1970s and 1980s continued this recognition. However, two newer themes were to emerge in some of the studies of the 1980s. In the first place there was a consideration of the impact of unemployment in the context of both the informal economy as well as the formal economy. Here, the general conclusion was that, contrary to some more optimistic predictions, there was no trade-off between loss of income and employment in the formal economy and increasing involvement in the informal economy (Pahl 1984). In the second place, there was a consideration of the impact of male unemployment on the sexual division of labour within the home. Again, more optimistic predictions based upon the recognition of increasing female labour-market participation and the possible differential impact of unemployment on men and women within particular labour markets seemed to suggest another kind of trade-off, this time within the household between men and women. However, while there would appear to be some local variations here, this optimistic prediction of some measure of role reversal does not seem to have been borne out by the facts. For a variety of reasons, often to do with the specific characteristics of local labour markets, unemployed men are not to be found increasing their participation in domestic and parental tasks to any significant extent (Harris and Morris 1986; McKee and Bell 1985; Morris 1985a, b). Again, a close examination of the household in the context of increasing rates of unemployment brings home the abiding economic character of marital relationships and the links between economic and domestic power.

One final issue to do with the economic significance of domestic relations has been the re-examination of patterns of homeworking (Allen and Wolkowitz 1987). This is a form of waged work, largely carried out by women, within the home which is often invisible in discussions of both the home and the economy. These patterns (which are worldwide) are not marginal or remnants of some earlier proto-capitalist form of economic organisation. They are certainly not to be dismissed as sources of 'pin money' for the women concerned. As a method of production, homeworking is as old as capitalism itself. It has never gone out of existence, but has rarely been visible (Allen and Wolkowitz 1987: 106).

To conclude this section, we have pointed to the increasing stress in sociological research on the economic significance of domestic relations. This stress has implicitly called into question a model of marriage seen purely in relational or emotional terms. However, it is likely that this focus of attention on the household presented its own particular difficulties. The stress on the household was sometimes at the expense of studies of the family and kinship, that is of relationships between households (Wilson and Pahl 1988). Yet it is clearly important to stress the economic dimension of marriage and domestic life. Such a recognition need not be at the expense of an understanding of the emotional and interpersonal dynamics of such relationships nor of a recognition of ties beyond the immediate household. One feature which was recognised in the focus on the economic aspects of family living right from the beginning was the way in which these aspects were closely bound up with issues of gender. It is to these that we turn in the next section.

CHANGING GENDER RELATIONS

The idea that marriages have been changing in the direction of greater equality between the partners has been a constant theme throughout the post-war period, as the two preceding chapters in this volume demonstrate. Indeed the aspiration for greater equality, reflected in the idea of companionate marriage during the 1950s, had turned into an assumption that equality between women and men in marriage was well on the way to being achieved by the 1980s (Burgoyne 1987). The Study Commission on the Family – a body whose work we shall discuss in more detail later – expresses this in its policy agenda for the family in the 1980s, by citing evidence that:

> there is a greater tendency today for couples to value qualities such as sharing, mutual adaptiveness, friendship and trust. In ideal terms at least, companionship and equality between women and men in families is considered crucial to a successful relationship'.

(Study Commission 1983: 3)

However, by comparison with the 1950s optimism that companionate marriage was becoming a widespread reality, the sociological writing of the 1980s was much more inclined to draw a sharp distinction between the aspiration and the lived reality. A focus upon this distinction introduces a streak of realism – sometimes of cynicism – into discussions of this issue, in a way which previously had been much more muted if not wholly absent. Undoubtedly this was due in large measure to the influence of feminism on researchers working on topics about family life during this decade. By the beginning of the 1980s, the feminist critique of the family as a key site of women's oppression was well established and widely discussed. As Scarlet Friedman puts it, for example, in her introduction to the collection which she co-edited entitled *On the Problem of Men*: 'The family has been recognised in the women's liberation movement to be a social institution which confines women, denies them the opportunity for independence, while at the same time it holds them responsible for "successful family life" ' (Friedman and Sarah 1982: 3).

The influence of this aspect of feminism on sociological research is probably best symbolised by the phrase 'the patriarchal family', which came to be widely used during the 1980s to describe the conventional nuclear-family household in which women play a subordinate and servicing role. It is a phrase which both describes this type of household and offers an analysis of the reasons for its existence – it exists to sustain the dominance of men. This analysis implies that one should look with great scepticism at apparent changes in gender relations which purport to give women greater equality. Why, as many feminists have put it, should men give up their power, and the material benefits which it brings them, without a considerable struggle?

Research in the 1980s differs from earlier work therefore in that it distinguishes more clearly between rhetoric and reality and has a tendency to be sceptical about whether gender relations are really changing significantly, whilst at the same time acknowledging the pressures which might make them do so. To illustrate this, we shall focus here on research concerned with two topics – the influence of women's employment upon gender relations in marriage, and the role of women and men as parents.

The effect of women's employment upon the marriage relationship has been a very significant theme in research in the 1980s, linked of course with the interest in the material and economic aspects of domestic life, which we discussed in the previous section. By contrast with parallel discussions in the 1950s, where women's employment was regarded as desirable provided it did *not* have any real effect on women's domestic roles (Finch and Summerfield, Chapter 1, this volume), research in the 1980s was more inclined to welcome adjustments in gender roles which might be consequent upon women's increased commitment to paid work. Researchers certainly were inclined to look for whether such adjustments were being made in reality and, to the extent that such adjustments were regarded as positively desirable, many must have been disappointed.

The clear evidence of research in the 1980s was that men's and women's respective domestic roles, and the gender relations which these embodied, had changed remarkably little. The most authoritative source of such evidence comes from the Women and Employment Survey, based on research from a representative sample of six thousand women (Martin and Roberts 1984). Although showing that men are somewhat more likely to take an active role in housework and child care if their wife has a paid job, none the less this study found that 54 per cent of women who work full-time, and 77 per cent of those working part-time did all or most of the housework (ibid 1984: 114). Even this is something of an underestimate, argue the authors, since they found that – when questioned about the division of labour in their marriages – women often did not report on the work that they did when their husband was out of the home, and they also 'counted' equally tasks which were more onerous and those that were less onerous, their husbands frequently doing more of the latter.

As Martin and Roberts wrote, many smaller-scale studies of the division of labour in marriage also support their findings. Susan Yeandle's (1984) work would be one example. Basing her research on detailed study of sixty-two women, Yeandle does indeed show that women still carry a double burden of paid work and unpaid household responsibilities. She documents a wide variety of strategies used by women to combine employment with domestic responsibilities, and also shows how women find different ways of making sense of their lives and the demands made upon them. In Yeandle's work, and other small-scale studies like it, the picture which emerges is not exactly static. It would be far too crude to say that women in the 1980s have just gone on carrying the domestic burden in the same way that they always have done. Such studies show a picture of creative adaptation, as women face new circumstances: increased demands for their own labour in some areas, reduced demands for men's labour, changing ideas about the role of women in society generally. But there is more than a hint that such adaptations tend to occur within the same basic parameters of gender relations – there is a sense that *something* is probably changing but there still seems a very long way to go before anything approaching real equality between women and men is achieved.

Other attempts to understand the changing (or unchanging) nature of gender relations have approached the matter from the other angle – the perspective of men. The growing number of studies in the 1980s which attempted to understand the position of men in modern society came to more or less the same conclusion (Chapman and Rutherford 1988; Hearn 1989; Hearn and Morgan 1990). There was certainly some evidence of change: those studies which highlighted the necessity of problematising issues of men and masculinities, together with some practical attempts on the part of men to confront sexism and violence, should clearly be included under this heading (see following section for further discussion of violence). However, the idea that we were seeing the rapid spread of a different form of life, the 'New Man', seems somewhat premature. Such a person is commonly defined as a man who contributes equally to house-work and the care of children, who shows greater willingness to express emotions and who eschews all forms of sexism in language and everyday practice. Optimism about the spread of these phenomena proved, in many cases at least, to reflect a confusion of style with real content. A con-siderable amount of effort on the part of sociologists and journalists ended up with relatively few sightings of this New Man.

This brings us to another important research area in the context of gender relations, namely research on parenthood, especially that which deals separately with mothers and fathers. Is this where the elusive New Man is most likely to be found – taking care of his children – even if he has yet to learn how to assume full charge in terms of running a household, or to change his personal attributes?

Certainly research on fatherhood suggests that men in the 1980s saw themselves as more active and more involved parents than had been the case in the past. For example, Bell and colleagues' (1983) study of men's practical support for their wives during childbirth and the early months of motherhood suggests that men see their place as in the home and taking active responsibility at this time. About three-quarters of the men inter-viewed thought that fathers should be entitled to statutory paternity leave, on full or basic pay, and indicated that they themselves would welcome the opportunity to be closely involved in the early weeks of their child's life.

Whether or not this represents a *real* change in the way most men relate to their children must remain open to debate. As McKee and O'Brien

(1982) show, in their discussion of the historical evidence about father-hood, the past seems to have been characterised by diversity at least as much as the present. In addition to evidence which confirms the con-ventional view that fathers in the past were remote figures who had little direct contact with their children, one can also find examples of fathers and children who seem to have developed warm and close relationships. What seems to have changed most clearly in the 1980s is public imagery, where a greater emphasis is placed upon the positive value of fatherhood. This in itself has created a greater legitimacy for those men who state openly that they wish to be more involved with their children.

But despite these indications that men in the 1980s were expressing more explicitly and more publicly their desire to take a more active role in parenting, the research evidence on this topic – like that on the effects of women's employment – offers plenty of reasons to be sceptical about how much things were really changing. In the introduction to their collection of articles on fatherhood, Lewis and O'Brien observe that: 'Despite the wave of optimism driving contemporary accounts (of the "new father"), the evidence for the existence of such a man is much less convincing' (Lewis and O'Brien 1987: 1).

One of the articles contained in this volume is about dual-earner couples, where women have stayed in their previous employment after having a child. It is here where one might expect the 'New Father' to be found, but it is striking that, even in such partnerships, overwhelmingly it was the wife who made arrangements for the care of their child during working hours and who continued to take the major responsibility for child care and housework when they were at home (Brannen and Moss 1987).

An important theme arising from this work, and considerably reinforced by studies of motherhood, is the question of where the *responsibility* for a child lies. Fathers may be much more inclined than in the past to put a child to bed, to entertain it on a Sunday morning, or to wash some nappies, but that is very different from being the person who has to ensure that the child's care is in some way 'covered' for every moment of the day and who is ultimately responsible for monitoring every aspect of its welfare. Such is the traditional role of mothers, and there is little evidence that there has been any change in this fundamental allocation of responsibilities. This analysis is borne out by research studies like Boulton's (1982). She care-fully documents differences in the way in which different women experi-ence motherhood and handle its practical consequences, showing a range from positive acceptance and enjoyment through to alienation. But what-ever kind of personal adjustments a woman makes, a common theme is that: 'a woman [has] sole and final responsibility for her children, responsibility which requires her to subordinate her own interests and to put the children first' (Boulton 1982: 209).

Another important piece of research on parenting during this period echoes a similar theme. Backett's (1982) work explored the experience of parenthood among a sample of middle-class couples with at least one pre-school child. The majority of these couples said that they saw motherhood and fatherhood as essentially similar activities, yet detailed study of their actual practice showed that they behaved very differently. In reality women were much more 'in the front line' in childrearing activities, and this meant that the ultimate *responsibility* also fell to them. For example, mothers were seen as people who developed specialist knowledge of childrearing in general, and of their own child's needs and responses. Therefore they took the ultimate responsibility in difficult situations for deciding how to handle a child, including how and when to discipline her or him. The basis of this knowledge was said to be the mother's more extensive involvement with the child, underscored by the presumption of 'constant availability' which applies to women but not to men. As one of the women in Backett's study put it: 'The only moment in my life when I feel *free* is when I'm asleep I reckon.... if someone else is looking after them you still feel responsible for them' (Backett 1982: 187, emphasis in original).

Changing gender relations was a dominant theme of research in the 1980s but the nature of that change remains elusive. Certainly researchers have positively embraced its desirability, but on the whole have succeeded only in showing how little has changed in reality. Where they have confronted the reasons for this, they have tended to identify quite large obstacles in the way of real change, typically pointing to the fundamental sexual division of labour in British society, which places women and men very differently in the socioeconomic structure, and which therefore sets severe limits upon the extent to which individuals can establish relationships of equality, however high their initial aspirations.

VIOLENCE IN DOMESTIC LIFE

We now turn to another way in which the term 'realism' might be understood: willingness to confront unpleasant or unpalatable truths. One of the concerns of sociological, especially critical sociological, studies of domestic life that were conducted in the 1970s and late 1960s was with some of the darker aspects of family living. This was clearly in opposition to the more optimistic presentations of functionalist theorists or the influential Penguin specials written by Fletcher (Fletcher 1966). In part this was a critique of some of the perceived 'anti-social' aspects of family living

(Barrett and McIntosh 1982), the way in which the family not only inhibited the aspirations of women but also stood in the way of any wider social or political engagement in society as a whole. In part it was a critique of the psychic damage done, especially to children, within the closed confines of the isolated nuclear family. Here, of course, the writings of Laing and Cooper were especially influential (Morgan 1975).

It is interesting to note, from the present vantage point, how much attention was focused in these critical assessments of family living on the psychic damage or symbolic violence that children were subjected to. Relatively little attention was paid to actual physical violence (and even less to sexual violence) inflicted on wives as well as children. However, Erin Pizzey's highly influential *Scream Quietly or the Neighbours Will Hear* was published in 1974 (Pizzey 1974) and increasingly feminist discussions focused on violences against women in the public sphere as well as in the private sphere of the home. A whole range of issues came to be placed on the agenda including rape within and outside marriage, sexual harassment, pornography, physical violence against wives and children and child sexual abuse. All of these concerns went beyond the confines of feminist or academic debate and entered into a variety of political agendas, perhaps the most dramatic illustration being the Cleveland investigations into child sexual abuse (see Morgan, Chapter 5, this volume).

This growing focus, certainly within feminist inspired research, on violences within the home may be seen as another aspect of the theme of 'realism' that informs this chapter. In place of the psychic or symbolic violence explored in the writings of Laing and Cooper we have actual physical violence, in a sense a parallel movement to the shift in the direction of a more material understanding of domestic living. There is another sense in which this focus on violence may be part of this 'realism'. Functionalist models as well as some critical accounts of the family focused on the home as a kind of haven or refuge from the increasingly impersonal or alienating features of modern life. However, this haven came to be seen, at least in some quarters, as something of an illusion, a place of possible threat and actual danger. For many women and children the family was, according to some researchers, 'the most violent group to which they are likely to belong' (Dobash and Dobash 1979: 7).

Research into these darker and dangerous areas of family living continued to grow during the 1980s, although it has to be recognised that sociological studies, at least in Britain, remain relatively scarce. However, it is clear that the research agenda is being mapped out and some of the key sociological issues are beginning to emerge. Of course, much of the work has been to try to map the range and extent of sexual and domestic violences. While it is doubtful whether we shall ever be able to measure the full extent of domestic violences and even more doubtful if we shall be able to gauge whether such violences have increased or decreased, what is significant is the way in which a variety of practices, previously hidden, marginalised or simply taken for granted have come under critical scrutiny. The focus on forms of sexual violence represents something of a paradigm shift, a new way of looking at or thinking about the everyday world, as much as a straightforward setting of a research or political agenda (Wise and Stanley 1987). In this context, Kelly's study has introduced two interesting innovations. In the first place, she introduces the idea of a continuum of sexual violence, ranging from a sense of being threatened by sexual violence to the occurrence of incest (Kelly 1988). Further, in drawing up this continuum she seeks to establish links and overlaps between different sexual violences, and the way in which they are understood or constructed, and between violences in public arenas and those in private places between intimates or family members. A similar kind of orientation informs Hanmer and Saunders' community study of violence against women (Hanmer and Saunders 1984).

In terms of more specific issues, it would seem that violence against women in the home has been most adequately covered in sociological research, although the number of detailed studies, at least in this country, remains very small. Of these, the best known and most widely quoted is the study by Dobash and Dobash (1979). Although referring to research conducted in the 1970s, this study was one of the most influential in developing a research-based, critical perspective on family life in the 1980s. In common with some other studies this discussion included accounts of societal responses to domestic violence as well as showing a willingness to place the discussion in a wider societal and historical framework. A more recent study considers the way in which spousal or partner violences were marginalised in debates about crime and crime statistics. The author argues that this process of marginalisation reflects the ways in which distinctions between the public and the private have been constructed (Edwards 1989). Issues of rape in marriage have increasingly become the subject of socio-legal debate although they did not form the subject of any major British study published before the end of the 1980s.

Studies of violence against children and child sexual abuse, adopting a sociological rather than a sociomedical or epidemiological perspective, continue to be relatively rare within Britain. Such studies that we do have tend to focus on the development of child abuse as a social and political problem (Parton 1985) or professional responses to and constructions of such events (Dingwall *et al.* 1983). Elsewhere, child sexual abuse may be treated as part of a continuum of violence against women (Kelly 1988) although of course it is not confined to the experience of women.

What does emerge in all the studies on this side of the Atlantic as well as in some of the American sociological studies of domestic violence is a rejection of a model of explanation that is based upon some notion of individual pathology. Domestic violences are to be understood, ultimately at least, in terms of the whole way in which the gender order is structured, the assumptions about what constitutes normal or legitimate behaviour for women and men. Most of all it is to do with issues of power and control within society, an argument well reflected in the subtitle of the Dobashes' book (1979) which reads: *A Case Against the Patriarchy*. For similar reasons there is a rejection of models of family pathology, often based upon the application of family-systems theorising. There is a desire to stress the normality of domestic violence in the context of patriarchy rather than its abnormality or pathology. Nevertheless, there would appear to be a need for accounts and models which stressed the interaction between the more micro-level interactions between intimates or family members within the home and more macro-level considerations to do with the distribution and maintenance of power relations between men and women in society as a whole. In short there needs to be a more systematic focus on the interplays between public and private in the sociological understanding of domestic violence, a project very close to the concerns of Jacqueline Burgoyne herself.

It has been argued that this focus on domestic violence may be seen as part of a move to a greater 'realism' in the understanding of family life, although as we shall argue one at some distance from other forms of familial realism. Indeed, we can see that there are direct, as well as meta-phorical, links between this focus on domestic violence and the interest in a more material understanding of marriage mentioned earlier. There are often clear links between the manifestations of physical power found in domestic violence and the wider framework of economic power which structures the household. Women who find themselves in a violent domestic situation may find their options limited by the economic constraints that structure marital relations (Pahl 1985). Closely related to these issues are the difficulties facing women after divorce (Maclean 1987) or single mothers (Graham 1987). It is clearly important to continue to see links between domestic violences and other aspects of marital and family living as part of the complex interplays between the emotional and the economic.

PROCESSES OVER TIME IN DOMESTIC RELATIONSHIPS

The fourth theme which we have identified in research on domestic life in the 1980s is more concerned with conceptual reorientations than with substantive areas of family life. It focuses upon the importance of seeing domestic relationships as changing over time, and their meaning and significance for individuals undergoing a series of modifications. In some ways this seems a very obvious point yet potentially it is an idea which has far-reaching consequences for the way in which we conceive of marriage and family life. Unlike the terms of popular discussion about 'the family' or 'family life' which present an undifferentiated image, these themes emerging from research direct us to a more subtle, a more complex – and therefore undoubtedly a more realistic – view of the way in which people's experience of these relationships changes over time. At its simplest, it reminds us that 'the family' can only mean parents plus young children for a relatively brief stage in any individual's lifetime.

The stimulus to seeing domestic life as a process over time – or more accurately as the product of several interlocking processes – comes in large measure from the influence of historical work. The development of family history (both in the United States and Western Europe as well as in Britain) in the 1970s had filtered through by the 1980s to have a considerable influence upon contemporary studies of family life. David Morgan has outlined this process and evaluated its significance in some detail elsewhere, and we will not repeat that discussion here (Morgan 1985:159–82). However, we will refer briefly to some of the main features which have been influential upon sociological work, drawing on this discussion. Essentially there are three main features of work in this tradition:

1 An emphasis on the need to see the development of domestic relationships as located in a particular set of historical circumstances, which both provide constraints and offer opportunities for particular forms of domestic relationship to flourish. The economic context of families and households is seen as particularly significant here. Treating domestic life as process has meant that individuals are seen as active beings who construct their own relationships out of those constraints and opportunities, and who may therefore come up with a variety of different forms. The concept of developing different 'strategies' has been used widely to express this.

2 A recognition that individuals who construct domestic relationships have both individual and shared agendas, and that these also change over time. The needs, desires and aspirations of men and women, parents and children, are not identical, though at different points in time they may come closer together than at others. From this standpoint domestic life needs to be viewed as an accommodation between individual and shared agendas – not necessarily always a successful one, but one which is bound to be subject to negotiation and renegotiation.

3 This perspective puts a considerable premium on the concept of the 'life

course' which embodies the perspective of time. The idea of the life course should be distinguished sharply from that of the 'life cycle', which appears both implicitly and explicitly in a good deal of research on the family and which implies that there is a predictable series of stages through which a 'normal' family will pass, from early marriage through to old age via family building, the empty nest and so on. The concept of 'life course' rejects any idea of fixed or predictable stages, replacing it with a much more fluid notion of change over time, in which individuals make their own domestic relationships in accommodation with others, timing their transitions from one form of accommodation to another in a way which takes some account of other people's needs but is never wholly shaped by them. The fixing of this process in historical time means that researchers who adopt the concept of the life course tend to develop a framework which focuses on the intersection between history and biography, and shows the diversity of forms of domestic life which are thus created.

Some of the historical work produced within this tradition has been far-reaching in its consequences for our understanding of contemporary family life. For example, Michael Anderson's writing, drawing upon demographic data over time, has raised very profound questions about the distinctive features of family life in the late twentieth century. He has shown that there is a distinctive 'modern life cycle', the key features of which are: the likelihood that most people will live well into old age; that almost everyone of both sexes will marry at least once and that they will do so in their twenties; that most people will have children and that the last child will be born within seven years of marriage; that most people's children will be married by the time they are in their early fifties and that most of their grandchildren will have been born before they are 60. Although this is experienced by most people as perfectly normal and unremarkable, in fact it is a life pattern which simply could not have occurred in earlier generations (Anderson 1985). A combination of increased life expectancy, the evening-out of the gender ratio in the population and different patterns of having and spacing children, have all made it possible for most people to experience the type of family life which people perceive simply to be 'normal': marrying, having children, seeing them grow up, knowing and enjoying grandchildren. Demographic conditions in the past meant that fewer people must have had an opportunity to experience this type of family life. It is therefore an interesting irony that this form of the family frequently is described as 'traditional'.

Sociological work informed by perspectives which emphasise processes over time began to emerge during the 1980s and some interesting examples are to be found in a collection edited by Gaynor Cohen (1987) and in a volume produced from the British Sociological Association conference in 1985, which took the life course as its key theme (Bryman *et al.* 1987). One effect is to make visible and sociologically interesting some domestic situations which hitherto had received little attention. One such is marriage in middle and old age, something which was regarded as of little interest in earlier studies of marriage and family when 'the family' meant essentially a unit which includes young children. The emphasis on life course and process highlights questions about how the meaning of marriage changes over time, and how its form gets renegotiated. Such questions are reflected explicitly in work contained in the BSA conference volumes, for example, Jennifer Mason's (1987) article, which discusses data from a study of long-married couples aged between 50 and 70. Mason shows, for example, that the theme of women's and men's essentially different *responsibilities* within marriage continues into middle and old age, although the form which these responsibilities take in practice is subject to change and renegotiation.

Another effect of a focus upon domestic life as process is to offer a context for analysing those situations which otherwise all too easily appear simply as a deviation from the norm. Processes of divorce, cohabitation and remarriage are important examples of this, and are areas in which Jacqueline Burgoyne herself made a particularly significant contribution in the 1980s. The study of stepfamilies which she and David Clark conducted (Burgoyne and Clark 1984) stands as a model of a piece of research which is informed by concepts of negotiation and mutual accommodation. Above all it sees the process of 'reconstituting' domestic relationships as integral to our understanding of contemporary family life, not as a deviation from it. David Clark, writing several years after the publication of this study, underlines the importance of the life-course perspective in understanding the constitution and reconstitution of marriage when he writes of the case studies of stepfamilies which they undertook:

> We see here intimacy and estrangement; growing together and growing apart; affection and violence; affluence and poverty; employment and unemployment; experience and inexperience. . . . To date there have been few attempts [in social science to understand] the integration of history and biography. Such an integration is essential for a full under-standing of marriage across the life course.
>
> (Clark 1987: 130–1)

Placing an emphasis on marriage and domestic life as process, to which change and diversity are necessarily integral, is one more way in which a sense of realism has been introduced into research during the 1980s. It produces understandings of family life which move well beyond the categories of normal and deviant by stressing individuality and variety. That variety is produced, however, not by a simple process of individual 'choice' – as perhaps the emphasis of the 1970s would suggest – but by interlocking social, economic and demographic processes which form the material out of which individuals must make their own lives. Such perspectives anchor our understanding of family life in material realities, in a way which is subtle and persuasive yet at the same time rather difficult to integrate with public debates about the family, which tend to be conducted in much more simple-minded terms.

CONCLUSION: REALISM AND RESEARCH IN THE 1980S

Research into marriage and the family, in common one might suppose with research into any other social phenomena, does not stand alone as some kind of detached and disinterested scholarly activity. It may be seen as part of a complex and dynamic triangular relation which includes social research, actual social processes and social and political ideologies. The 'actual social processes', what has actually happened to marriage and the family in the post-war years, have been documented and described at various points in this present volume (see in particular Elliott, Chapter 4, this volume). These would include rising rates of divorce and remarriage, increasing rates of cohabitation, the move away from falling age of marriage and so on. Such facts may be supplemented by various poll or survey data that indicate continuing high degrees of support for the argument that marriage is a normal and desirable stage in the adult life cycle. But clearly social research is not simply a matter of recording these 'facts' about marriage and the family. It is in part creating these facts (through the adoption of certain administrative definitions of marriage, for example), in part interpreting these facts (whether they are described as signs of change or continuity, for example) and in part contributing to, directly and indirectly, certain wider political debates.

What is being pointed to here are two sets of agendas and the possible tensions and relationships between them. In the first place, there are the research agendas, the subject of the main central part of this article. Here we have argued that the research agenda in the 1980s has included a greater emphasis on the economic aspects of marriage, a deepening awareness of gender relationships within domestic life, a slower but growing recognition of violence in the domestic sphere and a greater willingness to view family life in processual, life-course terms. In the second place are the political agendas, debates about the kinds and degrees of public intervention into family life that might be felt desirable. In this context we have noted that there has been an increasing politicisation of family and domestic life in the 1980s, that marriage and the family appear increasingly on certain public programmes. Britain is by no means unique in this respect; indeed in many respects it may be argued that Britain lags behind other countries in the development of overt and articulated family policies. However, overt discussion of these aspects of the 'private' sphere have increasingly entered into public debate and there is little doubt that social-research agendas may often be seen in an uneasy relationship with these political agendas.

The relationships and contrasts between the research and political agendas might be seen, first, in the debate about uniformity or diversity in domestic relationships, a debate referred to in earlier sections. In political terms, the debate was about whether too much attention had been paid to the various lobbyings on behalf of single parents, cohabitees and gay relationships at the expense of mainstream 'normal' family units. In research terms, the debate was about whether the 'conventional nuclear-family'-based household was now a minority phenomenon (and that socio-logical research should take account of this fact) or whether reading the same or similar data in a different way might reveal more abiding uniformities (Chester 1986).

Clearly these political and research agendas interacted and overlapped at various points. One point where this can be seen is in the work of the Study Commission on the Family, which became the Family Policy Study Centre in the course of the 1980s. Superficially, the work of this body would seem to argue for a more pluralistic view. More open to a diversity of political and social commitments and more willing to take a closer and often detailed look at actual processes, the Study Commission constantly warned against too ready an acceptance of the model of the 'stereotyped nuclear family', especially where issues of family policy were concerned. However, the authors of the various publications from this source did not seem to be willing to endorse a wholly pluralistic model: 'Even though the majority of parents, children and families still follow a fairly traditional pattern, the minority who do not is growing, and this raises substantial policy questions' (Rimmer 1981: 63).

A recognition of the diversity of family forms may have influenced the sense of caution shown in arguing for family policy (the emphasis tended to be more on a family-based perspective or possibly a family-impact statement rather than a full-blown family policy) although clearly most of the authors seemed to feel that any deconstruction should take place within recognised limits.

Similarly, the social-research agendas dealt with in this chapter would seem to be arguing on the side of diversity. However, it should be stressed that such diversity that might emerge may well be a function of the questions being asked and the overall frameworks of interpretation being adopted. It is true that scholarly research often, perhaps characteristically, argues in favour of complexity and against simplification and that the research questions outlined here point in the direction of diversity. But it can equally be argued that they suggest a measure of uniformity in, for example, underlining some of the widespread and persisting patterns of gender inequalities within the home or for the wide degree of acceptance of marriage as a desired state.

One area where a research agenda might make a contribution is in terms of problematising the notion of 'the stereotypical nuclear family'. Both critics from the Left and defenders on the Right deploy this term but appear to use it in a variety of overlapping ways. In some cases it may refer to a form of household composition, normally including both adults and children although sometimes including just a 'conventionally' married couple. The most restrictive understanding would include a married couple where the husband is in full-time paid employment and where the wife stays at home together with two children. What we often seem to be dealing with is not simply a stereotype but a stereotype of a stereotype, one as far removed from actual family experiences as it is from serious research practice. The research agendas would seem to be less concerned with adjudicating as to whether there 'really' is diversity or uniformity than in spelling out the ways in which such uniformity or diversity might be seen and the possible consequences of this different perspective. The research agenda is, in this sense, pluralist but not simply in terms of arguing straightforwardly for a plurality of family forms and practices.

A similar tension between research and political agendas might be seen in terms of another opposition that runs through this chapter, indeed many of the chapters, and that is the one between continuity and change. The research perspectives outlined earlier have argued for both change and continuity. They have argued against simple evolutionary models of the family such as those that posit a shift from institution to relationship in marriage (see Morgan, Chapter 5, this volume) and have argued in favour of continuities in terms of such questions as gender relations and the centrality of economic activities within marriage and the household. But they have also argued for new perspectives or new emphases in the analysis of domestic life, these including a recognition of violence within intimate relations and a more sophisticated sense of process within domestic living. But again these are shifts in ways of seeing domestic relationships rather than simple shifts in actual practices.

In considering the interplay between these research agendas and political agendas we may take a closer look at the idea of 'realism' mentioned at various points in this chapter. In using the word 'realism' here we are closer to the popular understanding of this term than to more specialised philosophical definitions. One conventional understanding of 'realism' in family studies, one to some extent shared by those of the Right and on the Left, is in terms of an adjustment to the realities of 'Thatcherism' and a move away from the more permissive agendas of the 1970s and late 1960s (Richards and Elliott, Chapter 2, this volume). Visions of equal and freely chosen sexual, personal and domestic relationships and a liberation from the binding ties of the conventional nuclear family faded, so the story goes, in the light of increasing unemployment, the debates about AIDS and the deeper insertion of conservative ideology. The Right's model would seem in part to be a kind of familistic realism, one stressing the centrality of normal family living. Most people, the argument went, expected to enter into normal married domestic situations, a fact not necessarily challenged by increasing divorce rates.

The kind of realism that seemed to emerge out of the research agendas was of a somewhat different order. In the first place, it would claim to be a less idealised set of understandings than some of these which preceded, such as those stressing the relational or symmetrical aspects of marriage. Hence, for example, the stress on the economic dimensions of everyday domestic life or the recognition of violence as a central, and by no means pathological, aspect of intimate relations. In the second place, there would be a claim that such perspectives were more 'realistic' in so far as they came closer to reality. This would be true, for example, in the case of the continuing stress on gender inequalities and the desire to see domestic life in processual terms. Hence, the bottom line would seem to be that these are not, in some post-modernist way, simply different perspectives but that they do come closer to the ways in which family living was actually experienced and with what was actually happening in society.

The tension between continuity and change and between research and political agendas may be seen in the FPSC's publication, *Inside the Family* (Henwood *et al.* 1987). The cover shows an almost stereotypical 'New Man', bare-chested but in such a way that suggests vulnerability rather than masculinity, holding a baby. Yet the text, exploring the actual divisions of labour between women and men in parenting and in the home, suggests much more continuity in terms of the 'traditional' model than is suggested in the cover.

Clearly the 'realisms' outlined in this chapter are not all of a piece and the competing claims on realism reflect different research agendas, different political agendas and differences between research and political agendas. Indeed, to conceptualise the 1980s as an 'age of realism' is to provide yet further illustration of the ideological deployment of time discussed elsewhere in this volume (Morgan, Chapter 5, this volume). To provide an adequate account of domestic life in any period of time we need, among other things, to tease out the range of competing definitions and understandings within that time period and to assess their consequences for everyday family living.

REFERENCES

Allen, S. and Wolkowitz, C. (1987) *Homeworking: Myth and Realities*, Basingstoke: Macmillan.

Anderson, D. and Dawson, G. (eds) (1986) *Family Portraits*, London: The Social Affairs Unit.

Anderson, M. (1985) 'The emergence of the modern life cycle in Britain', *Social History* 10(1): 69–87.

Askham, J. (1984) *Identity and Stability in Marriage*, Cambridge: Cambridge University Press.

Backett, K.C. (1982) *Mothers and Fathers. A Study of the Development and Negotiation of Parental Behaviour*, London: Macmillan.

Barrett, M. and McIntosh, M. (1982) *The Anti-social Family*, London: Verso.

Bell, C., McKee, L. and Priestley, K. (1983). *Fathers, Childbirth and Work*, Manchester: Equal Opportunities Commission.

Berger, P. and Kellner, H. (1964) 'Marriage and the construction of reality', *Diogenes* 46: 1–24.

Boulton, M.G. (1982) *On Being a Mother: A Study of Women with Pre-School Children*, London: Tavistock.

Brannen, J. and Collard, J. (1982) *Marriages in Trouble: The Process of Seeking Help*, London: Tavistock.

Brannen, J. and Moss, P. (1987) 'Fathers in dual-earner households – through mothers' eyes', in C. Lewis and M. O'Brien (eds) *Reassessing Fatherhood: New Observations on Fathers and the Modern Family*, London: Sage.

Brannen, J. and Wilson, G. (eds) (1987) *Give and Take in Families*, London: Allen & Unwin.

Bryman, A., Bytheway, B., Allatt, P. and Keil, T. (1987) *Rethinking the Life Cycle*, London: Macmillan.

Burgoyne, J. (1987) 'Rethinking the family life cycle: sexual divisions, work and domestic life in the post-war period', in A. Bryman, B. Bytheway, P. Allatt and T. Keil (eds) *Rethinking the Life Cycle*, London: Macmillan.

Burgoyne, J. and Clark, D. (1984) *Making a Go of It: A Study of Stepfamilies in Sheffield*, London: Routledge & Kegan Paul.

Chapman, R. and Rutherford, J. (eds) (1988) *Male Order: Unwrapping Masculinity*, London: Lawrence & Wishart.

Charles, N. and Kerr, M. (1988) *Women, Food and Families*, Manchester: Manchester University Press.

Chester, R. (1986) 'The myth of the disappearing nuclear family', in D. Anderson and G. Dawson (eds) *Family Portraits*, London: Social Affairs Unit, pp. 19–29.

Clark, D. (1987) 'Changing partners: marriage and divorce across the life course', in G. Cohen (ed.) *Social Change and the Life Course*, London: Tavistock.

Cohen, G. (ed.) (1987) *Social Change and the Life Course*, London: Tavistock.

David, M. (1986) 'Moral and maternal: the family in the Right', in R. Levitas (ed.) *The Ideology of the New Right*, Cambridge: Polity Press.

Dingwall, R., Eekelaar, J. and Murray, T. (1983) *The Protection of Children: State Intervention and Family Life,* Oxford: Blackwell.

Dobash, R.E. and Dobash, R. (1979) *Violence Against Wives: A Case Against the Patriarchy,* London: Open Books.

Edwards, S. (1989) *Policing 'Domestic' Violence,* London: Sage.

Finch, J. (1983) *Married to the Job,* London: Allen & Unwin.

Fitzgerald, T. (1983) 'The New Right and the family', in M. Lovey, D. Boswell and J. Clarke (eds) *Social Policy and Social Welfare,* Milton Keynes: Open University Press.

Fletcher, R. (1966) *The Family and Marriage in Britain,* Harmondsworth: Penguin, revised edition.

Friedman, S. and Sarah, E. (eds) (1982) *On the Problem of Men,* London: Women's Press.

Graham, H. (1987) 'Being poor: perceptions and coping strategies of lone mothers', in J. Brannen and G. Wilson (eds) *Give and Take in Families,* London: Allen & Unwin.

Hanmer, J. and Saunders, S. (1984) *Well-Founded Fear: A Community Study of Violence to Women,* London: Hutchinson.

Harris, C.C. and Morriss, L.D. (1986) 'Labour markets and the position of women', in R. Crompton and M. Mann (eds) *Gender and Stratification,* Cambridge: Polity Press, pp. 86–96.

Hearn, J. (1989) *The Gender of Oppression,* Brighton: Harvester.

—— and Morgan, D.H.J. (1990) *Men, Masculinity and Social Theory,* London: Unwin Hyman.

Henwood, M., Rimmer, L. and Wicks, M. (1987) *Inside the Family: Changing Roles of Men and Women,* London. Family Policy Studies Centre, occasional paper no. 6.

Kelly, L. (1988) *Surviving Sexual Violence,* Cambridge: Polity Press.

Land, H. (1980) 'The family wage', *Feminist Review* 6: 55–77.

Lawson, A. (1988) *Adultery: An Analysis of Love and Betrayal,* Oxford: Blackwell.

Lewis, C. and O'Brien, M. (eds) (1987) 'Constraints on fathers: research, theory and clinical practice', in *Reassessing Fatherhood: New Observations on Fathers and the Modern Family,* London: Sage.

McKee, L. and Bell, C. (1985) 'Marital and family relations in times of male unemployment', in B. Roberts, R. Finnegan and D. Gallie (eds) *New Approaches to Economic Life,* Manchester: Manchester University Press.

McKee, L. and O'Brien, M. (eds) 'The father figure: some current orientations and historical perspectives', in *The Father Figure,* London: Tavistock.

Maclean, M. (1987) 'Households after divorce: the availability of resources and their impact on children', in J. Brannen and G. Wilson (eds) *Give and Take in Families,* London: Allen & Unwin.

Mansfield, P. and Collard, J. (1988) *The Beginning of the Rest of Your Life? A Portrait of Newly-wed Marriage,* London: Macmillan.

Martin, J. and Roberts, C. (1984) *Women and Employment: A Lifetime Perspective,* London: HMSO.

Mason, J. (1987) 'A bed of roses? Women, marriage and inequality in later life', in P. Allatt, T. Keil, A. Bryman, and B. Bytheway (eds) *Women and the Life Cycle,* London: Macmillan.

Morgan, D.H.J. (1975) *Social Theory and the Family,* London: Routledge & Kegan Paul.

—— (1985) *The Family, Politics and Social Theory*, London: Routledge & Kegan Paul.

Morris, L.D. (1985a) 'Renegotiation of the domestic division of labour in the context of male redundance', in B. Roberts, R. Finnegan and D. Gallie (eds) *New Approaches to Economic Life*, Manchester: Manchester University Press.

—— (1985b) 'Local social networks and domestic organisation', *Sociological Review* 32(2): 327–42.

Pahl, J. (ed.) *Private Violence and Public Policy: The Needs of Battered Women and the Response of the Public Services*, London: Routledge & Kegan Paul.

—— (1989) *Money and Marriage*, London: Macmillan.

Pahl, R. (1984) *Divisions of Labour*, Oxford: Blackwell.

Parton, N. (1985) *The Politics of Child Abuse*, London: Macmillan.

Pizzey, E. (1974) *Scream Quietly or the Neighbours Will Hear*, Harmondsworth: Penguin.

Rimmer, L. (1981) *Families in Focus: Marriage, Divorce and Family Patterns*, London: Study Commission on the Family, occasional paper no. 6.

Roberts, B., Finnegan, R. and Gallie, D. (eds) (1985) *New Approaches to Economic Life*, Manchester: Manchester University Press.

Smart, C. (1987) 'Securing the family? Rhetoric and policy in the field of social security', in M. Lovey (ed.) *The State or the Market*, London: Sage.

Study Commission on the Family (1983) *Families in the Future: A Policy Agenda for the 1980s*, London: Study Commission on the Family.

Wilson, P. and Pahl, R., (1988) 'The changing sociological construct of the family', *Sociological Review* 36(2): 233–72.

Wise, S. and Stanley, L. (1987) *Georgie Porgie: Sexual Harassment in Everyday Life*, London: Pandora.

Working Party on Marriage Guidance (1979) *Marriage Matters*, London: HMSO.

Yeandle, S. (1984) *Women's Working Lives: Patterns and Strategies*, London: Tavistock.

Part II

Demographic trends

Introduction

For the second part of the book, B. Jane Elliott has produced an enormously useful summary of key demographic trends in the years 1945–87 and has succeeded in bringing together a number of previously uncombined data sets. This chapter serves as a valuable resource in making sense of the key themes explored in detail in parts I and III. The author begins by setting out major changes in patterns of marriage over the period. She shows how from the 1940s an equalisation of the sex ratio created the conditions in which a higher proportion of men and women in the population would get married. This was accompanied up to the end of the 1960s by a trend towards earlier marriage. However, from 1970 age at marriage began to increase and was associated with a drop in rates of marriage. It remains unclear to what extent falling marriage rates and rising levels of cohabitation represent a movement away from the institution of marriage. Divorce, however, clearly increased over the period, particularly between 1960 and 1980, though divorce rates remained fairly constant during the 1980s. Divorce rates also varied considerably in different parts of the United Kingdom and in England and Wales a clear association between divorce and social class was demonstrated. Between 1950 and 1987 the proportion of all marriages taking place which were remarriages for one or other partner increased from 20 per cent to 36 per cent. This was entirely the result of increasing numbers of divorced men and women marrying again.

There were two 'baby booms' in the period, the first in 1947 and the second in 1964, but during the late 1970s the number of births dropped below replacement levels for the first time since the start of civil registrations. From 1950 to the late 1970s the large majority of births took place inside marriage. Thereafter, the proportions of illegitimate births rose significantly, though it appears that many of these children were born to cohabiting couples and by 1986 some 70 per cent of such births were registered jointly by both parents. Elliott also draws attention to the dramatic changes which have taken place in patterns of women's employment since the Second World War. In 1951 men outnumbered women in the paid workforce by two to one, but by 1981, 40 per cent of the workforce were women and by 1987 the proportion had risen to 45 per cent. However, there was little change in women's participation in full-time employment; most of the growth came in part-time work and women with dependent children remained significantly less likely to be economically active than other women.

Jane Elliott concludes her chapter by highlighting the consequences of these trends for the way in which we think about families across the life course. She suggests that for the purposes of empirical research we might place a greater emphasis upon tracing *individuals* through their life histories in order to better understand patterns of family formation, dissolution and reconstitution.

4 Demographic trends in domestic life, 1945–87

B. Jane Elliott

In this chapter I will focus on the main population characteristics which have affected the experience of marriage and family life over the four decades since the end of the Second World War. My aim is to piece together information and statistics from existing fragmented sources and to construct from these a more complete and integrated picture of changes in domestic life. The topics covered will include: cohabitation; the number and age of people who marry; patterns of fertility; divorce; remarriage; and women's participation in the labour force.

MARRIAGE

The two main constraints on the extent of marriage in any society are the number of couples who choose to formalise their relationships in this way, and the availability of equal numbers of men and women. For a long time there were more women than men in the population available for marriage. The Finer report noted that: 'in mid Victorian England, almost one third of the women aged 20 to 44 had to remain spinsters because differential mortality rates and large scale emigration so depleted the reservoir of men, that there were not enough to go round' (Finer Report 1974: 23). The sex ratio became less distorted in the early twentieth century as emigration slackened off, but the deaths of nearly a million young men during the First World War meant that by 1921 there were only 894 bachelors for each 1,000 spinsters in the age group 15–54. Hence marriage rates were higher for men from the turn of the century until the late 1940s and it was not until 1961 that men outnumbered women in the 16–44 age-group. As Finer put it: 'Ever since working class "teddy boys" began in the late 1940s to ape the mufti and hairstyle of Edwardian Guards' officers, the cosmetic habits of young men have testified to women's new found equality of opportunity to marry' (Finer 1974: 25).

A more equal sex ratio in the marriageable age groups has therefore allowed an increase in the proportion of men and women in the population who get married. Figure 4.1 shows that from the 1940s, after a temporary dip in marriage rates during the war, up until the beginning of the 1970s there was indeed an increasing overall propensity to marry in Britain, which reached its peak in 1970. In 1941 the general first-marriage rate was 78 per 1,000 single men and this rose by about 10 per cent to 86 per 1,000 in 1970. The corresponding increase for women was even more pronounced, a 30 per cent rise in marriage rates from 74 to 100 marriages per 1,000 single women over the same thirty-year period. Indeed it can be seen from Figure 4.1 that women's marriage rates have been consistently higher than men's since the early 1950s. This is due in part to the unequal sex ratio mentioned earlier, but also to the fact that divorced men are more likely to remarry than divorced women. In other words, single women have a larger number of potential marriage partners available to them than do single men. Clearly the sex ratio is not the only factor which influences the extent of marriage; despite a constant sex ratio in the marriageable age groups, marriage rates did not stay constant in the 1970s and 1980s.

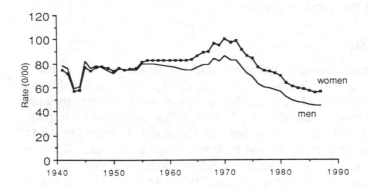

Figure 4.1 General first-marriage rates (per 1,000 population aged 16 and over), England and Wales, 1941–87
Source: OPCS Marriage and Divorce statistics 1974, 1985, 1987

After 1972 first-marriage rates for both men and women began to fall quite steeply. So that by 1987 the level of female first-marriage rates was half what it had been at the 1970 peak and was similar to the lowest levels during the war, with only about one in twenty single women marrying in a year. For men the first-marriage rates dropped even lower, with only about one in twenty-five single men getting married in 1987.

These general first-marriage rates are rather unreliable measures of marriage intensity, however, because they are affected by changes in the age structure of the single population. For a more detailed analysis of marriage behaviour, it is necessary to examine the age-specific first-marriage rates, which control for the age distribution of the population and provide insights into the marriage experiences of different age groups over time. The first-marriage rates for men and women are shown in Figures 4.2a and 4.2b. The marriage rate has been calculated as the ratio of first marriages to the single population in a particular age group thus giving a measure of how likely someone in a particular age band is to get married.

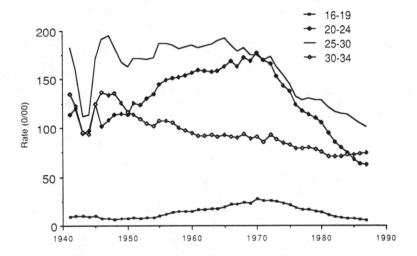

Figure 4.2a Male, nubile first-marriage rates (per 1,000 population)
Source: OPCS Marriage and Divorce statistics 1985, 1987; Registrar General's
　　　　Statistical Review 1973, Table H1

It can be seen that from the end of the Second World War until 1970 there was a trend towards earlier marriage for both men and women, with an increase in marriage rates for the under twenty-fives and relatively stable marriage rates in older age groups. For men, in their early twenties, the marriage rates rose rapidly throughout the 1950s and 1960s from a level of 125 per 1,000 in 1951 to 177 per 1,000 in 1970, an increase in the order of 40 per cent. For women, however, it was the increase in teenage marriage rates which was particularly marked.

The tendency to marry at progressively younger ages during the 1950s and 1960s is also demonstrated by the fall in the median age at marriage for

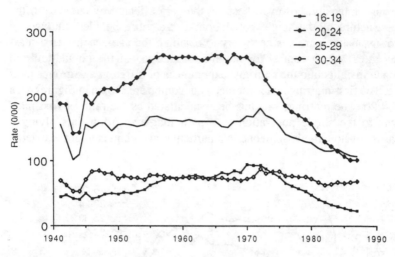

Figure 4.2b Female, nubile first-marriage rates (per 1,000 population)
Source: OPCS Marriage and Divorce statistics 1985, 1987; Registrar General's
Statistical Review 1973, Table H1

bachelors and spinsters. In 1951 this average age of first marriage was 26.8
years for men and 24.6 for women; by 1971 these figures had both dropped
by about two years to 24.6 and 22.6 respectively. Thus the increase in the
general first-marriage rates during these two decades, which could be seen
in Figure 4.1, may be largely attributed to the marriage behaviour of the
16–24 age group.

Further examination of Figures 4.2a and 4.2b reveals that the fall in
general first-marriage rates after 1970 was also largely due to the marriage
behaviour of men and women aged under 25. For men in the 20–24 age
band there was a decline from a peak yearly rate of 170 marriages per 1,000
in the late 1960s to a rate of only 80 marriages per 1,000 in the early 1980s,
while for women the corresponding drop was even more dramatic from 261
to 123. Teenage marriage rates have also fallen, so that in 1970 about one
in forty teenage men and one in ten teenage women were married, while in
1987 the figures were more like one in 200 teenage men and one in forty
teenage women.

Part of the initial drop in marriage rates in the early 1970s may be
attributed to the 1969 Family Law Reform Act, which came into effect in
1970. This legislation reduced the age at which people could get married
without parental consent from 21 years to 18 years. In response to the act
many people who would have married in their early twenties were now able

to marry before age 21. This resulted in a borrowing of marriages from the future – a peak in teenage marriages in 1970, followed by a fall in marriage rates for the 20–24 age group in the early 1970s.

The rise and fall of general first-marriage rates since the 1940s can therefore be seen as largely due to the marriage patterns of the younger section of the population. What is not yet clear is whether the recent decline in marriage rates in this younger age group is due to young people marrying at progressively older ages, or from an increasing section of the population rejecting marriage altogether.

Since the end of the Second World War, trends in the marriage rates of Scotland and Northern Ireland have been very similar to those for England and Wales described earlier. Throughout the United Kingdom there was an increase in the incidence of marriage, especially at younger ages, during the 1960s followed by a trend towards postponement of marriage in the 1970s and 1980s. The average age at which couples currently get married is also remarkably similar throughout the United Kingdom. Crude marriage rates do, however, tend to be slightly lower in Northern Ireland than in Scotland and England and Wales.

However, the proportion of marriages solemnised by a religious, as opposed to a civil ceremony, differs markedly between different parts of the United Kingdom. Civil ceremonies are most common in England and Wales with 48 per cent of marriages having been solemnised this way in 1987, compared to 42 per cent in Scotland and only 13 per cent in Northern Ireland. Although the proportion of civil ceremonies has increased in all these places since the end of the Second World War, the trends have shown rather different patterns over time. In both Scotland and in England and Wales the major decline in religious services occurred during the 1960s and early 1970s, whereas in Northern Ireland there was actually a slight increase in the proportion of religious ceremonies during the 1960s, but then this was followed by an increase in civil ceremonies during the 1970s. Proportions of civil ceremonies have stayed relatively constant throughout the United Kingdom during the 1980s.

COHABITATION

From the early 1970s onwards, a growing number of couples have chosen to live together as husband and wife without formalising their union with a marriage ceremony. In response to this increasingly common domestic arrangement, the family information section of the General Household Survey was expanded in 1979 to include questions on current and past experiences of cohabitation. An analysis of this newly collected data

(Brown and Kiernan 1981) showed that in 1979, 9 per cent of single, never-married, women aged between 18 and 29, were cohabiting and that cohabiting couples represented 6 per cent of the total number of 'first unions' (first marriages plus cohabiting single women) in this age group. More recent data from the General Household Survey shows that in 1987, over 11 per cent of all women aged 18–24 were cohabiting compared with 5 per cent of those aged 25–49 (CSO 1989a).

As 1979 was the first year of the General Household Survey in which information about cohabitation was elicited, we have no directly comparable data on how common such living arrangements were in the past. However, there is evidence of stable, non-marital, relationships including childrearing in earlier periods, and it is probably only the more temporary, premarital, type of cohabitation which should strictly be viewed as a contemporary phenomenon (Brown and Kiernan 1981).

In addition to collecting information about current household composition, the 1979 General Household Survey asked women who were married or who had ever been married, whether they had lived with their husband as 'man and wife' prior to their wedding day. As we would expect, evidence was found of a marked increase in the incidence of premarital cohabitation during the 1970s. Of the first marriages solemnised in the period 1971–73, 7 per cent were reported as having been preceded by cohabitation, compared to 19 per cent of those solemnised between 1977–79. By the early 1980s this figure had risen still further to around 26 per cent. The incidence of premarital cohabitation is even higher for second marriages (when either one, or both partners have been married previously), with 60 per cent of such couples who married in 1979 reporting that they had lived together before the wedding (Brown and Kiernan 1981).

Data from the General Household Survey suggests that the length of premarital cohabitation has increased during the 1970s and 1980s. The median duration amongst couples marrying for the first time was ten months in the 1970s, whereas in the 1980s the median duration is in the order of thirteen to fifteen months (Kiernan 1989). Assuming that premarital cohabitation is likely to prolong the time between a couple meeting and their wedding day, if premarital cohabitation becomes more popular or increases in duration, then we would expect delays in marriage leading to further declines in marriage rates for the younger age groups. Indeed, cohabitation was probably an important part of the reason for fewer young people getting married in the 1970s. Estimates show, however, that a maximum of 50 per cent of the reduction in proportions married between 1973 and 1980 can be explained in this way (Kiernan and Eldridge 1987).

DIVORCE

The incidence of divorce in England and Wales increased substantially during the two decades between 1960 and 1980. From a yearly rate of only two divorces per 1,000 married persons in the quinquennium 1956–60, the divorce rate increased sixfold to a rate of twelve per 1,000 in 1980. Figure 4.3 shows this upward trend in the context of the last forty-five years. It can be seen that the divorce rate initially increased quite slowly during the early 1960s, so that by 1968 the rate had only climbed to 3.7 per 1,000, a figure exactly comparable with the 1946–1950 post-war rates. During the 1970s, however, the increase in the divorce rate was much more rapid.

It is interesting to note that the sharp rise in the divorce rate which corresponded with the implementation of the 1969 Divorce Reform Act in 1971, was accompanied by a significant increase in the median length of marriages ending in divorce. This would suggest that the temporary 'blip' in the divorce rate in 1972 may best be explained by the backlog of long-finished marriages which could at last be formally terminated as a result of the new provisions of the act.[1]

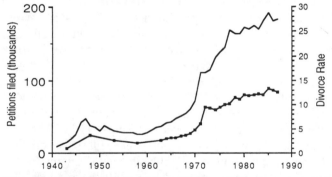

Figure 4.3 Petitions filed each year (000s) and divorce rates per 1,000 married population, England and Wales, 1941–87
Source: OPCS Marriage and Divorce statistics 1974, 1985, 1987, Table 2.1

Since 1978 the incidence of divorce has remained relatively stable and the median length of marriages ending in divorce has been fairly constant at just over ten years. In 1985, after the 1984 Matrimonial and Family Proceedings Act came into force, the divorce rate temporarily rose again, and the median length of marriage dipped from 10.1 years in 1984 to 8.9 years in 1985. This is not surprising as the new act reduced the time limit for divorce from three years of marriage to only one year of marriage, and so we would expect the median length of marriage to reduce as some very short marriages would be included in the calculation for the first time. Over six thousand more couples obtained decrees following petitions filed in the last three months of 1984 compared with the number who successfully filed petitions in the previous three months. Of these extra couples, the majority had been married for only two years (Haskey 1986). What is more interesting perhaps is that in 1986 and 1987 the median length of marriage did not remain constant but increased to 9.4 years and 9.5 years respectively, which might suggest that some newly-weds were actually encouraged to divorce very early in their married lives by the 1984 act. It will be interesting to see what happens to the median length of marriages in the future.

It should be remembered that length of marriage has not always been so largely determined by the incidence of divorce. The high levels of marital dissolution due to the divorce rates of the 1980s may be viewed in a different light if a more long-term historical perspective is taken, and changes in life expectancy are considered.

Going back to the 1890s, approximately 30 per cent of the cohort of couples married in 1896 experienced marital break-up before their twentieth wedding anniversary due to the death of their spouse. Assuming current divorce rates the extent of marital break-up is remarkably similar for couples in the 1980 marriage cohort. The latest estimates (Haskey 1989) show that 32.0 per cent of those marriages contracted in England and Wales in 1987 are likely to end in divorce during the first twenty years, and ultimately nearly four out of every ten marriages will have ended in divorce before the thirty-third wedding anniversary.

In Scotland divorce is slightly less prevalent than in England and Wales, with a 1987 divorce rate of 10.2 per 1,000 married couples (compared with 12.6 for England and Wales). These figures contrast sharply with Northern Ireland, where the 1987 divorce rate was approximately 6 per 1,000 married couples (CSO 1989b). It is unclear which factors create these differences. Although the Roman Catholic religion might be thought to inhibit divorce in Northern Ireland, research by Trent and South (1989), in which they analysed data from sixty-six different countries, found that religious participation was not a significant structural determinant of divorce rates except in so far as it might influence the law.

In addition to an overall increase in the number of petitions filed for divorce, the four post-Second World War decades have more specifically seen an increase in the number of petitions filed by wives as opposed to husbands. In the quinquennium 1946–1950 just under half (45 per cent) of petitions filed were by women; this proportion rose virtually monotonically to a level of 73 per cent in 1977 (the only aberrant year being 1971 when the proportion fell from 64 per cent in 1970 to 60 per cent). Since the end of the 1970s the proportion of divorces legally initiated by wives has stayed fairly constant at 71 to 73 per cent. The grounds given for divorce also show a gender imbalance. The 1987 figures show that 45 per cent of the divorces which were granted to husbands were on grounds of adultery and about 25 per cent on the grounds of two years' separation. Whereas grounds of behaviour accounted for 52 per cent of divorces petitioned for by wives, and only 25 per cent were on grounds of adultery. Clearly these are all only legal definitions and we can make no assumptions about which partner really initiated the dissolution of the marriage or why. However, even if the figures are only indicating the way that men and women use the law to end their marriages it is still interesting that such a marked difference exists.

The socioeconomic characteristics of divorcing couples have seldom been studied, largely due to the lack of readily available information from national records of divorce. Although the husband's occupation is recorded for every decree made absolute in England and Wales, this information is not coded and entered into the computer at the Office of Population Censuses and Surveys with the other legal and demographic information, primarily because of the cost involved.

Haskey (1984) analysed a sample of 2,164 divorces in England and Wales in 1979, representing just over 1.5 per cent of the total during the year. The forms were extracted and the divorced husband's occupation coded according to the 1980 OPCS classification of occupations. Estimates of the number of married men in England and Wales by age, occupation, social class and socioeconomic group were obtained from the 1979 Labour Force Survey. From these two sets of figures an age-standardised divorce ratio was calculated for each different social class.

It can clearly be seen from Table 4.1 that except for social class 3, there is a social-class gradient in the standardised divorce ratios (SDRs), with those in the professional and intermediate classes having a much lower risk of divorce than those who have been coded as unskilled or partly skilled. The risk of divorce in cases where the husband is in the armed forces, or where the husband is unemployed appears particularly high. Gibson (1974) obtained similar findings when he analysed a national sample of 723 divorcing couples who obtained decrees absolute in 1961, with the white-collar workers of social class 3 and the unskilled manual workers having the highest divorce rates. Gibson attributes this association between social class and divorce to the financial condition of the marriage, particularly as it affects housing conditions. His analysis does not, however, include a consideration of couples where the husband is in the armed forces. Indeed, Haskey's finding that this occupational group are particularly prone to divorce would suggest that economic factors cannot be the sole explanation for the current differentials between divorce rates in different social classes.

Table 4.1   Social class and socioeconomic differentials in divorce

Social class of husband	Number of divorces	SDR	Median length of marriage
1 Professional	55	47	8.3
2 Intermediate	350	83	10.1
3n Skilled non-manual	220	108	9.4
3m Skilled manual	685	97	9.0
4 Partly skilled	295	111	10.2
5 Unskilled	149	220	8.7
6 Armed forces	41	270	7.7
Inadequately described	96	—	12.3
Not economically active	273	—	7.7
Unemployed	142	225	7.9
All social classes	2,164	100	9.2

Source: Courtesy of Haskey 1984, Tables 3, 7

REMARRIAGE

At the beginning of this chapter I discussed first marriages, but about a third of the marriages solemnised each year are second marriages for either the bride or groom or both. If we consider Table 4.2 we can see that the majority of remarriages in 1987 involved one divorced spouse, and within that, remarriages involving both spouses who have been divorced are the largest single component. Twelve per cent, or roughly one in eight of all new marriages involve both spouses who have been divorced.

Table 4.2   Marriage and remarriage, typology, England and Wales, 1987 and (1950)

Groom	Bride		
	Single	Divorced	Widowed
Single	64% (80%)	9% (4%)	0.5% (0.5%)
Divorced	10% (5%)	12% (2%)	1% (1%)
Widowed	0.5% (3%)	1.2% (1%)	1.4% (3%)

Source: Courtesy of OPCS Marriage and Divorce statistics 1974, 1987
Note: All new marriages – proportion of brides and grooms who married spouses of different marital statuses

By comparing the 1987 figures with the corresponding values for 1950 we can see that the increase in the proportion of remarriages as a percentage of all new marriages from 20 per cent to 36 per cent is wholly due to the increase in divorced persons remarrying. The close relationship between trends in remarriage and divorce can be seen clearly in Figure 4.4, with the remarriage and divorce curves running almost parallel to each other until 1980. The first peak in divorce rates, immediately after the war, is mirrored by a peak in remarriage rates for both men and women and the second peak in divorce rates which occurred in 1971 after the Divorce Reform Act is also reflected in the remarriage rates.

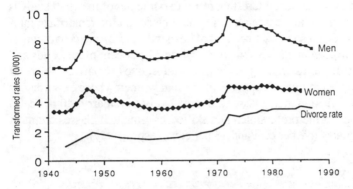

Figure 4.4 Remarriage and divorce rates, England and Wales, 1941–87
Source: OPCS Marriage and Divorce statistics 1974, 1985, 1987
Note: *The remarriage and divorce rates have been transformed using the
square root the operation in order that the three curves may all be
represented on the same graph, i.e. a figure of 6 on the graph represents
an actual rate of 36 per 1,000

Marriage statistics do not directly provide information on the proportions of divorced people who ultimately remarry or on the time interval between divorce and remarriage. However, we do have information on a sample of 1,000 couples who divorced in 1973 (Leete and Anthony 1979). This record linkage study of divorce and remarriage traced the second marriages contracted by the sample up until the end of 1977. It was found that in only 233 out of the 1,000 couples had neither party remarried during this period, while 56 per cent of the men and 48 per cent of the women remarried over the four-and-a-half year period. As divorce often occurs in order for a second marriage to take place, it is not surprising that within a year of the divorce 60 per cent of the men and women who were to remarry by the end of the study, had already done so. After this first year the proportions who remarried declined rapidly. As one might expect, remarriage was found to be more common among the younger divorcees, for example, 60 per cent of women who were under 30 at the time of their divorce remarried, compared to only 32 per cent of women aged 40 and over at divorce.

A second, more recent, and more detailed linkage study was carried out on a sample of over 1,000 couples who divorced in 1979 (Haskey 1987). As was shown in Figure 4.4, the remarriage rate declined slightly for both men and women during the 1970s, and this is reflected by a decrease in the proportions of men and women remarrying in this second study. In the first two years after divorce, 29 per cent of divorced wives and 32 per cent of divorced husbands from the 1979 sample had remarried, compared with 39 per cent of divorced wives and 42 per cent of divorced husbands in the 1973 sample. Perhaps the most interesting result to come out of the 1979 study is the finding that social class has a differential effect on the remarriage rates of men and women so that 41 per cent of husbands and 27 per cent of wives from the non-manual classes remarried, while 31 per cent of husbands and 35 per cent of wives from the manual social classes remarried. If social class is analysed in more detail, it is found that women whose ex-husbands were in the skilled manual classes are most likely to remarry (40 per cent) and husbands in the professional and skilled non-manual classes are most likely to remarry (44 per cent and 45 per cent, respectively).

FERTILITY

This section focuses on fertility and explores the changes in patterns of family building which have occurred over the last forty-five years. Figure 4.5 presents the overall fertility rate (i.e. the number of live births per thousand women aged 15–44) and also shows the trends in age-specific fertility rates. After a sharp peak in 1947 following demobilisation after the Second World War, the overall fertility rate remained reasonably constant in the early 1950s and then rose steadily to a maximum rate of 94 births per 1,000 women in 1964. This was the 'baby boom' of the early 1960s. The fertility rate then declined gradually to a level of 85 per 1,000 in 1971 and dropped more steeply to a low point of 59.3 in 1977.

Historically the number of births in any one year has always exceeded the number of deaths, but in 1976, 1977 and 1978 the number of births dropped below replacement levels for the first time since the start of civil registrations. During the decade after 1977, the live birth rate remained reasonably constant with about 60 babies being born per 1,000 women aged 15–44 each year.

For a more detailed analysis of fertility we need to look at the age-specific birth rates. Among teenage women, fertility rates are substantially lower than for women in their twenties or early thirties, and although the trend is similar to that of the overall fertility rate there are some important differences. First, the same post-war peak in fertility is not exhibited by this age group; there is a gentle 'bump' in the later 1940s but the peak occurs

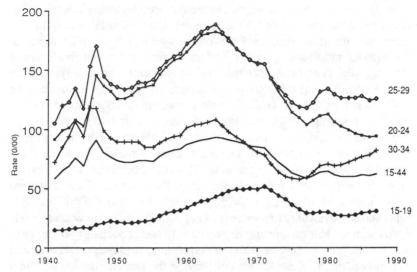

Figure 4.5 Age-specific fertility rates (total births per 1,000 women in each age
          group), England and Wales, 1941–87
Source: OPCS Birth Statistics 1974, 1987

after that of other age groups (in 1949 rather than 1947). The 'baby boom'
of the early 1960s also appears to be delayed in teenage fertility rates, with
the peak coming in 1971 and just over one in twenty teenage women giving
birth to a baby in that year. This compares with only about one in fifty
teenage women giving birth to a baby in 1945.

For the other three age groups in Figure 4.5 the trends in fertility can be
seen to be virtually identical. The curves for the 20–24 and 25–29 age
groups run together from about 1955 to 1970 while in the later 1940s and
early 1950s the fertility rate was slightly higher for women in their late
twenties. This pattern is repeated after 1971 when the fertility rate dropped
more steeply for women in their early twenties than for women in any other
age group. In other words, from the early 1950s until around 1970 there was
a gradual shift towards earlier childbearing, with increases in the fertility
rates of the under twenty-fives. However, since 1970 there has been a
tendency for women to postpone having children. This is exhibited by the
fact that during this period it was fertility rates for the youngest age groups
which fell most steeply while from 1975 onwards fertility rates in the 30–34
age group have risen considerably.

The two factors which have the biggest effect on the fertility rate in any
one year are the quantity of fertility (or family size), and the timing of
fertility (or family spacing). On the first count there is indeed evidence

from surveys that the number of children desired by married women has fallen since the early 1960s. One example is a follow-up survey of 350 couples married in Hull in 1965–66 in which 312 couples were re-interviewed and their experience of fertility during the first five years of marriage was compared with their initial intentions on family building (Peel 1972). Among these couples, intended family size was found to be 2.61 children on average in the first interview, but had been revised downwards to an average of 2.23 children five years later. In other words the 312 couples had originally wanted a total of 813 children, but this had now declined to only 697 children. The most common reasons given for these changes in intentions were economic (55 out of 106 couples who revised their ideal number of children downwards). The contraceptives most commonly used were found to be the condom (35 per cent), the pill (31.7 per cent) and withdrawal (21.6 per cent). Peel highlighted the new control that contraceptives had given parents over family size, concluding on an optimistic note: 'people now have almost complete control over their behaviour in family planning. Couples are now having the families they want rather than making the most of what they get' (Peel 1972: 345).

Table 4.3 Fertility rates by cohort and age group

	Fertility per 1,000 women in each age group				
Period during which child-bearing started	*15–19*	*20–24*	*25–29*	*30–34*	*35–39*
1941–45	16	134	140	96	**50**
1946–50	21	135	164	**106**	41
1951–55	22	159	**184**	90	26
1956–60	31	**180**	165	67	20
1961–65	**41**	165	138	53	
1966–70	49	135	127		
1971–75	44	108			
1976–80	31				

Source: Courtesy of OPCS Birth Statistics 1974, 1985, 1987

It is more complex to understand how the timing of childbirth for different cohorts affects the yearly fertility rate, but consideration of the data as laid out in Table 4.3 may help to explain this phenomenon. In this table the rows indicate the fertility experiences of different cohorts as they progress through the life course so that we can see, for example, that the cohort who started childbearing in 1951–55 were the last cohort whose peak childbearing age was 25–29 and that for subsequent cohorts it has been younger (20–24). By looking down the first column we can also see that from the early 1950s each cohort in turn experienced greater rates of teenage childbirth until the 1970s.

Each diagonal running downwards towards the left in the table represents a snapshot of fertility during a particular quinquennium. The diagonal representing the five years 1961–1965 has been highlighted, and it shows quite clearly how the baby boom was brought about. Women in their early twenties were having families unusually early at the same time that the previous cohort was going through their period of maximum fertility in their late twenties; teenage fertility rates were higher than they had ever been, and the fertility rates in the older age groups (30–34, 35–39) were also relatively high, presumably because the war had disrupted their early fertility experiences. Thus we can see how the differential timing of fertility for different cohorts of women brought about the baby boom of the early 1960s.

ILLEGITIMACY

From 1950 to the end of the 1970s the vast majority of births (over 90 per cent) took place within marriage, and therefore in the previous section by discussing fluctuations in the total birth rate we have largely been focusing on legitimate births. This section will specifically consider illegitimate births. Figure 4.6 shows the trends in both the absolute number of illegitimate births during the period 1941 to 1987 and also in the illegitimacy ratio (that is the proportion of all births which are illegitimate).

The first peak in the number of illegitimate births can be seen to occur approximately two years earlier than for the total birth rate, i.e. during rather than after the last stages of the Second World War.

After this wartime peak, when 10 per cent of all births were illegitimate (a total of 63,000 births in 1945), the illegitimacy ratio dropped to a relatively low value of 5 per cent and stayed fairly constant during the 1950s. From 1960 levels of illegitimacy began to rise steadily, to a ratio of 8.4 per cent in 1968. On 27 April 1968 the 1967 Abortion Act came into effect, which for the first time permitted termination of pregnancy by a registered medical practitioner, subject to conditions other than purely medical ones[2]. This new legislation can be seen to have arrested the rise in the illegitimacy ratio for about another eight years. Indeed if we look at the total number of illegitimate births they can be seen to decline fairly rapidly from a total of 70,000 in 1968 to 54,000 in 1976. Over this same period the number of abortions performed on residents of England and Wales increased from 22,000 in the last eight months of 1968 to 102,000 in 1976 (about half of these were carried out for single women). Thus the number

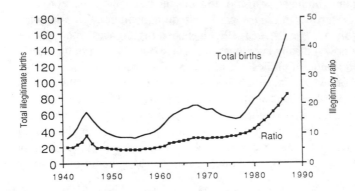

Figure 4.6 Illegitimate births and the illegitimacy ratio in England and Wales,
         1941–87
Source: OPCS Birth Statistics 1974, 1987

of births to single women declined by 16,000 compared with a 40,000
increase in abortions over the eight years from 1968 to 1976, which would
suggest that the number of conceptions to unmarried women continued to
increase at approximately the same rate as it had been increasing before the
Abortion Act.

From 1976 the number of illegitimate births and the illegitimacy ratio
rose steeply again, and both show no signs of levelling out. However, from
the late 1970s onwards, with the increase in cohabitation and a decrease in
first-marriage rates, it may be argued that the meaning of illegitimacy
changes[3]. Many couples are now having children out of wedlock intentionally, so that an illegitimate child may be born into a *de facto* family.
Information on the birth certificate as to whether a child is registered by
only the mother (sole registration), or by the mother and father (joint
registration), may be used as a proxy to indicate the circumstances of the
child's birth.

If we look at the two pie charts in Figure 4.7, which show the outcomes
of extramarital conceptions in 1986 compared with 1976, we can see that
over this decade there has indeed been a change in the nature of
illegitimacy.

Whereas in 1976, 35 per cent of women who conceived outside marriage
decided to have the baby, but not to get married, in 1986 this figure had
risen to 50 per cent: of these illegitimate births, just over 50 per cent were

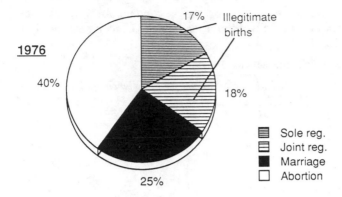

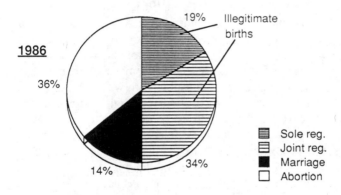

Figure 4.7 Outcome of conceptions outside marriage for women of all ages, England and Wales
Source: OPCS Birth Statistics 1987, Table S19

joint registered in 1976 but by 1986 the proportion was nearly 70 per cent. In other words joint registration seems to be replacing marriage as a response to pregnancy for a growing number of couples.

WOMEN'S WORKING PATTERNS

These changes in British families, since the Second World War, have been accompanied by some dramatic changes in women's employment patterns.

Table 4.4 summarises some of these changes in women's paid work. At the 1951 census, there were twice as many men in the paid workforce than women, by the 1981 census the ratio approaches even numbers with women making up 40 per cent of the workforce, and by 1987 this figure had risen to 45 per cent (Joshi 1989).

Table 4.4 Women's economic activity, 1951–81

	Economically active women as a % of all women aged 20–64			Women of all ages as % of labour force
	Total	Full-time	Part-time	
1951	36.3	30.3	5.2	30.8
1961	42.2	32.1	9.1	32.5
1971	52.3	32.8	18.0	36.5
1981	61.1	30.4	27.1	40.2

Source: Courtesy of Joshi 1989, Table 10.1

It can be seen that although the participation rate of women of working age increased dramatically between 1951 and 1981, there has been very little change in women's participation in full-time work. All of the post-war increase in women's employment is accounted for by the increase in part-time jobs. These changes mean that whereas before the war a woman's career as part of the labour force usually ended when she got married and work outside the home was seen as incompatible with wifely duties, in the period after the war the birth of a first child replaced marriage as the appropriate time to leave paid work, and many women returned to work once the youngest child was of school age. The increase in participation rates can largely be accounted for by married women returning to the labour market at shorter and shorter intervals after child bearing.

Table 4.5 Women's economic activity by age of youngest child

		Age of youngest child			
	Childless	0–4	5–10	11–15	16+
Full-time	78	7	16	31	32
Part-time	6	20	48	45	34
'Unemployed'	9	4	4	5	5
Economically inactive	7	69	32	19	29

Source: Courtesy of Martin and Roberts 1984, Table 2.6

Despite the substantial increases in women's economic activity, the majority of women are still directly responsible for most of the care of their children until they start school, and thereafter outside school hours and during school holidays. Martin and Roberts (1984) found that the age of the youngest child in the family was a better predictor of women's economic activity than the number of children aged under 16.

Table 4.5 clearly shows that women with dependent children are significantly less likely to be economically active than those with no dependent children, and that as those dependent children get older, a growing proportion of women go out to work full-time rather than part-time.

These changes in female employment are often invoked as explanations for the changing patterns of family formation and dissolution which have been observed since the end of the Second World War. Maire Ni Bhrolchain (1986a, b) has investigated the associations between women's employment and birth spacing in life-history data from the 1946 cohort and the 1976 Family Formation Survey. She suggests that women with a high commitment to the labour market may adopt one of two different strategies. They may either shorten their birth intervals in order to minimise the total amount of time spent out of the labour market caring for small children. Alternatively, they may lengthen birth intervals in order to return to work between periods of childbearing and child care. Thus two effects of women's employment on fertility are hypothesised: current work exerting a negative decelerating influence and prospective employment a positive accelerating influence. Ni Bhrolchain concludes that during the 1950s and 1960s prospective job opportunities gave women an incentive to accelerate their fertility, and that during the 1970s this mechanism was reversed, in that more women were returning to the labour market between births which tends to lead to longer gaps between babies. In addition, she highlights the important role played by improvements in contraception giving women choice and control over their fertility patterns. We should also note the advances in maternity care which decrease the medical risks to women giving birth at later ages.

Women's increased labour-force participation has also been offered as one of the possible structural determinants of the divorce rate (Trent and South 1989). Women's increased economic activity may make them less dependent on husbands' income, and thus provide the requisite independence for dissolving unhappy marriages. Trent and South analyse data from a sample of sixty-six different countries to investigate the societal-level correlates of the divorce rate. Their results show that there is a curvilinear (U-shaped) relationship between female labour-force participation rates and the divorce rate. So that the divorce rate first decreases and then increases with the increase in the proportion of women in paid employment.[4]

In a multivariate analysis of the Women in Employment sample of 5,320 women (Martin and Roberts 1984) Ermisch (1989) found that women with more work experience at a given duration of marriage were more likely to get divorced subsequently, and this result was maintained independent of the effects of fertility and age at marriage. He also suggests, however, that there may be aspects of reverse causation, in that women who perceive a high risk of divorce may seek paid employment as an 'insurance' against the financial consequences of divorce. But it seems unlikely that the effect could be completely explained in this way.

CONCLUSIONS: FUSION AND FISSION – WHAT BECAME OF THE NUCLEAR FAMILY?

In the four decades since the end of the Second World War there have clearly been, and continue to be, changes in the nature of the family, and changes in the experiences of the individuals within the family. It could be argued that we have seen the demise of what is believed to be the typical family unit, namely a 'nuclear family' consisting of a married couple and their legitimate children living together as a single, discrete household. As Table 4.6 shows, married-couple families with dependent children made up less than one-third of households in 1987.

Table 4.6 The distribution of household types in 1961 and 1987

	1961 %	1987 %
One person		
under pensionable age	4	9
over pensionable age	7	16
Two or more unrelated adults	5	3
Married couple with:		
no children	26	27
1–2 dependent children	30	23
3+ dependent children	8	5
adult children only	10	9
Lone parent with:		
dependent children	2	4
adult children only	4	4
2+ families	3	1
All households	100	100

Source: Courtesy of CSO 1989a Social Trends 19, Table 2.3

However, we can also see that even in 1961 when marriage and fertility rates were relatively high and the divorce rate was low (at one-sixth of the rate for 1987), only 38 per cent of households matched the description of a typical nuclear family described earlier. Indeed if we compare the percentage of lone-parent families we can see that between 1961 and 1987 this figure only increased from 6 to 8 per cent. The most noticeable change in household composition is that in 1961 only one-eighth of households contained one person living alone compared with one-quarter of households in 1987.

The problem with such figures is that they can only provide a snapshot of the distribution of different types of households at any one time. It is therefore more informative to consider changes in the family in terms of its life course. In 1947 Glick described the life cycle of the family in a classic article as follows:

> From its formation until its dissolution, a family passes through a series of stages that are subject to demographic analysis. Typically, a family comes into being when a couple is married. The family gains in size with the birth of each child. From the time when the last child is born until the first child leaves home, the family remains stable in size. As the children leave home for employment or marriage, the size of the family shrinks gradually back to the original two persons. Eventually one and then the other of the parents die and the family cycle has come to an end.
>
> (Glick 1947: 164)

The mid-1950s with long life expectancy and very low divorce rates was perhaps the first and last time historically that the family life cycle could be described in these terms. The family can no longer be seen as coming into being 'when a couple is married', as in the 1980s we see an increasingly differentiated process of family formation with cohabitation often preceding legal marriage, and a growth in the number of children born into these *de facto* unions. As a result of the high divorce and remarriage rates, children no longer only join families by being born, and parents no longer only leave the family by dying.

Indeed, the reason that the proportion of lone-parent households has not increased more markedly since the early 1960s, despite the rise in divorce, is the high incidence of remarriage. At virtually the same rate as families are splitting up, new 'reconstituted' families are being formed. In the introduction to his book *Marriage, Divorce, Remarriage* Andrew Cherlin (1981) describes the following hypothetical life history.

> When Bill was ten, his parents separated. He lived with his mother and saw his father every Saturday. Four years later, his mother remarried,

and Bill added a stepfather to his family. At eighteen, Bill left home to attend college, and after graduation he and his girlfriend moved in together. A year and a half later they married and soon afterwards they had a child. After several years, however, the marriage began to turn sour. Bill and his wife eventually separated with Bill's wife retaining custody of the child. Three years later Bill married a woman who had a child from a previous marriage and together they had another child. Bill's second marriage lasted 35 years until his death.

(Cherlin 1981: 1)

During his lifetime Bill had lived in eight different households (making the same distinctions between categories as in Table 4.6). Clearly not everyone can expect to pass through all the events in this example, but although in the 1950s someone with a family history as complicated as this would have been rare, in the 1980s it is no longer so unusual.

The identity of a family is now more diffuse as it is increasingly likely to undergo a series of transitions; metamorphoses involving both fission and fusion. This makes it more difficult to identify and follow the life cycle of a single family and necessitates focusing on the life histories of individuals instead, as they join and leave these more transitory family units.

NOTES

1   The 1969 Divorce Reform Act effectively dismantled the concept of a matrimonial offence. The new provisions of the act meant that a petition for divorce could be presented to the court by either party to a marriage on the ground that the marriage had broken down irretrievably. In order to prove that the marriage has broken down irretrievably the petitioner must convince the court of one of the following facts:
   (a) That the respondent has committed adultery and the petitioner finds it intolerable to live with the respondent;
   (b) that the respondent has behaved in such a way that the petitioner cannot reasonably be expected to live with the respondent;
   (c) that the respondent has deserted the petitioner for a continuous period of more than two years immediately preceding the presentation of the petition;
   (d) that the parties to the marriage have lived apart for a continuous period of at least two years immediately preceding the presentation of the petition and the respondent consents to a decree being granted;
   (e) that the parties to the marriage have lived apart for a continuous period of at least five years immediately preceding the presentation of the petition.
2   The conditions of the 1967 Abortion Act were that a legally induced abortion must be (a) performed by a registered medical practitioner, (b) performed, except in an emergency, in an NHS hospital or in a place approved for the purposes of the act, (c) certified by two registered medical practitioners as necessary on any of the following grounds:

(i)   The pregnancy causes a risk to the woman's life
(ii) There is a risk to the physical or mental health of the woman
(iii) There is a risk to the physical or mental health of existing children
(iv) There is a substantial risk of the unborn child suffering from such physical or mental abnormalities as to be seriously handicapped.

The majority (90 per cent) of abortions are carried out on ground number 2 alone.

3   Recent changes in family law (such as the 1987 Family Law Reform Act) have removed the remaining differences in the legal rights of children born in and outside of marriage. The term 'illegitimate' may no longer be used in legal documents.

4   The sex ratio, a late average age at marriage, and an index of socioeconomic development were also found to be significantly related to the divorce rate in Trent and South's study (1989).

REFERENCES

Brown, A. and Kiernan, K. (1981) 'Cohabitation in Great Britain', *Population Trends* 25: 4–10, London: HMSO.

CSO (1989a) *Social Trends*, London: HMSO.

—— (1989b) *Annual Abstract of Statistics*, London: HMSO.

Cherlin, A. (1981) *Marriage, Divorce, Remarriage*, Cambridge, Massachusetts: Harvard University Press.

Ermisch, J. (1989) 'Divorce: economic antecedents and aftermath' in H. Joshi (ed.) *The Changing Population of Britain*, Oxford: Blackwell.

Finer Report (1974) *Report of the committee on one parent families*, London: HMSO.

Gibson, C. (1974) 'The association between divorce and social class in England and Wales', *British Journal of Sociology* 25: 79–93.

Glick, P. (1947) 'The family life cycle', *American Sociological Review* 12: 164–74.

Haskey, J. (1984) 'Social class and socio-economic differentials in divorce in England and Wales', *Population Studies* 38: 419–38.

—— (1986) 'Recent trends in divorce', *Population Trends* 44: 9–16, London: HMSO.

—— (1987) 'Social class differentials in remarriage after divorce: results from a forward linkage study', *Population Trends* 47: 34–42, London: HMSO.

—— (1989) 'Current prospects for the proportion of marriages ending in divorce', *Population Trends* 55: 34–7, London: HMSO.

Kiernan, K.E. (1989) 'Family formation and fission', in H. Joshi (ed.) *The Changing Population of Britain*, Oxford: Blackwell.

—— and Eldridge, S.M. (1987) 'Inter- and intra-cohort variation in the timing of first marriage', *British Journal of Sociology* 38: 44–65.

Joshi, H. (ed.) (1989) 'The changing form of women's economic dependency', in *The Changing Population of Britain*, Oxford: Blackwell.

Leete, R. and Anthony, S. (1979) 'Divorce and remarriage: a record linkage study', *Population Trends*, 16: 5–11, London: HMSO.

Martin, J. and Roberts, C. (1984) *Women and Employment: a lifetime perspective*, London: HMSO.

Ni Bhrolchain, M. (1986a) 'Women's paid work and the timing of births: longitudinal evidence', *European Journal of Population* 2: 43–7.

—— (1986b) 'The interpretation and role of work-associated accelerated child-bearing in post-war Britain', *European Journal of Population* 2: 135–54.

Office of Population Censuses and Surveys (OPCS) (1974) *Birth statistics*, London: HMSO.

—— (1974) *Marriage and Divorce statistics*, London: HMSO.

—— (1985) *Birth statistics*, London: HMSO.

—— (1985) *Marriage and Divorce statistics*, London: HMSO.

—— (1987) *Birth statistics*, London: HMSO.

—— (1987) *Marriage and Divorce statistics*, London: HMSO.

Peel, J. (1972) 'The Hull family survey II: family planning in the first five years of marriage', *Journal of Biosocial Science* 4: 333–46.

Registrar General's Statistical Review (1973) London: HMSO.

Trent, K. and South, S.J. (1989) 'Structural determinants of the divorce rate: a cross-societal analysis', *Journal of Marriage and the Family* 51: 391–404, Nebraska: NCFR.

Part III

Private troubles, public issues

Introduction

In this third part of the book we move away from the narrative and chronology of emerging social and historical processes surrounding marriage and domestic life over four decades. We now consider some of the underlying themes which have come to preoccupy family researchers in recent decades – notions of the public and the private, of institution and relationship, of structure and agency and of intervention in family life. We look at the role of ideology in shaping how we make sense of family life and experiences within it. We consider some of the differing frameworks for understanding marriage and the intimate world, particularly those deriving from sociological, psychodynamic and social-work theories. In much of this, from whichever perspective, the concern is with ways in which the private experiences encountered in marital and family relationships are shaped and given meaning in relation to external events and circumstances.

David Morgan's theme is that of the ideologies which surround marriage and family life. He begins by contrasting 'family talk' as it is constituted by both 'lay' persons and 'professionals' and suggests that the concept of ideology is helpful in understanding this distinction. Ideologies, however, should not be seen merely as the products of elite groups, and sociologists should be alive to the dangers of reifying family ideologies. Such ideologies are often linked to constructions of the past and the imputation of differences between past and present. Morgan highlights the irony of ideological constructions of the family which portray it as a natural, immutable domain but which at the same time raise anxieties about the degree of unwelcome change taking place in family life. The notion of a shift from marriage as institution to marriage as relationship embodies some of these contradictions and as Morgan shows, such an ideology can be used to mask important differences within marriage, for example, those based on gender or ethnicity.

David Clark is also concerned with differences in marriage, particularly in the early months of matrimony. Drawing on the concerns of phenomenological sociology and of feminism, he goes on to present the kind of approach to understanding marriage and domestic life which was referred to at various points in the first part of the book. This is a qualitative perspective in which the focus is upon the constitution of the marital world in the early months. Using data from a study of fifty couples, conducted in Aberdeen in the early 1980s, he explores a range of emergent experiences. Clark presents a four-part typology of early marriage in which the dominant metaphors are of couples *drifting, surfacing, establishing* or *struggling*. He refers to the problems of this kind of typology but argues that qualitative methodologies have enormous importance for our understanding of the range of experiences taking place within the 'private' domain of marital and familial relationships.

Christopher Clulow develops this theme of understanding the internal aspects of marriage, in a chapter where he draws upon his own clinical experience in order to illustrate the contours of a psychodynamic under- standing. The psychodynamic model gives special attention to the role of unconscious motives in behaviour and makes connections between a person's earliest experiences and later relationships in adult life. It there- fore has a great deal to offer those who, like Clulow, seek to understand how marriages are made, broken and remade. Men and women are por- trayed here as 'selective historians, unwittingly emphasising certain features and obscuring others as they interpret experience'. We see some of the psychodynamic factors which shape how and why spouses choose one another, the mutual satisfactions and disappointments which can occur in their relationships and some of the ways in which these are dealt with. Focusing on the consequences of break-up, Clulow draws attention to the several strands of the marriage relationship which come apart at this point and he shows how the psychodynamic perspective is also alert to the wide range of external issues, such as property and legal factors, which can determine psychological reactions at this time. He also looks at the longer- term emotional consequences of divorce and the ways in which it can shape the experience of remarriage, both for adults and children. The inclusion here of a chapter written from a psychodynamic perspective is a significant reminder of the progress which has been made in recent years towards a multidisciplinary understanding of marriage in society.

Janet Walker's chapter explores the full range of social work and psycho- therapeutic interventions in family life in the period since the Second World War. Ranging over the broad sweep of legislative change sur- rounding social work in this period, she explains the relationship between statutory and voluntary social-work provision within the welfare state and draws attention to the varying roles of specialism and genericism in social- work practice. In an exploration of the 'best interests' philosophy, Walker then focuses on social work with children, including those 'in trouble' through their own actions and those 'in care' because of their wider social circumstances or risks to which they are exposed in the home. She then looks at the major implications of changing patterns of family formation and dissolution, particularly divorce, for social work with families: in marriage guidance, family conciliation and family therapy. She concludes with a discussion of the limits which surround state intervention in family life, and uses the 1989 Children Act as an illustration of the new emphasis upon balancing autonomy with protection. Walker's account shows social work with families undergoing a number of crises and transitions as it struggles to understand and intervene in situations of immense personal, political and structural complexity.

In his chapter on 'pretended family relationships' Jeffrey Weeks returns us to the theme of ideology, reminding us of how alternatives to conventional family life are but weakly articulated within our culture. He takes a fascinating case study to illustrate this: the debates surrounding Clause 28 of the 1987 Local Government Bill, which sought to prevent local authorities 'promoting' homosexuality. Weeks sees this piece of legislation as a heavily over-determined example of the New Right's preoccupation with the 'crisis' surrounding conventional family life, an opportunity to strike back against those alternative movements which were inexorably lapping around its base. Through a discussion of the commune movement of the 1960s, as well as subsequent alternatives to the conventional family, Weeks moves on to explore the significance of the later pluralisation of family life within academic and policy discourse. He describes a variety of 'subterranean social orders' which might contain authentic alternatives to family relationships: in particular 'moral communities' in which 'mutual support and need give rise to value systems in which the community itself becomes the focus of attachment and the location for the growth of intimate relationships', and he cites communal responses to HIV and AIDS as an example of this. Weeks is preoccupied neither with finding alternatives to family life, nor with stretching the concept of 'family' to include all intimate relationships. He concludes with an uplifting appeal for the development of an 'ethical pluralism' which recognises that the achievement of happiness and personal fulfilment need not be restricted to those who inhabit the world of the family.

5 Ideologies of marriage and family life

David Morgan

Whatever the actual status of marriage and the family as institutions there can be little doubt that talk about these topics remains a popular activity. The talk, of course, varies considerably in terms of level of abstraction and degree of formality ranging from the speech at a party political conference or the scholarly paper to everyday talk about particular weddings, baptisms or funerals and the complex and shifting nexus of relationships and obligations that come to the fore on such occasions. The differences between these two sets of practices might be characterised as approximating to the differences between a speech and a conversation. In both cases words are uttered but in the case of the conversation these words are exchanged and conducted with all the interplays between verbal and non-verbal cues, modifications and qualifications and hesitations that characterise inter-personal encounters generally. Exchange is not absent in the former case, of course, although it may be conducted more formally, through question and answer mediated through a chair or through verbal and written exchanges through the mass media, exchanges that do not require the direct co-presence of the other.

The set of problems that I want to consider here concerns the relation-ships that exist or might be assumed to exist between these two sets of practices. Both sets of practices would seem to focus on similar topics; in both cases we would seem to be considering 'family talk'. However, in what sense can it be maintained that the two different sets of actors are in fact talking about the same thing or set of things? For a start, it would seem likely that everyday talk around these topics (including the everyday talk of politicians, clergy or sociologists when they are, as it were, off duty or in civilian dress) rarely addresses 'The Family' or 'Marriage'; rather, they talk about Uncle Norman's illness, Daphne's divorce or the problems that Steve and Di are having with the twins. A third party, often a sociologist, is required to constitute these utterances and exchanges as 'family talk'. A further set of questions arises when we consider the possible linkages between the two sets of practices, even if we agree that they are both in some sense examples of 'family talk'.

Other chapters in this book deal with questions of change that have actually taken place in marriage and the family during the latter part of this century. I am not here so concerned with these changes. Rather, I am more concerned with versions or accounts of such changes, with the stories that people, lay and professional, tell about what has happened to these institutions over time. They may be comparing their own experiences with the experiences of their parents or grandparents, or talking about changes within their own lifetimes or they may be making comparisons with even more remote and less well-defined times in the past. Ultimately, of course, social change and talk about change cannot be separated; each constitutes the other. Another way of considering the theme of this chapter is to do with the troublesome word 'ideology' and the ways in which ideological constructions of marriage and the family are bound up with ideas of stability and change, with comparisons between the way we were and the way we live now. I want both to explore the problems and potentialities of the use of the concept of 'ideology' in this context and to explore the ways in which 'family talk', however formalised or elaborated, becomes part of everyday marital and family living.

THE CONCEPT OF IDEOLOGY

Ideology, as has often been noted, is one of the most troublesome words in the sociological lexicon (Williams 1983). This is not the place for a full literature survey although we do need a little more than a bare definition. What I attempt to do here is to explore a set of issues, tensions or ambiguities in the use of the term 'ideology' in sociological discussion, noting in particular the relevance of these debates for the study of marriage and the family.

1 In the first place there is the question of with what ideological statements or representations are being compared, in other words what might be said to count as a 'non-ideological' statement. In some cases this is seen as a question of the relationship between 'science' and 'ideology', one which, in many versions, is often seen in oppositional terms. Indeed, it is often maintained, part of the application of science is towards the exposure, the bringing out into the open, of ideology. But what if science is itself ideological?

   In the case of family and marital relationships we can see the tension at its clearest in the case of various professional and therapeutic interventions into domestic life and the theories and research that support and derive from such interventions. Here we are considering the various traditions and derivations from Freudian psychoanalysis, communications theory and systems theories. On the one hand we can see all these as providing genuine insights into the nature of family and domestic life, into the unconscious motivations that influence behaviour, into the processes that not only shape or distort interpersonal communication within marriage and the family but which simultaneously mask or inhibit the recognition of these processes by the individuals involved. Such insights may be drawn upon by therapists and counsellors to increase self-awareness on the part of family members or to alleviate some of the pain associated with family crises such as bereavement or divorce. On the other hand, a more sceptical perspective may see these developments as part of processes which involve increasing professional and state surveillance into areas of private life and the increasing privatisation of 'problems' in an advanced capitalist society. In place of a progressive and broadly humanistic view of science as rationally derived understanding applied for the alleviation of marital or family problems we have a perspective which emphasises the role of these 'problems' and sees the development of these discourses as contributing to the reproduction of a wider capitalist or patriarchal order.

The tension does not end there. What of those perspectives, sociological, Marxist or feminist, which claim to cast doubt on to the scientific insights into domestic life? Are these to be viewed as genuine scientific insights or as alternative ideological perspectives? This is, of course, a relatively familiar dilemma in the sociology of knowledge (see, for example, Merton 1957: 456–88) and one that cannot simply be resolved by fiat. Part of the process of resolution will include the recognition that all knowledge is socially located and has social consequences, both recognised and unrecognised, but that this does not in itself necessarily entail the absolute denial of the knowledge under consideration. It will also need to be recognised that 'ideology' itself is not a thing or a process detached from human agency but itself represents a critical perspective on society, a perspective which is similarly socially located. Thus it is clear that the growing insights into 'marital problems' that have developed since the Second World War and which, in Britain, have been associated with the theory and practice of Marriage Guidance have enabled individuals to gain insights into their own relationships and into the relationships of others while at the same time contributing to the very construction of certain aspects of relationships between spouses as constituting 'marital problems' in the first place. Such constructions have further consequences in, for example, the blurring of gender, class or ethnic divisions. Any concrete analysis must be careful, detailed and historical, prepared to recognise the shifting claims and counterclaims between ideology and science and to recognise the complexities, ambiguities and ironies involved not only in these social processes but in the process of investigation itself (for examples see Brannan and Collard 1982; Clark and Haldane 1990; Reiger 1985).

2 A second set of problems is to do with the question as to whether we are concerned with a unified ideology, associated with and possibly functional for, a given social order, or whether we are dealing with a plurality of ideologies, attached to a variety of social groups, each with its own special interests. In this chapter I shall be arguing for a modified plural version. I shall argue that there are a variety of interested parties in matters to do with marriage and the family and that these do not necessarily form a simple or seamless unity. Thus we can talk about a range of professionals, of political interests or religious leaders without assuming that all these interests converge in some kind of automatic harmony.

However, this should not lead us to suppose that there is a completely open market in these matters. Unities may be complex and contradictory as well as mutually reinforcing and harmonious. It may, indeed, be possible to argue that the very deployment of the concept of 'ideology' may itself, on occasions, over-simplify or mask contradictions and tensions within the ideologies.

I have two examples, taken from the post-Second World War period, which may serve to illustrate this complex and sometimes contradictory unity. The fourth issue of a publication called *Getting Married*, a special edition of the popular medical magazine, *Family Doctor* and published by the British Medical Association, was the subject of a certain amount of scandal and concern at the time of its publication. This included an article by Eustace Chesser under the title 'Is chastity outmoded?' (Chesser n.d.). This piece appeared alongside articles by the anthropologist, Ashley Montague, Joseph Brayshaw of the National Marriage Guidance Council, Marjorie Proops (a well-known advice columnist), a Methodist minister (the Rev. Peter Ainsworth), another anthropologist (Kenneth Little) and a legal expert (Elaine Gee). As might be expected, the bulk of the articles came from people with medical qualifications and dealt with such subjects as mothers-in-law, sex within marriage and whether it would be possible to determine the sex of a child in advance. The pieces were short, down to earth in style and supported by photographs, cartoons and short, humorous articles. There were more 'commercial' pieces on cooking, furnishing and generally setting up home. We find more or less the same picture in 1960, which also includes pieces by Marjorie Proops, Ashley Montague and Joseph Brayshaw, the church this time being represented by the celebrated Methodist preacher,

Dr Leslie Weatherhead. Weatherhead was certainly no supporter of the relatively modest permissive proposals being advanced by Chesser in the earlier publication.

Another illustration comes from a couple of publications dealing with divorce and coming from the Church of England. *Putting Asunder* (1966) presented the Church's conclusions (in a group appointed by the Archbishop of Canterbury) in arguing for the substitution of the concept of 'marriage breakdown' for the older legal idea of 'matrimonial offence'. This publication had an appendix on the psychological aspects of marriage, referring extensively to the work of Dr H.V. Dicks, closely associated with the Tavistock Institute. There was also an Appendix on sociological aspects by Professor Donald Macrae. Oral evidence came from Lady Ormrod (London Marriage Guidance Council), Gerald Sanctuary (National Marriage Guidance Council), Justice Ormrod and, again, Dr Dicks. Some of the implications of the divorce reforms largely set in motion by this report were considered in another publication. *Marriage and the Church's Task* (1978). Here the General Synod Marriage Commission considered oral evidence from, among others, Nicholas Tyndall on behalf of the NMGC, a representative of the Institute of Marital Studies and Jack Dominian. Perhaps of special interest is Appendix 6, which gives two examples of work with married couples, a workshop on marriage education which included references to the very influential work of Virginia Satir and a marriage-enrichment group. In the latter programme, key books were by David and Vera Mace, Eric Berne, Jack Dominian, T.A. Harris (*I'm OK, You're OK*), Carl Rogers and Virginia Satir.

The point about these two examples is that they both may be understood as adding up to a positive endorsement of marriage. Yet this unified view can only be seen as a complex one, bringing together individuals, groups and interests which should not be seen as constituting a simple unity and who certainly had different kinds of involvement or interest in marriage itself. The fact that many of the British contributors to these two sets of publications may have been loosely linked through those kinds of metworks that often connect 'the great and the good' should not obscure the possible differences. There were certainly contradictions (Chesser versus Weatherhead, for example) and differences between majority and minority views. Further, the views represented in these publications were not necessarily the views of all the members of the various organisations and professions represented in these discussions. Nevertheless, we can see all these writings as constituting an overall endorsement of the centrality and importance of marriage while recognising the various social and legal changes that had been taking place, including a growing questioning of premarital chastity and the desire for the reform of the divorce laws.

3 Closely associated with this previous point is a distinction between general and specific aspects of ideology and the hypothesised relationships between them. In the present case, at the more general level there is the promotion of understandings about marriage and the family which, it might be argued, underline their centrality, naturalness or basic quality. In a variety of papers, Bernardes has argued forcefully that the very use of the term 'family' (including its use by sociologists) tends not simply to a process of reification whereby the family takes on a thing-like status but also gives endorsement to conservative ideologies which treat the family in naturalistic, basic and ahistorical terms (Bernardes 1985, 1986). Doubtless, similar arguments might be made in relation to the usages of the term, 'marriage'. It can be argued that the constant use of the word 'family' in contexts such as 'family policy', 'family doctor', 'family viewing' or 'family sized' all tend in the same direction, that is towards taking the institution of the family out of its social and historical context and reinforcing a naturalistic and essentialist set of understandings. Weeks' analysis of the phrase 'pretended family relationships' (Chapter 9, this volume) may be seen as an illustration of this process.

However, ideology may be concerned with more specific issues such as 'sex before marriage', the sexual division of labour within the home or whether the Church should remarry divorced persons. Here, there is much more room for contradiction and disagreement and much more ambiguity about the very nature of an ideological utterance or text. Chesser's arguments against rigid premarital chastity were very much presented in a kind of scientific discourse, considering, for example, the harm that might be done to individuals or to society as a whole through too dogmatic an insistence on virginity (Chesser, n.d.). With hindsight, however, it is possible to reread his arguments as having ideological significance through their ultimate endorsement of marital relationships, of sexuality within such heterosexual relationships to the overall support of the institution of marriage in a changing world. The emphasis was as much on the 'marital' as the 'pre-'.

What is being suggested in this argument is a set of possible links between specific 'messages' or 'talk' about marriage and the family and more general ideological constructions of these institutions. It is possible, for example, for people to argue for quite different positions in relation to the sexual division of labour within the home or the advisability of the employment of mothers but to refer these specific arguments back, equally, to more general conceptualisations of the family.

Further, such statements and arguments need not refer solely to questions of marriage and the family; they may also refer to issues of sexualities and normal sexuality, to questions of work and employment or to the wider organisation of gender relations. Specific utterances on sex before, within or outside marriage may draw upon and reinforce more general notions of marriage and the family. However, these links cannot be taken for granted. These assumed links should be recognised as hypotheses or theoretical constructions, as guides to further research and analysis. For example, there has been much valuable work conducted around the ways in which individual couples or family members make use of more general notions of 'family' and 'normality' in coming to terms with or making sense of their own particular and very concrete domestic situations. This might include such situations as dealing with a handicapped child (Voysey 1975) or 'making a go' of remarriage (Burgoyne and Clark 1984).

4 A further issue, again overlapping with the previous ones in the analysis of ideology, concerns the extent of its influence. Most of the discussion up to now has concentrated on various elite or professional groups within contemporary British society; senior members of the Church of England and other religious bodies; marital counsellors, paid or unpaid; politicians, members of the medical profession and so on. To delineate ideology as originating in such groups is, as we have seen, itself no straightforward task. To assume that this ideology is disseminated throughout the general population is a even more complex matter. Indeed, Abercrombie and colleagues (Abercrombie *et al.* 1980) argue that often ideology functions not so much as a means of incorporation of the subordinate classes into the wider social order but rather as a mechanism contributing to the unities of various elite groups themselves. If, as would seem to be the case in matters to do with marriage and the family, non-elite members continue to give silent or vocal endorsement to the wider social order, this may not be a consequence of ideological indoctrination but through the 'dull compulsion' of everyday economic life. In the case of marriage and the family, this may be translated in terms of the relative lack of viable alternatives.

Whether or not we accept this position in its entirety, there is undoubtedly a question of some importance about the wider dissemination of professional or official constructions of marriage and the family or the extent to which there is consensus between lay and professional views. In asking such questions, we again confront complexities. For example, professionals often maintain that one of the problems of modern marriage, indeed one of the contributory factors in higher divorce rates, is the fact that couples have unrealistic expectations about marriage. If this be the case, from where do these expectations arise? Popular candidates are often the 'media' or romantic novels. If these be sources of un-realistic expectations (and it is by no means certain that they are) this is a further suggestion that ideologies around marriage and the family do not form a coherent whole since these popular over-endorsements of marriage might conflict with other professional models. However, some research would suggest that individuals do in fact have more or less down-to-earth expectations about marriage and marriage partners (Callan and Noller 1987; Gorer 1955; Mansfield and Collard 1988). Indeed, the picture becomes more confounded. It is possible that experts' construc-tions of the expectations of married couples may be more unrealistic than these expectations themselves. Nevertheless, as Mansfield and Collard show, young couples do worry about external images of mar-riage and whether their marriage conforms to constructions of a 'proper marriage' (Mansfield and Collard, 1988: 4–5). Ideology begins to be-come more and more elusive; it is everywhere and nowhere.

We may begin to explore, if not to solve, these problems by noting that Mansfield and Collard's study of young married couples placed some stress on the all-important difference between 'beliefs' and 'what actually happens' (ibid: 38–9). This is not to say that beliefs are irrele-vant to action, merely to make the well-established point that the relationship between the two is more complex than might at first be supposed. In other words, what people do and the accounts people give of their actions are both important but belong to two different areas of analysis and their straightforward interconnection cannot be assumed in advance. Another way of considering this, one very close to the interests of Jackie Burgoyne, is in terms of the distinction between 'public' and 'private' accounts (Cornwell 1984). These again exist at different levels, the former being more open to professional or ideological influences than the latter. In public accounts, individuals may refer to their ideal expectations of marriage and marital partners; in private accounts they may refer to their own marriages, their own partners as these 'really are' and not as put out for public consumption. It is important not to arrange these distinctions in any kind of hierarchy; 'public' accounts are not necessarily any less 'true' than 'private' accounts. Rather, they both belong to different orders of 'truth'.

I should like to suggest a model which stresses an interplay between public accounts, between elite constructions and everyday construc-tions. One of the possible difficulties with Abercrombie *et al.*'s (1980) reformulation of the dominant-ideology thesis is that it may deny ordin-ary people – non-specialists – the capacity as ideology producers in their own right. Ideology as a form of theorising is not confined to specialists;

it is part of the business of everyday life. Thus it is just as likely that professionals and elite members will draw upon popular ideologies in their more formal elaborations as that lay people will incorporate and be influenced by professional accounts, including accounts disseminated through mass publications. Clearly, there is never a complete fit between popular accounts and professional elaborations, between everyday talk and public speech, but the interplay between them must be part of the focus of any study of ideology.

5 One final set of problems concerns the relationship between ideologies about marriage and the family and yet more general ideologies prevalent in a particular society. This is a further elaboration of the relationship between the general and the particular, in this case with marriage and the family becoming the latter rather than the former. In some Marxist formulations, of course, the general ideology is related to a general mode of production with other ideologies and modes of production being articulated with these general modes in relationships of some complexity. (See Eagleton 1976 for how this might work in the case of literature.) Thus it is often argued that certain models of marriage and the family are consistent with, reinforce or maintain wider legitimations of a capitalist or a patriarchal order. To give an over-simplified example, freedom of choice in marriage is linked with freedom of choice in the market and notions of the home as a private sphere reinforce ideologies of private property. This would seem to be an area where there is more speculation than research although some historical work has begun to explore the linkages between domestic ideologies and business ideologies (Davidoff and Hall 1987). One theme which is worthy of further exploration is the extent to which certain constructions of marriage and the family, constructions which stress universality, naturalness and centrality, serve to smooth over or minimalise social divisions (between genders, classes and races) within society as a whole. Marriage and the family as 'central life interests' are held to override class or ethnic divisions; against these timeless experiences, such divisions might seem to be of relatively minor significance. While feminist research has contributed much to the analysis of the ways in which this works in relation to gender (classically Bernard 1973) there is much to be done in relation to these other divisions.

To conclude this section, any discussion of ideology in relation to marriage and the family should take into account these points: the complex interplay rather than opposition between science and ideology; the distinction and relationships between the pluralities and unities of ideologies; the distinction and relationships between the general and specific aspects of ideology; and the interplays between lay and professional, public and private accounts. We should note, finally, that the very use of the term 'ideology' is double-edged. By bringing to the surface that which was once apparently concealed, the deployment of the concept of ideology is part of the critical tradition of sociology. But by prematurely imposing an artificial unity or solidarity on something which may be much more diffuse and contradictory, the sociological intervention may be contributing to a wider process of reification.

IDEOLOGY AND THE USES OF THE PAST

It may be argued that all ideologies in some measure address themselves to questions of time, whether it be in looking back to some golden age, forward to a glorious future or through the elimination of a sense of change altogether in favour of unchanging verities. These foci on time and change become particularly important in the case of the family where time is built into understandings and constructions of domestic relationships. This is not simply a question of individual or household life cycles but also a reminder that generations and family-based households are linked over time. More-over, there are often strong links between family time and historical time; one of the first ways in which individuals come to have a sense of history is through hearing older relatives talking about 'the olden days'.

As already indicated, three possibilities present themselves. In the first place it may be argued that, in matters to do with family living, nothing of significance changes very much. Copulation, birth and death remain fun-damental facts of nature, people will always fall in love, 'this nobody can deny'. Mansfield and Collard provide a quotation from Plutarch and we are invited to read this as an example of a 'modern' understanding of marriage (Mansfield and Collard 1988: 61). Mount, in his conservative defence of family relationships attacks the ideas of the social construction of love and family sentiments and seeks to provide examples across the centuries, emphasising a fundamental familistic nature that neither church nor state can destroy (Mount 1982).

It is relatively straightforward to consider the ways in which theologians might argue that the spiritual truth of marriage and family relations abides despite the social changes that they recognise as having taken place or the ways in which conservative thinkers work from the bedrock of biology to the necessity and unchanging nature of social institutions. It is more interesting, perhaps, to consider the ways in which other scientific dis-courses downgrade history and culture in favour of deep-rooted psycho-dramas echoing back through the ages, from generation to generation. Thus there is, perhaps, no paradox in finding Church of England publications which recognise the changing nature of marriage while finding support in

psychotherapeutic literature and practice for a relatively unchanging understanding of the relational properties of marriage.

This is not the place to assess these arguments, although it may be
appropriate to signal here my own perspective. This is well summarised by
Frykman and Löfgren in their study of Swedish bourgeois culture:

> The cult of love became a major theme in bourgeois family ideology, but
> for us to understand this we must bear in mind that such words as love,
> tenderness and intimacy, although they reflect universal human needs,
> are formed or deformed by culture.
>
> (Frykman and Löfgren 1987)

Thus, whatever weight we might wish to assign to relatively abiding
features of human life it is important to argue, at the same time, that these
features are never fully detachable from particular historically located
ideological discourses. Theological, biological and, more recently, some
psychoanalytical perspectives may converge to provide for a powerful
sense of continuity in marital and family relationships although these points
of convergence should not be taken as signs of some overall conspiracy. At
the very least, however, it would seem that conservative thinkers would
appear to have a relatively easy time when it comes to defending marriage
and the family.

A second deployment of time in family ideology is to talk in terms of
decline or loss. This, too, makes relatively effortless connections between
popular nostalgia and conservative (and Conservative) ideologies. As
Aldous and D'Antonio note, nostalgia and the construction of the past are
an important element in ideologies about the family (Aldous and
D'Antonio 1983: 10–11). Mansfield and Collard begin their study of the
hopes and aspirations of young marrying couples with a reference to media
constructions of 'marriage under siege' (Mansfield and Collard 1988:
16–19). The implied contrast in these formulations is to a time when
marriage was more accepted or less open to challenge. The lines of argument are familiar although the details will vary with each account. In 'the
past', there were fewer divorces, the extended family was stronger, there
was more respect for parents, family members cared more for each other
and so on. Sociologists or historians who argue or seek to demonstrate that
most of these assumptions are open to question sometimes feel that they
have a difficult time in getting a hearing.

Again the sources for these models of the past and the construction of this
sense of decline or loss are various. Chronicling such a decline has, of
course, been part of a strand of religious prophecy for many centuries and
often comes easily to political as well as to Church leaders. However, we
may also note certain sociological accounts which elaborated sharp

contrasts between a pre-industrial world of communal ties and obligations with the anomie and the alienation of modern society. A variety of accounts from diverse and even contradictory sociological traditions may point to a certain lack of wholeness, a sense of fragmentation and loss.

A third ideological construction of the past would appear to be quite different. Consider the following two quotations, both taken from one of the *Getting Married* publications mentioned earlier:

> Our grandfathers used to make the decisions and our grandmothers accepted them. This dependence of the women was enforced by both economic necessity and social customs.
>
> Today, modern marriage is, we believe, much richer and fuller by being a partnership between equals.
>
> (B. Sandler in *Family Doctor* (n.d.))

In place of the golden age we have the bad old days. Here, and in numerous other publications from a variety of diverse and contrasting sources, we have a construction of the family of the past as patriarchal, undemocratic and constraining, especially for women. This is contrasted with a modern sense of partnership and a growing equality brought about by the contraceptive pill and expanding employment opportunities for women. This is a major aspect of the 'Institution/Relationship' contrast, explored in the next section. We find this especially stressed in matters to do with sexuality where, as compared with the past, we are more willing now to talk about the most intimate details and more willing to acknowledge the multiple pleasures of the body. The ironies of the Foucauldian perspective have effectively called into question this straightforward model of steady liberal enlightenment (Foucault 1979) and what might be said of sexuality might also, with little difficulty, be applied to these progressive models of marriage and the family. Even without the critical perspective of Foucault it can be seen that such models of the past can be deployed in a conservative direction; models of progressive emancipation and enlightenment can be used as arguments against feminists, sexual radicals and others who wish to 'go too far'.

The Thatcherite project (to use a highly simplified formulation of a complex set of political and ideological processes) provides an interesting variation on this deployment of time. As a modern version of Conservatism (with the emphasis upon the modern) it cannot simply rely upon straightforward nostalgia or a re-assertion of traditional values. This is because the modern Conservative project often entails attacks, whether directly or indirectly, on some of those institutions centrally identified with tradition or 'entrenched interests': the universities, some of the older professions, sometimes even the Church and the monarchy. The sense of decline or loss in this version is of relatively recent origin and is characterised by the interconnected themes of the erosion of personal responsibility through collectivism and the erosion of moral responsibility through permissiveness. Thus the 1960s and the early 1970s are seen as the source of many of the present social ills of today and are contrasted with a model of Victorian times, a combination of evangelical morality and free enterprise. The recent past, then, in this version, represents a distortion of the highest and the most natural human sentiments.

Thus, ideologies around marriage and the family operate with a variety of constructions of time and the relationships between past, present and future. Such constructions are not simply popular sentiments writ large but neither are they a form of mass indoctrination. They can be seen as arising out of the constant interplay between popular understandings and felt experiences and political and professional projects. They are part of 'what everybody knows' and routinely enter into everyday family talk. They are also part of the stock in trade of speechmakers and, not infrequently, social scientists. They may be linked to more general concerns; for example, sexual morality is often taken as a measure of 'social health' as a whole. They often provide a bridge between private concerns (fears about *my* adolescent children or *my* marriage) and public debates.

On the surface these constructions of time would seem to have little in common. Logically, it would seem that a belief in the unchanging bedrock of human relationships would meet uneasily with a belief in the decline in the quality of such relationships or, alternatively, a growing enrichment of such relationships. Yet all these constructions of time, in their different ways, focus upon marriage and the family as a site for a complex and dynamic unity of fears, hopes and anxieties. And just as the parent who, perhaps ironically, sighs for the days when 'children were seen and not heard' is perhaps combining a sense of loss with a recognition of positive change, these apparently conflicting constructions of time merge into the flexible multisited unity of family ideology. Having one's cake and eating it may be a logical impossibility, but it is perhaps an ideological necessity.

FROM INSTITUTION TO RELATIONSHIP

To illustrate some of these issues in the study of ideology, and in particular the ways in which ideology deals with questions of past and present, I shall focus specifically upon marriage and on one particular story that is told about marriage. This is the argument that western societies (at least) have witnessed a long-term shift in marriage which might be characterised as a shift from institution to relationship. This may be seen as an ideological construction in a variety of ways.

In the first place, it is not so much a falsification as a one-sided accentuation or over-simplification of a complex set of changes. In the second place, this construction, although gaining wider currency, can be identified with particular sets of professionals with a special interest or expertise in marriage and marital problems. Further, it can be understood as having the consequence, if not necessarily the aim, of smoothing over contradictions within marriage in our society and may play a part in the re-affirmation of marriage in a complex society. In short, the theme of the shift from institution to relationship represents a particular simplified story which has social consequences.

The statement that 'marriage was once an institution but is now a relationship' occurs at the beginning of a recent promotional video on behalf of *Relate* (formerly, the *National Marriage Guidance Council*), and it provides the main organising principle for *Marriage Matters*, a Government-sponsored publication outlining the availability and delivery of marriage guidance in Britain (Working Party on Marriage Guidance 1979; Morgan 1985: 21–32). Aspects of this theme may be found in the writings of Young and Willmott and Berger and Kellner, although the origins of this distinction almost certainly go much further back, certainly to Blood and Wolfe and Burgess and Locke but also to the classic sociological tradition, especially Durkheim. The structure of the argument, whatever the origins, is relatively straightforward: there is a contrast between some previous state and the situation in which we now find ourselves and a more-or-less linear progression from the former to the latter. In current formulations, while there may be some recognition that this shift has presented some societal and personal difficulties, there is more than a hint of approval for these changes.

That there are ambiguities and complexities with this formulation will be readily apparent. What, for example, is the time period under consideration? Is it a statement about how marriage was seen or understood – 'marriage used to be *seen* as an institution' – or a statement about the actual nature of marriage in times past? Certainly, close examination of our own time suggests an interplay between the institutional and the relational, rather than a simple accentuation of the latter as against the former. Mansfield and Collard, for example, see this contrast as being in part related to another kind of distinction between the public and the private and suggest a kind of co-existence: 'the public institution of marriage is being privatised' (Mansfield and Collard 1988: 4). Among their respondents, they find the powerful image of marriage as 'One-ness' (ibid: 161), but although this idea of marriage as a relationship appears to be all-important, the couples still seek institutional recognition. The public and the private, the institutional and the relational, meet in the wedding ceremony.

It is possible to begin to isolate some of the elements of this construction of 'marriage today' as being a relationship rather than an institution:

Marriage as choice

Marriage is something which is freely chosen and based upon love. It is likely that this idea of marriage as choice (including not only the actual partner but, theoretically, whether to marry or not) is strongly linked to notions of individualism. While religious teaching, especially Protestant- ism, may have experienced something of a tension between traditional constructions of marriage and notions of individualism, this tension would seem to have been largely resolved in favour of the latter (Hargrove, 1983). Even where institutional aspects are recognised, the institution is for the benefit of the individual and not the other way around.

Marriage, love and sexuality

Relationships, with a capital 'R', have come to be a dominant cultural theme and at the same time have come to be focused upon marriage. Marriage is not a simple relationship, it is *the* Relationship; the major thread is love. This is not, as many commentators are at pains to point out, a romantic view of marriage; it is more one which stresses the idea of companionship and growth (Mansfield and Collard 1988: 20–1). Courtship, Mansfield and Collard point out, becomes a period of testing out a relationship rather than a signalling of serious intent to the rest of the world. Perhaps the abolition of the idea of 'breach of promise' reflects a legal recognition of the shift from institution to relationship (ibid: 74).

Important in this period of testing is sex. The ready acceptance of heterosexual experience as part of a relationship that will, most likely, end in marriage is no longer the occasion for frissons of disapproval. Chesser, for example, wanted to see 'the expression of a deep and lasting genuine relationship as the true test of the morality of the sexual act, not the formal institution of marriage' (Chesser n.d.: 40). And if sex is seen as important in the premarital relationship it takes on an increasing centrality within marriage itself. Christian manuals on marriage deal with sex in a manner and to a degree that might have been regarded as pornographic in earlier decades (Woodward and Salholz 1982) and therapy becomes an important part of marital therapy and marriage guidance.

It is perhaps here that we see the deployment of a particular construction of the past at its sharpest. The past is characterised as patriarchal, prudish and ignorant. Recent research, in contrast, has tended to emphasise another picture of the Victorians, one which allowed for a considerable amount of tenderness and playful sensuality within marriage. However, the point is not so much one of the accuracy or otherwise of our representations of the private lives of our ancestors. It is more to do with the construction of these lives and the ways in which our 'enlightenment' is established in contrast to these darker, patriarchal days.

Just as the idea of marriage as a relationship is seen as preceding the actual wedding ceremony, so, too, does it continue after a particular marriage has come to an end through divorce. The members of the *Putting Asunder* Working Party did not see the doctrine of marital breakdown as being incompatible with a 'covenant of lifelong intention' (Church of England 1966: 18). They rejected the kind of zero-sum game in which one party was seen as innocent and the other as guilty and were more prepared to recognise divorce for what it is: 'a failure of the marital two-in-oneship' (ibid). The members of this Working Party drew upon a wide range of sociological literature for their analysis of modern marriage and for the elaboration of a theme which argued that increasing divorce rates reflected higher relational expectations between partners who were becoming increasingly equal in status. This, of course, has become something of a sociological orthodoxy.

Yet, as Mansfield and Collard note, there is a built-in contradiction within this modern construction of marriage. They note a formal incompatability between the themes of togetherness and the theme of self-realisation (Mansfield and Collard 1988: 180). Similarly, Askham has explored a tension between identity and stability within marriage (Askham 1984). Couples faced with this kind of tension attempt to work out some kind of compromise. At the ideological level, however, we should note that the ideology of 'Relationship', which might under certain circumstances be seen as smoothing over certain contradictions, seems to open up new contradictions.

Marriage as security

This is a word which crops up time and time again in studies of marriage and marital expectations. In Mansfield and Collard's study, for example, it can be linked to themes of privacy and the development of a 'place of one's own' (Mansfield and Collard 1988: 55–6). A small sample of American men found security an important theme in their expectations of marriage (Nordstrom 1986). Security may be seen as having a very tangible physical embodiment in the purchase of a house; private property and emotional security converge. Yet again, perhaps there is a contradiction here. Security, in emotional terms, may be very much part of the wider theme of Relationship yet, in its more prosaic forms, it may work against themes of personal growth. Security may lack excitement and challenge. Individuals may find themselves 'saddled' with mortgage responsibilities which, in times of high unemployment, may become a source of insecurity. Again there are possible unresolved contradictions within the ideological construction of marriage as a Relationship.

Marriage as stability

This is closely associated with the idea of marriage as security but may be distinguished from it. Stability has both a relational and an institutional aspect. The stability can refer to the individuals concerned, with a growing sense of identity and direction. Or it may refer to the establishment of a stable, domestic unit within a wider social fabric. The associated idea of 'maturity' (Mansfield and Collard 1988: 54) similarly points in both directions at once. Society 'needs' stable, mature individuals just as individuals 'need' a sense of maturity and stability.

Marriage as natural

This might be seen at some distance from the construction of marriage as a Relationship, especially where the latter emphasises individualism, growth and choice. To say that marriage is 'natural' would seem to imply that the single status is 'un-natural' and this construction alone would seem to provide powerful pressures on behalf of the marital status. Yet, at the same time, 'natural' does have other connotations which are more compatible with the idea of marriage in relational terms. 'Natural' may be identified with spontaneity and openness. To enter into a 'natural' relationship, then, should not be seen as a constraint or a compulsion; rather it is being true to 'one's nature'.

These, then, are some of the themes implied in the idea of marriage as a Relationship. There are, empirically speaking, considerable doubts that may be raised as to whether the transitions in marriage could ever be described in terms of a straightforward ideal–typical institution/ relationship contrast. Marriage is probably best understood as having different mixes between the two at different times and in different sections of society. It is, however, the case that there is a greater tendency to describe marriage in these terms and it can be argued that this reflects more of a shift in the groups or the parties interested in marriage than in any change in the social institution itself. Predominant among these we would note marriage guidance counsellors, marriage and sexual therapists and some social scientists. These groups may be seen as part of a wider therapeutic and counselling culture. With the growth and crystallisation of a body of knowledge and professional practice, comes the definition and redefinition of the object of study and concern. What is involved here (and the same may be said of experts in industrial relations or educational psychology) is the focusing upon and the isolation of a set of relationships and practices as an object of study and intervention.

The focus here has been upon marriage. This focus may reflect changes whereby marriage actually becomes the most important adult relationship or it may reflect different ways of viewing sets of relationships. However, from time to time, writers on marriage (especially from the Christian perspective) feel obliged to remember the wider sets of relationships within which marital partners are enmeshed. For example, a contributor to one of the *Getting Married* booklets stressed: 'Marriage is something much more than a purely personal relationship between two people' (Davey, in *Family Doctor* n.d.: 93). He is referring here to the fact that each partner has her or his own set of kin and friends and that marriage establishes new communal and societal identities. Nevertheless, the relatively high profile of marriage, as opposed to other domestic or interpersonal relationships is something to be pondered.

It is clear that the construction of marriage as having undergone a shift from the institutional to the relational may be seen as a scientific sum-mation from one set of perspectives and as an ideological representation from another. It is certainly possible to argue that this understanding is broadly consistent with wider sets of values to do with choice, individual realisation and personal development. What perhaps is less clear is the extent to which this understanding is shared by the population as a whole although there are some suggestions that everyday perceptions (as opposed to professional elaborations) are more mixed. It would be interesting to speculate, for example, whether traditions of working-class 'fatalism' (Purcell 1988) might be seen as representing a stoical acceptance of the more institutional aspects of marriage. It is certainly possible to argue that a stress on the institutional aspects of marriage, with the emphasis on rights, duties and boundaries, *can* leave space for the elaboration of other ties of friendship or neighbourhood thereby modifying the exclusivity of the mari-tal relationship.

UNITIES AND DIVISIONS IN MARRIAGE: GENDER AND ETHNICITY

It would appear that the formulation of marriage in terms of a shift from institution to relationship is intended to have a very broad application. It would certainly seem to apply to the population of England and Wales as a whole but probably is also seen as applying to 'the west' more generally.

Indeed, in as much as this formulation may be seen as a variation on Goode's 'world revolution', a shift to the conjugal-based family, this account may be seen as having, at least ultimately, a more global referent (Goode 1970).

It is often argued that one of the things ideology 'does' is to smooth over social contradictions, divisions and potential tensions and that, hence, such a global formulation may also be seen as having these ideological effects. We may see this, first, in the case of gender. Part of the orthodoxy associated with the treatment of marriage as *a* or *the* relationship is the assumption that the relationship itself has become more equal. The *Getting Married* publications repeated this theme in a variety of places: 'Marriage in this country for women today is in some ways better than it has ever been, because the wife is more and more accepted by her husband as his comrade and partner in all spheres of life' (Mary Macauley in *Family Doctor* 1960: 34).

More ambiguous are the contributions from Ashley Montague. He writes of the prejudices of the 'masculine dominated world' (*Family Doctor* 1960: 36) and elsewhere refers to the joint and complementary roles of men and women within marriage (ibid: 36). However, he is also a believer in woman's 'natural qualities' which make her appear to be the more valuable partner within the relationship. Women, he writes, are 'natural lovers'. While all the publications that deal with the marital relationship in the full sense stress the impact of family planning and employment outside the home as major factors transforming marriage itself, the practical extent and implications of this transformation in terms of the gender division of labour within the home are rarely spelt out. In most cases it would seem to be assumed or taken for granted that the woman remains the prime carer.

However, a continuing stream of feminist and feminist-inspired research and scholarship has indicated persisting patterns of inequality between men and women in practically every sphere of domestic life, certainly within marriage. Thus a major contradiction would seem to be between the ideology of relationships which stresses the Relationship over and against the experiences of the gendered individuals who make up that relationship and their everyday practices. As Mansfield and Collard write: 'The language of marital relationships denies differences; the reality of married life defies sameness' (Mansfield and Collard 1988: 194).

There are, as several of the contributors to a recent collection on fatherhood point out (Lewis and O'Brien 1987), a variety of reasons why relationships within the home and involvements in parenting in particular, continue to be unequal, despite ideological premises to the contrary. These would include the various involvements of men in the public sphere, the practices of unions and managements, social arrangements to do with child care and parental leave and so on. The contradictions between the premises and assumptions of equality (and the growing use of the word 'parenting' in place of mothering or fathering may be doing the same work as the increasing use of the word 'relationship' to describe marriage) may be yet one further source of tension and strain within a marriage. Certainly we have reason to believe that understandings of marriage in terms of the institutional/relational mix may be different for men and for women. The construction of marriage in relational terms would certainly seem to have different consequences for men and women, with the latter perhaps being held more responsible for the emotional and interpersonal side of that relationship.

The ways in which constructions of marriage – whether in institutional or relational terms – have often masked differences in the actual experiences of men and women are now relatively widely understood, at least within social science literature. Less explored are the ways in which constructions of marriage and family life may also smooth over, ignore or stereotype differences in terms of nationality or ethnicity. Indeed it may be suggested that accounts of marriage and the family in modern Britain either ignore questions of ethnic differences altogether or, where they are taken into account, tend to catalogue them simply as sets of static differences rather than exploring all these variations within a framework that emerges from a historical discussion of the processes of imperialism, racialism and immigration. Thus we may have brief accounts of 'Sikh families', 'Muslim families', 'Jewish families', 'Chinese families' and so on but all in the context of an implied contrast with white (and often middle-class) families.

Two processes may be seen as taking place more or less simultaneously. In the first place, there is a construction of difference or of 'otherness'. Thus in the construction of marriage as a relationship with its emphasis upon freedom of choice, there is an implied contrast with other groups who do not (yet) see marriage in these terms. 'They' have arranged marriages, 'their' marriages are more unequal or more patriarchal and so on. In some cases, these ascriptions of patterns of domestic life on to other groups may not necessarily be pejorative. I have often heard many rather wistful references to the stronger sense of family obligations and family loyalties that are thought to exist among 'Asian' families, for example. However, even such favourable references may carry more than a hint of 'orientalism', conveying a sense of strangeness, alienness or otherness.

This is not to say that differences between families and marriages may not be characterised in such terms and that such differences may not be mapped on to groups or categories with different ethnic or religious origins. These differences are a matter of closer empirical observation. But it is to suggest that constructions such as 'the Muslim family' carry with them a double reification (of an ethnic group and of the idea of 'the family') detached from any wider historical considerations. Further, such constructions silently imply another double reification, that of 'the white family' or 'the British family', but one which remains outside critical investigation.

At the same time, accounts of family and marital life may also be presented in such a way as to smooth over or to ignore any such differences altogether. Thus again, the construction of marriage in relational terms by implication refers to everyone within the British Isles. Differences in ethnic-group experience, as with differences in gender or class experiences, are held to be of relatively little significance as compared with the deep relational experience that constitutes all marriages. Ideological constructions of marriage and family life may therefore have no small part in the construction of a national identity.

Paradoxically, therefore, ideological constructions of marriage and the family may simultaneously construct national unities as well as ethnic or religious differences. Again, logical near-impossibilities become ideological normalities. It may also be noted at this point that in recognising the presence of such differences and of the ideological propensity to smooth over or to ignore such differences that there is a danger of taking a male, white and middle-class perspective as being the prism through which all other patterns are explored and problematised. Thus 'gender' is often coded as 'women', 'ethnicity' as 'black' and 'class' as 'working-class' or 'poor'. The categories of 'men', 'white' and 'middle-class' or 'wealthy' remain relatively unexplored and unproblematised. This is, of course, not uniformly true. We do have a growing number of accounts of men in families (Lewis and Salt 1986; Morgan 1990) just as we do have accounts of middle-class family life (Bell 1968; Edgell 1980), although the theme of class may not be problematised as much as it might. But the problematisation of 'white' marriages and family life remains almost completely unexplored.

CONCLUSION

To return to my point of departure, it may be argued that questions of ideology deal, in some measure, with the point of intersection between everyday talk about marriage and the family and public speech or discourse. The focus here has been largely on certain aspects of public speech, the way in which issues to do with marriage and the family have become the topic for a range of professional discussions, practices and interventions. In particular, I have looked at understandings of the way in which marriage has changed from being an institution to a relationship and how this broad understanding has pervaded a wide range of professionals and specialists, including therapists, ministers of religion and journalists, who would not normally have been bracketed together. Thus even differences over whether couples should have sex before marriage became subsumed under wider agreements over the importance of marriage as a relationship. To describe these professional theories and practices as ideological is to indicate a particular and partial way of viewing these practices; it is not necessarily to deny their potential importance for understanding the nature of marriage in our own times or for bringing comfort or self-realisation to those who turn to such professionals for help and guidance.

This discussion has inevitably focused on publicly available texts – books, articles, speeches and so on – since these are necessarily the most accessible media for the analysis of ideology. The more everyday under-standings of marriage and the family are less accessible to us although there is probably enough evidence to suggest that we should beware of assuming too readily a congruence between public speech and private talk about the family. We also know enough, theoretically and empirically, to eschew the 'hypodermic' model of ideology where it is being perceived as injected into routine understandings of persons in their everyday lives. Clearly, pro-fessional understandings are available, and increasingly available, to a wide range of non-professionals; the *Getting Married* publications and the debate about Chesser's article in one of these, provide just one such example. But we should see these publicly available statements as being part of an array of resources which are used by people in domestic situa-tions as they go about their daily lives.

Further, the 'hypodermic' model presents too stark a contrast between lay and professional and obscures the ways in which professionals may themselves be influenced by routine and everyday assumptions about family, marriage and gender. Professionals of all kinds are gendered indivi-duals and have family relationships and experiences and while their train-ing may sometimes encourage them to look critically at these, it would be unusual if their accounts of the nature of marriage and the family were not coloured in some measure by their own experiences. Certainly construc-tions about the family in terms of 'nature' and the 'natural' almost inevit-ably point to an overlap between professional and lay understandings. Similarly, there is a congruence, an affinity, between professional accounts of the contrasts between 'then' and 'now' in terms of the changing nature of marriage and the family and the everyday tales told by parents and grandparents and woven into routine family talk. Ideology involves the interplay between public and private accounts, with neither being wholly determined by the other.

Opportunities to explore the interplay between public and private and between lay and professional (the two oppositions are, of course, not synonymous) may be found in public scandals and dramas around issues of sexuality and the family which periodically crop up in our history. Such examples may include the Abdication crisis, the Profumo affair and the Parkinson scandal. Certainly, the continuing interest in the marriages, divorces and separations of members of the Royal Family may provide some useful material although the regret must be that we have so much more of media accounts and relatively little of the understanding of and the responses of individuals to these dramas. Perhaps one of the best illustrations in recent years is the debate around child sexual abuse following the Cleveland revelations and enquiries (Campbell 1988). Here we have the meeting point of many of the actors and themes in debates and constructions about marriage and the family in Britain in the 1980s. These include social workers, doctors and medical practitioners, the police, the church, politicians, journalists and the media. The themes include relationships between adults and children, between men and women, the boundaries between the public and the private as they apply to the family, debates about feminism and about professional interventions. What is important about the Cleveland case, perhaps more than any of the other public scandals which seem relatively trivial in comparison, is that it highlights real divisions and contradictions in understandings of the family which cannot be subsumed under overarching constructions of the symmetrical family or marriage as a relationship. It is here, perhaps, that we may begin to understand the limits of ideology.

REFERENCES

Abercrombie, N., Hill, S. and Turner, B.S. (1980) *The Dominant Ideology Thesis*, London: Allen & Unwin.
Aldous, J. and D'Antonio, W.V. (1983) 'Introduction: families and religions beset by friends and foes', in W.V. D'Antonio and J. Aldous (eds) *Families and Religions: Conflict and Change in Modern Society*, Beverly Hills and London: Sage.
Askham, J. (1984) *Identity and Stability in Marriage*, Cambridge: Cambridge University Press.
Bell, C. (1968) *Middle-Class Families*, London: Routledge & Kegan Paul.
Bernard, J. (1973) *The Future of Marriage*, New York: Souvenir Press.
Bernardes, J. (1985) 'Do we really know what the 'family' is?', in P. Close and R. Collins (eds) *Family and Economy*, London: Macmillan.
—— (1986) 'Multidimensional developmental pathways: a proposal to facilitate the conceptualisation of "Family Diversity" ', *Sociological Review* 34: 590–610.
Brannen, J. and Collard, J. (1982) *Marriages in Trouble: The Process of Seeking Help*, London: Tavistock.

Burgoyne, J. and Clark, D. (1984) *Making a Go of It: A Study of Step-families in Sheffield*, London: Routledge & Kegan Paul.

Callan, V.S. and Noller, D. (1987) *Marriage and the Family*, North Ryde, Australia: Methuen.

Campbell, B. (1988) *Unofficial Secrets. Child Sex Abuse: The Cleveland Case*, London: Virago.

Chesser, E. (n.d.) 'Is chastity outmoded?' in *Family Doctor* 'Getting Married' (4th issue), London: British Medical Association, pp. 38–41.

Church of England: Group Appointed by the Archbishop of Canterbury (1966) *Putting Asunder*, London: SPCK.

Clark, D. and Haldane, D. (1990) *Wedlocked? Intervention and Research in Marriage*, Cambridge: Polity Press.

Cornwell, J. (1984) *Hard-Earned Lives*, London: Tavistock.

Davidoff, L. and Hall, C. (1987) *Family Fortunes. Men and Women of the English Middle Class 1780–1850*, London: Hutchinson.

Eagleton, T. (1976) *Criticism & Ideology*, London: Verso.

Edgell, S. (1980) *Middle Class Couples*, London: Allen & Unwin.

Family Doctor (n.d.) *Getting Married* (4th issue), London: British Medical Association.

Family Doctor (1960) *Getting Married*, London: British Medical Association.

Foucault, M. (1979) *History of Sexuality: An Introduction*, London: Allen Lane.

Frykman, J. and Löfgren, O. (1987) *Culture Builders: A Historical Anthropology of Middle Class Life*, New Brunswick & London: Rutgers University Press.

General Synod Marriage Commission (1978) *Marriage and the Church's Task*, London: C10 Publishing.

Goode, W.J. (1970) *World Revolution in Family Patterns*, New York: Free Press.

Gorer, G. (1955) *Exploring English Character*, London: Cresset Press.

Hargrove, B. (1983) 'Family in the white American Protestant experience', in W.V. D'Antonio and J. Aldous (eds) *Families and Religions*, Beverly Hills and London: Sage.

Lewis, C. and O'Brien, M. (eds) (1987) *Reassessing Fatherhood*, London: Sage.

Lewis, R.A. and Salt, R.E. (eds) *Men in Families*, Beverly Hills and London: Sage.

Mansfield, P. and Collard. J. (1988) *The Beginning of the Rest of Your Life? A Portrait of Newly-Wed Marriage*, London: Macmillan.

Merton, R.K. (1957) *Social Theory and Social Structure*, Glencoe, Ill.: The Free Press, revised edition.

Morgan, D.H.J. (1985) *The Family, Politics and Social Theory*, London: Routledge & Kegan Paul.

—— (1990) 'Men in families: issues of critical sociological theory', in J. Sprey (ed.) *Theorizing About the Family*, Beverly Hills and London: Sage.

Mount, F. (1982) *The Subversive Family*, London: Jonathan Cape.

Nordstrom, B. (1986) 'Why men get married: more and less traditional men compared', in R.A. Lewis and R.E. Salt (eds) *Men in Families*, Beverly Hills and London: Sage.

Purcell, K. (1988) 'More in hope than anticipation: fatalism and fortune telling amongst women factory workers', University of Manchester Sociology Department, *Studies in Sexual Politics* no. 20, Manchester: Manchester University Press.

Reiger, K. (1985) *The Disenchantment of the Home*, Oxford: Oxford University Press.

Voysey, M. (1975) *A Constant Burden: The Reconstitution of Family Life*, London: Routledge & Kegan Paul.

Williams, R. (1983) *Keywords*, London, Fontana, second edition.

Woodward, K.L. and Salholz, E. (1982) 'The Bible in the bedroom', Newsweek, 1 February, p. 41.

Working Party on Marriage Guidance (1979) *Marriage Matters*, London: HMSO.

6 Constituting the marital world
A qualitative perspective

David Clark

It will be apparent from all the chapters in this book that marriage and marital relationships touch on many other aspects of social life, such as family and kinship, social class, employment and unemployment, housing, leisure and lifestyle, and in particular that marriage holds a place within wider debates about gender. It is surprising therefore that there have been relatively few studies in Britain which have focused specifically on the social construction of the marriage relationship, describing in detail the ways in which the intimate worlds of marriage connect with the more public territories of social structure. There are a number of possible reasons for this. Marriage can be a subject which makes sociologists uncomfortable: too much attention to it may be interpreted as being 'pro-marriage' in some ideological sense, or as being insensitive to the several ways in which marriage serves to disadvantage wives in favour of husbands. At the same time, the discipline, at least in its 'malestream' form, has not been particularly sensitive to ways of tapping into and exploring the internal worlds of marriage. Thoughts, feelings and emotions have tended to be off-limits to many social researchers, who have been either indifferent to them as a valid domain for enquiry or lacking in the appropriate skills to make the attempt. It has therefore only been since the mid-1970s that a number of studies have emerged which both focus on marriage and treat the accounts of husbands and wives as the primary source of data, paying special attention to the use of qualitative methods. In a comparatively short period of time, however, these studies have made a significant impact upon our understanding of marriage in British society, if only of mainly white groups within it.

Although relatively unconnected, the twin intellectual influences on this pattern of development within sociology were, on the one hand, the writings of phenomenologists, and on the other, the growing body of feminist research, theory and practice. The main contribution of phenomenological theory to this process was in the writings of Berger and Kellner (1964) as well as Berger and Luckmann (1967), all of whom derived much of their thinking from Schutz (1964). Berger and Kellner's famous paper on 'Marriage and the construction of reality', referred to at several points in this volume, was particularly influential in describing the marriage relationship as a shield against *anomie*, a dramatic coming together of 'strangers' who through the construction of a joint biography give meaning to their lives and to the social world (Berger and Kellner 1964: 5). Marriage from this perspective was seen as a vehicle for self-actualisation, for personal growth and for self-expression through intimacy, conversation and sexual fulfilment. Such notions are a useful reminder of the ways in which social science may frequently serve to bolster and promote, rather than debunk or deconstruct, the dominant ideological and cultural forms of the age: they owe much to a male, middle-class and white view of what marriage in the 1960s ought to be like. Subsequent debates would seriously challenge these ideas of marriage and family life as a 'haven in a heartless world' (Lasch 1977) and Morgan (1981) offered a detailed critique of what had come to be known in the literature as the 'Berger and Kellner thesis', showing how the argument suffered from a one-sided emphasis on the *relational* aspects of marriage and from a failure to consider marriage also as an institution, subject to varying understandings between social classes and in particular between men and women.

The main purpose of *feminists* was to treat the social construction of the marriage relationship as a *gendered* phenomenon, linked also to structural factors existing outside of marriage, which powerfully influence individual experience within it. Writers such as Barrett and McIntosh (1982) drew attention to the dynamic interplay between the public and the private aspects of marriage and domestic life, showing how the personal, psychological and material needs of husbands could so often predominate over those of wives within the so-called marriage 'partnership'. As Jessie Bernard (1973) pointed out, *two* marriages – his and hers – exist within every marriage relationship, so that husbands and wives 'explain' themselves in different ways, arising out of their contrasting biographies and the expectations which surround them. As we saw in Finch and Morgan's earlier chapter, feminism exposed the intimate world of marriage as a potential and actual prison in which women might be physically and emotionally incarcerated. Feminists held a mirror up to marriage and showed within its 'private' arenas many of the external rules governing male–female relationships in the 'public' world outside.

As practical frameworks for researching marriage, however, phenomenology and feminism were not incompatible. Indeed they were to be successfully combined in a number of studies which have proved central to recent understandings of marriage and domestic life. What all of these studies have in common is a commitment to qualitative methods, a reliance on small samples (sometimes including a case-study approach), a willingness to engage in careful analysis of detailed accounts of married life and the active promotion of depth interviewing as a reflexive tool for sociological enquiry. This approach has great strengths, creating the opportunity for rapport and understanding to develop within the research process and allowing the micro-worlds of marriage to be recorded and subjected to careful analyses in which individual men and women are central rather than peripheral to the argument. This is a sociological tradition which places the human actor at the core of things, always recognising how the wider world of structure can bear in and shape individual experience. The approach is not without its drawbacks, however, and raises a number of practical and ethical issues for those who adopt it: who takes responsibility for the unintended outcomes of this type of research, what are the limits to confidentiality, how appropriate is it to encourage disclosure within the context of a research, rather than a therapeutic interview? These and other aspects of this question have been explored in more detail elsewhere (Clark and Haldane 1990).

Such problems require continuing debate, but do not invalidate the method as such, which has produced an important body of research. Examples which stand out are the work of Backett (1982) on parenting, of Lewis (1986) on fatherhood, of Forster (1987) on the effects of unemployment on families and of Cunningham-Burley (1987) on grandparenthood. Whilst all of these studies have something to say about marriage, others focus more specifically on marriage relationships. Askham (1984) has explored the conflicting tendency which arises when marriage is seen as both a source of identity and of stability. Burgoyne and Clark (1984) looked at the special characteristics of second marriages and Mason (1987) has focused on the specific issues of marriage in later life. Hart (1976) portrayed the experiences of men and women who were members of a club for the divorced and separated; and Brannen and Collard (1982), in a work which provides a striking juxtaposition of feminist theory with phenomenologically influenced methodology, have examined the processes of help-seeking for couples experiencing marital difficulties.

In this chapter I want to focus on a very specific aspect of this qualitative tradition, by referring to some work on the *early stages of marriage* which I carried out in Aberdeen in the early 1980s. Before turning to the detail of that data, however, I shall briefly sketch in some of the broad issues concerning early marriage which have been identified in two previous qualitative studies. My purpose is to shed further light on the pivotal experiences involved in the early period of getting and being married, a process which I refer to as *constituting the marital world*.

The phenomenon of *youthful* marriage, as B. Jane Elliott points out in Chapter 4, reached the peak of its popularity during the late 1960s and was a source of both public and academic concern. Demographic and survey evidence showed how teenage marriage was associated with pregnancy, high fertility, living in shared accommodation and an increased risk of divorce, plunging young couples into what one writer called 'the vortex of disadvantage' (Ineichen 1977). However, during 1968–69 Diana Leonard carried out fieldwork in Swansea among a group of young newly-wed couples, with the specific intention of developing an account of *their* experience of courtship and marriage and with no particular emphasis on a social-problems perspective. Using a broad range of anthropological methods, and in a carefully contextualised local study, Leonard looked at the weddings of thirty-four couples who had been married in church and twenty who had been married in a civil ceremony; she interviewed husbands and wives at varying times before and after the marriage, made observations at weddings, and talked with a number of vicars, priests and registrars. Her work, which was not published until some time later (Leonard 1980), had four main preoccupations: (1) the extent to which courtship dominates young people's (and especially young women's) lives, (2) the importance of moral decorousness in achieving and maintaining status change through marriage, (3) the importance of courtship events in determining differences in standards of living attained at marriage and their possible long-term influences on lifestyles, (4) the complexity of rituals used to celebrate marriage, but the relatively attenuated ways in which respondents explained these rituals (Leonard 1980: 256).

It was not until a decade later that another project on the period of early marriage was carried out in Britain, when in 1979 staff at the Marriage Research Centre began the 'Early Years Study' involving sixty-five couples who had married in the London area (Mansfield and Collard 1988). In this case, problems of access limited the study group to those who had married in church, but unlike Leonard the researchers were able to interview each husband and wife separately, recording the sessions for later transcription and analysis. A particularly important feature of this study was the intention to follow up the couples after a period of five years (see Mansfield and Collard forthcoming). Much more explicitly committed to the detailed analysis of individual accounts, though lacking some of the contextual elements of Leonard's work, this study presented a 'portrait of marriage' from the experience of being 'ready for marriage' to 'becoming a couple'. Mansfield and Collard were particularly concerned to understand how *future orientations* within these marriages could be used to explicate aspects of the marriage relationship. They identified three forms of individual orientation within their study group: planners, roamers and venturers.

The *planners* were described in the following terms: 'not only were they deciding what to do (and what *not* to do) but they seemed to be planning *who they would be*' (Mansfield and Collard 1988: 206, emphasis in original). A second group, the *venturers*, emphasised the role of luck and chance in their lives, but were in general optimistic and confident about the future (ibid: 207). The *roamers*, however, had a 'relatively weak sense of the future' and had 'neither plans nor strategy' (ibid: 207). These authors concluded that marriage as a strategy for handling 'the rest of your life' will have a variety of outcomes according to the profile of that strategy. Some marriages may be contracted, for example, in relation to short-term aims and are therefore unlikely to endure, whilst in others an assiduous planning orientation may act as a shield against the stresses occasioned by major changes occurring at various points in the life course.

My own study of the early period of marriage was conducted in Aberdeen in 1980–82 and has been reported in detail elsewhere (Clark 1982a, 1982b, 1987, 1989). Unlike the Swansea and the London studies, however, this project set out to include equal proportions of *first* and *subsequent* marriages in a total of fifty couples interviewed twice, in both month one and month six of their marriages. In the first interview spouses were seen individually, whilst the second interviews included both individual and joint sessions. All interviews were tape-recorded and transcribed in large part (Clark 1989: 119–27). As in the London study, a primary concern was to develop a narrative of the process of getting and becoming married, focusing on the major themes of meeting, developing a relationship, deciding to engage and/or cohabit and the method by which the marriage was formalised (just over a half, most of them first marriages, had occurred in church). The study also looked at a number of key themes during the early period of marriage: stress, worries and intimacy; plans, thoughts and circumstances in relation to having children; and in particular, the relationships between paid employment, domestic labour and material lifestyles among the fifty couples.

Drawing on this data, I want to focus here on a further typology of the early phases of marriage in which I have sought, like Mansfield and Collard (1988), to capture clusters of meanings and experiences which emerge from husbands', wives' and couples' accounts of constituting the marital world. I have done this by trying to group the couples, across a range of themes and issues, in ways which are both consistent with the 'unique' elements of their own accounts but which also portray common circumstances and shared characteristics. My purpose is to use this typology in a grounded way,·by reflecting the concerns of those who took part in the study.

The construction of this kind of 'emergent' typology runs a number of risks. It is not an exercise in multivariate or cluster analysis; it remains an interpretive process; and it is about predominant themes rather than fixed categories. Of course not every couple in each group will manifest all of the attributes which go to make up the group. And as I have indicated, there are a number of marginal cases where assignment to a particular place in the typology has been especially problematic. There are also a number of phenomena which do not readily belong in any part of the typology, but which are in a sense all-pervading: sexual divisions, the domestic division of labour, gender stereotypes, sexual behaviour and patterns of intimacy (for full details see Clark 1989). Furthermore, it is also possible that some may object to a typology of *couples*, on the grounds that such an approach masks these important gender differences. Mansfield and Collard's (1988) typology of newly-weds, for example, takes this into account and categorises *individual* orientations, recognising that these do not always produce a neat fit between marriage 'partners'. Here, however, I am choosing to focus on the *couples'* relationships, and so have tried to classify them accordingly.

I hope it will also be clear that my purpose is not simply to contrast the experiences of first marriages and remarriages within the study group. For the most part my aim has been to identify the plurality of experiences encountered in getting married, recognising that often there can be no clear distinction between 'marriage' and 'remarriage', not least among those couples where only one of the spouses has been married before (this was true in fifteen of the twenty-five remarriages in the study). One category within the typology is entirely made up of remarriages, but for the rest the groups are mixed. I hope this will serve to remind us that *remarriages* should not be too readily problematised and that a range of experiences, emotions, values and meanings are common to both first and subsequent marriages, telling us something in turn about *marriage*, in what Morgan (1981) calls the 'strong' sense. The typology should therefore give some insight into the range of ways in which marriages within our society are constituted, enabling us better to understand some of the marital 'outcomes' which may ensue.

FOUR IMAGES OF EARLY MARRIAGE

The typology I shall describe emerged out of innumerable readings of the interview transcriptions, coding and analysing a range of variables. It has four parts: *drifting, surfacing, establishing* and *struggling*. Whereas the latter two groups were clearly emergent from the data and together made up three-fifths of those interviewed, the first two groups, particularly the one I have termed *drifting*, are more enigmatic and rather more problematic to describe; I shall therefore deal with these first in setting out the typology. I will also show how the marginal cases sometimes display characteristics which overlap more than one of the categories.

Drifting (n = 11)

These eleven couples seemed for the most part unclear about how they would like their lives to develop and had what might be regarded as a relatively weak 'future orientation'. Conscious planning and preparation for the future appeared fairly unimportant to them. Their relationships and circumstances could contain some contradictions, even complications, but these were not sufficient to be constructed as problems within the marriage. Likewise, getting married was unlikely to have been seen as a watershed, more as a further development in their relationship. Courtships among this group had a rather haphazard quality, with delays and postponements being quite common. Drifting couples were generally unclear on future plans about children, housing, work, but not in ways which troubled them to any great degree. They were likely to have only partially formed views about how marriage would be and how it would affect their relationship. Un-ambitious about lifestyle, they may have some hobbies but not an elaborate portfolio of activities. These couples were without any obvious financial problems, but even when earning considerable sums, were likely to adopt a disinterested viewpoint on money matters. Some wives in this group were not in paid employment, but were unclear about how to describe their role.

Drifting *into* marriage was a characteristic of some of the accounts in this group. Alec Firth (21),[1] an offshore oil worker, talked about the decision to get married:

> Just right out of the blue . . . 'cos we'd arranged about three times to get married and then just kept changing it . . . all of a sudden I just decided it was time.

Later he described his views of what marriage might be like:

> D.C.: What sort of plans did you make for marriage, how did you envisage your life working out?
> Alec: Well, just thought we'd be a lot happier on our own, in our own house. . . . I hadn't really thought too much about it, just thought we'd get a house and see what happens day to day, sort of thing, it's working out fine just now.

Judith Ferguson (24), a full-time student, described her thoughts at the time she started living with Kevin (30), a prison officer:

> I think I knew then that we'd probably end up getting married. It was

something we never discussed, no, in fact he never asked me to marry him, we just both knew, I think.

In the case of the Fords, a long-standing friendship, begun at school, gradually developed into a stronger relationship. Tim Ford (20), another student:

> It just seemed the natural progression.
> D.C.: Mm . . . when did you begin to think in terms of marriage?
> Tim: Eh, I can't really answer that question, there wasn't a specific time on it . . . it must have been the summer after I asked her out, 1978, 1979, no 1980 . . . I think it was '79, '80.

Linda Ford (20), a nurse:

> D.C.: What about the decision to get married, how did that come about?
> Linda: Eh . . . I think we more or less fell into it, we didn't really see the point of waiting, though everyone told us we wouldn't have enough money and all the rest of it, we should wait until we were more settled, but we just carried on.

Another couple gave very attenuated descriptions of their attraction to one another; their accounts of deciding to marry were equally constrained, with each of them seeing little difference between living together and being married. In two cases there was little time for reflection of any sort and the couples began living together soon after meeting, but with no clear expectations of permanence or plans to marry. For one couple in this group involvement in a religious sect was the predominant theme in their accounts of the relationship; indeed it appeared that he had committed himself to the sect simply in order to pursue his relationship with her. When he was asked about how he had imagined married life would be, he acknowledged 'not thinking past the marriage bit', whereas in reply to the same question his wife stated that she had been more preoccupied with 'getting the big event over'. Jackie Fitzpatrick (18), a telephonist, described her experience in almost surreal terms:

> D.C.: So what about the decision to get married, how did that come about?
> Jackie: Well . . . just sort of one night when we was arguing . . . it was the first argument we'd really had, and he just asked me to get engaged to him . . . and I said no. And then he says, 'Maybe if I ask you another time will you say yes?' I said 'Maybe, you can ask me again sometime', and he says, 'When will I ask?' And I says, 'Please yourself.' And he asked me again there and then and I said yes. It was useless saying no really.

But it is perhaps the account of Beatrice Fisher (23), a dental assistant, which exemplifies the drifting perspective:

> D.C.: How soon did that come up as something between you, the idea of marriage?
> Beatrice: I still don't know how that came about (laughs) we just started talking about it and we thought 'Great, we'll get a flat' and we sort of went into it without really thinking about it, I think (laughs). We just sort of . . . 'OK, we'll get a flat' (laughs) not thinking of what will the parents think and what effect will it have on us.

At the same time, pragmatism seems to play a part in the drifting orientation. One couple drifted into marriage for purely contingent reasons: it would enable them to rent a house from her employer. Similarly, another thought that marriage and sharing accommodation with her grand- mother would help in their application for local authority housing. In the case of the Fergusons, already referred to, there were concerns that he would not be further promoted in his job until they were living together as husband and wife. The Reeves illustrated this pragmatic attitude at the level of relationships. Daniel Reeves (23), another offshore oil worker, preferred to 'forget about' his first marriage, which lasted just a year, describing it as a 'bad time in my whole life'. Fiona Reeves (25), a part-time domestic assistant who had not been married before but had an illegitimate daughter, extended this pragmatism to thoughts about the future in a passage where she had been describing the problems of starting to live with someone who has been married before:

> I'm not a person . . . I sort of take life day to day. I mean if he walked out on me tomorrow I'd just say 'Oh well, back to social [security] or whatever.' I mean I'm just nae that type to worry about what's going to happen in the future. I mean, once it's done, it's done. It does nae bother me.

Only two couples in this group had clear views about when they wished to have children, and in both cases described themselves as 'trying' to have a baby. Several others gave accounts which further emphasised their drift- ing orientation. One remarried couple were 'vaguely considering' a rever- sal of her sterilisation, but had done nothing about it by the second interview. Another young woman in her first marriage had never used any form of contraception during the relationship, and when asked about the risks of pregnancy stated that she had 'never really thought about it happening'. Tim Ford declared himself opposed to the idea of planned parenthood:

D.C.: Is planning a family important to you?

Tim: How do you mean, planning?

D.C.: Well, rather than just leaving it to chance.

Tim: Eh . . . I don't like the idea of having a planned family . . . I would rather have, it's strange (laughs) . . . I don't like the idea of deciding 'Right, we'll have a baby next September . . . '. I think I would prefer it to be chance when we want it to be chance.

The Fitzpatricks also seemed to be adopting this line of thought; both gave interestingly vague accounts about having children. Ray (25), a garage fitter:

D.C.: And would you be thinking about starting a family soon or not?

Ray: Trying just now . . . if nothing happens, aye y' ken, we just decided to start now about two weeks after we got back from our honeymoon. If nothing develops this month, she'll just go back on the pill again, 'ken, 'til next year or something, February next year. Just give us a bittie more money in the bank and get things . . . stupid starting a family just now.

D.C.: But you said you were trying.

Ray: Aye, we're trying . . . we were just speaking about it last week, thinking about all the money you would need and things . . . if it comes around, ken . . . I'll manage to work out. But hopefully . . . nae really worrying if she is having a bairn just now.

Jackie Fitzpatrick (18), a telephonist, put it this way:

D.C.: So when are you thinking of starting a family?

Jackie: I don't really know, I just keep changing my mind . . . we were going to start to have a family . . . to start trying straight away . . . and then we changed our minds, thought we'd wait until next year, but just now I don't think we can really make up our minds.

D.C.: So you haven't stopped taking the pill or anything yet?

Jackie: Actually, eh . . . I forgot to take it, so I left it for this time and then I'm going back on it again, so we decided we're just going to . . . I'm going to stay off it this time and if we change our minds, say 'Oh well we'll go back on.' I don't really know . . . it's just . . . I mean he decides one thing, I decide on the opposite and he decides the opposite and I . . . '

Only three of the couples in this group were purchasing their own homes at the time of the first interview. Although these drifting couples did not regard home ownership as unimportant, they clearly lacked the powerful desire to have a place of their own, which, as we shall see, was such a feature of those in the *establishing* group and also of some of those who were *surfacing*. Drifting couples were also unclear about other life goals and plans. Judith Ferguson (24) thought it was too difficult to make plans while she was still a student. Elaine Firth (25), who said she had feared being 'left on the shelf' before she met Alec, had given up her job as a shop assistant to be at home with her newly purchased dogs and her hopes of pregnancy. Two couples both expressed vague ideas about emigrating, but had no clear plans in that area. Most of these couples indeed had no clear picture of what their lives might be like in the years to come.

Some were clearly reticent about sharing too much of their feelings in the interviews, such as the couple who dropped out before the second stage of the study, and with whom a chance encounter later revealed that they were having difficulties in their relationship and considering separation. Fiona Reeves also refused to take part in the second interviews, though her husband was willing. Another couple, though loquacious, often treated my questions flippantly and refused to elaborate their answers. Four others were distinguished by the way they replied straightforwardly, but in little detail. I hope however to have demonstrated that the notion of drifting in the period of courtship and of early marriage is not purely an artefact of the respondents' willingness to talk. There is evidence here to suggest that drifting into marriage and through its early months is one definable pattern among the fifty couples who took part in the study. Drifting should not be regarded as a residual category nor as a negative one; it might rather be seen as a purposive strategy whereby the marital world is constituted in such a way that both emotional and material expectations are limited, kept in check, and shielded against the possibilities of disappointment. These couples were indeed adept at hedging their bets, hoping to get by on a judicious mix of pragmatism and capriciousness.

Surfacing (n = 9, including 3 marginal cases)

This group consisted entirely of remarried couples, particularly those who had experienced a range of difficult circumstances in previous years. Spouses in this category were in general in their thirties or older, rather than their twenties. These couples constructed themselves as being 'not out of the wood yet', but were in general on an upturn: materially and emotionally. They may not yet have disposed of all material legacies, which continued to intrude from a former marriage, such as problems over ownership of the former matrimonial home or household goods from within it, but were actively working towards this. They may have encountered some early difficulties in courtship, which had now been resolved. Their accounts contained a growing sense of confidence, however, as in the early months they embarked upon a planned programme, over which they felt increasing levels of control. For the most part one or other partner was sterilised and they were mainly content to have no more children. Among these couples ideas and expectations about marriage would be consciously tempered by experience of earlier marital relationships, but they were, in general, eager to demonstrate an improving lifestyle, especially in material terms.

A number of women in this group described former marriages marked by material hardship and psychological distress. Jane Rattray (36), a cleaner, had experienced violence and poverty in her first marriage; for some years after her separation she was unable to form any relationships with other men, and lived with her children, toiling on a low income. She described her relationship with Daniel (54), a porter, as crucial to a process of personal and material reconstruction: 'He brought me out of myself .. totally changed my outlook on life.' Pamela Rankin (39), by the time of the study a self-employed shopkeeper, had also had a long, violent and frightening marriage and although she was beginning to establish some improvement in her material life before she met Ronald, it was he who helped her psychological recovery:

> Ron always described me as a person behind a wall, he said I had a wall there, a defence mechanism . . . Ron's that kind of person, he likes to talk things through, y' know, if there's something bothering you, 'Let's sit down and talk about it.' Whereas I tended to bottle things up. And I still tend to do that a little y' know, but nothing in comparison to what I used to do. I used to sweep my feelings under the carpet, y' know . . . safer. I'm a much more stable person now than I was, emotionally, and I think that has all to do with Ron's influence.

One woman had a first husband who frequently beat her and who received psychiatric treatment for his problem drinking. After the separation she was afraid of living on her own at first, but since starting to live with a new partner, her life had 'changed completely'. Another had not endured material hardship in her first marriage, but had attempted suicide when her husband left her for another woman. Soon afterwards she returned to Aberdeen from the south of England, lived with her mother for a while and started a new relationship with a man who had not been married before. As she began to rebuild her life she got a job, bought a flat using money from the divorce settlement and began living with her new partner. In her case, surfacing from the legacies of the past seems to have hinged around the subsequent experience of becoming pregnant and deciding to get married.

In the cases of the Rennies and the Reynolds, both husband and wife shared some common earlier experience that had a strong bearing on their subsequent relationship. Ernie Reynolds (47), a freelance consultant in the oil industry, had been married for over twenty years when he first met Fiona (46); she had recently divorced her husband after twenty-one years of marriage. In his first marriage Ernie had travelled the world in a succession of jobs; Fiona's first husband had been in the Navy and was frequently away for several months at a time. In their separate interviews each described themselves as having 'failed' in marriage. When Ernie and Fiona met, they were both working hard to establish their own businesses, and it was this joint preoccupation that seems to have been an organising principle in their attempts to overcome past difficulties. Success in business seemed to provide the foundation for both self- and mutual respect. Ernie:

> It's made me more aware . . . I have a totally different relationship with Fiona than I had with my ex-wife . . . it really is totally different. We're very, very close . . . and I don't think I was ever as close as that with my ex-wife. But we also have this independence as well, you know, she is a person in her own right . . . just because she's married me and taken my name, she's not subordinate to me. You know, she is a person and she has the right to be a person and have her say, do her thing if she wants, so long as her say is something we both want. And I'm almost certain that's the way she feels about me.

Angus Rennie (44) and Caroline Rennie (33) were both employed in local government and had met at work; Caroline's ex-husband had worked in the same office for a time. Angus and Caroline both told poignant, though differing, stories of their unhappiness in first marriage. Angus appears to have had an 'empty shell' marriage which lasted over twenty years before he 'took the coward's way out' and deserted his wife, leaving a note on the kitchen table. Though materially comfortable, he had been deeply unhappy for a number of years, finding interests outside the marriage in voluntary work and hobbies. Caroline's experience had been more dramatic, with a husband who was manic depressive. Angus and Caroline's courtship was not without its difficulties, as they struggled to build a relationship which went beyond their contacts at work and he summoned up the resolution to leave his wife. This was a classic case of consciously building a new relationship in the shadow of divorce. Following the sale of former matrimonial homes, and meeting the costs of their divorces, the Rennies found themselves better off than previously. Angus was able to look forward to the ending of maintenance payments to his daughters when they left school over the next few years. He described himself as functioning more effectively at work. Caroline spoke of a variety of 'projects' they were undertaking in the home: decorating, gardening and buying furniture. One of the few couples in this group who were not sterilised, their continuing uncertainty about whether to have a child in the remarriage appeared as one of the factors impeding them as they gradually surfaced from an earlier period of unhappiness.

Three couples in this group fit less easily, however, into the surfacing category and should be regarded as marginal cases: Rowe, Riddoch and Rowan. Jonathan and Denise Rowe (both 40) met whilst married to their respective first spouses and living in North America, where they were working for multinational companies; the two couples set up a *menage* in which they swapped partners at weekends. There followed a lengthy period of stress and unhappiness as this arrangement broke down and the couples each decided to separate. Subsequently they all returned to Europe, divorced and eventually remarried, formalising the earlier relationships in the *menage*. By the time of the interview Jonathan and Denise had been living together for two years, had established joint-custody arrangements with their respective children and former spouses, and were enjoying the benefits of his high-earning job and a large house in the country. It might be argued that they had already surfaced from the legacies of the past and could be better described as *establishing* the marital world, relatively un-cluttered by emotional or material baggage from earlier years.

By contrast, the Riddochs were perhaps more *struggling* than surfacing, and for reasons entirely due to the ways in which his first marriage continued to intrude upon this one. Ray Riddoch (41) met Diane Riddoch (35) through their work in advertising. She was unmarried, but it was some considerable time before he separated from his wife. Subsequently, he was to pay his former wife substantial amounts in aliment and maintenance and while he continued to live nearby was often called upon to intervene in routine family problems. This pattern of close contact continued even after his remarriage to Diane, and was only broken when they moved to take up new jobs in another Scottish city; even then these tensions with his former wife almost resulted in Diane leaving him at one point during the first six months of the marriage. The Riddochs had some financial worries, but were in general surfacing from a difficult and tense period in their relationship, subject only to further ways in which the emotional legacy of his former marriage might continue to intrude upon their relationship.

Finally, the Rowans were a *surfacing* couple, who bordered on the *drifting* category. Gerry Rowan (43), a factory worker, was widowed with no children and Lorraine Rowan (40), a works supervisor, had been married twice before and had a teenage daughter living at home. Gerry had lived alone for some time after his wife had died, and following early difficulties in which he had drank heavily and generally 'neglected' himself, he had gradually adjusted to her loss. For Lorraine, however, two previous marriages had left a major legacy, chiefly in the form of a distrust of men. During the early weeks of marriage, with no major real worries and relations between her daughter and new husband apparently going well, she voiced only one significant anxiety:

> D.C.: Do you have any particular fears or worries having just got married?
>
> Lorraine: I'm scared it doesn't last, that's an awful confession. I'm scared, I keep saying that to Gerry, I'm scared that somebody pokes me and says it's nae happening to me, I cannae believe that I've got somebody like Gerry. I can relax, can sit and watch TV, I dinnae have to worry that he's looking over my shoulder. I dinnae have to worry that he's going away to sleep with someone else. It's great, super, absolutely great. I'm just scared it doesn't last.

Setting this aside, the rest of the Rowans' account of early marriage was closer to the *drifting* category. With no major plans or preoccupations and in the absence of any clear material or financial obstacles, Gerry and Lorraine seemed content to drift into the future. I asked how they saw their lives in five or ten years time.

> Gerry: I never think about it.
>
> Lorraine: No I dinnae think about it either. I enjoy each day, I enjoy it . . . I think it's the best thing that ever happened to me. I've never regretted it, not for a minute, have you?
>
> Gerry: No, never even think about it. (laughs)

Establishing (n = 15)

These fifteen couples appeared to have no major legacies to impede their successful construction of the marital world during the early period, though they did encounter some problems, typically described as 'adjustment difficulties'. As a group they were likely to be without significant financial worries, but could be committed to major programmes of expenditure. Both spouses were likely to be in paid employment and for these couples the home formed an important focal point for the development of the marriage relationship, through the aquisition of material goods. They were likely to have clear views about what marriage could and should be like. First marrieds amongst them had been engaged, had saved, planned and obtained independent accommodation. Remarrieds appeared relatively un-constrained by issues of custody, access, maintenance, property disputes or emotional difficulties emanating from a former marriage; they were also likely to be living in separate accommodation from that of the first marriage. These couples planned to have children fairly soon, but only when material circumstances allowed. *Establishing* couples were likely to have active lifestyles, organised leisure and shared activities. They were conscious of qualitatively different relationships with parents since getting married.

Couples in this group exemplified the process of self-consciously establishing the marital world as a domain which could be moulded, manipulated and fashioned according to choice. To a greater or lesser degree, they had been successful in this during the early months. It is perhaps not surprising, therefore, that more first than second marriages were to be found in this category. For these couples there were few material or emotional legacies to thwart attempts at establishing marriage and domestic life. Indeed, in several cases there were also a variety of supports and sources of help to further assist them: notably those coming from parents who provided financial and other assistance. For these couples, material wellbeing was constructed as the foundation upon which marital happiness was to be built.

Among the first ten marriages in this group, only one couple had lived together beforehand and only two had not purchased their own accommodation. But in both cases this was part of a deliberate strategy for the future. Whilst the Forrests lived first of all with her mother and then moved into a rented flat during the first six months, their primary intention was to build their own home, through a self-help building scheme. A similar pattern of deferred gratification was observable among the Fowlers, who planned to return to his home in Australia, also to build a house of their own and settle there. All of the other first-married couples were living in their own homes, usually tenement flats purchased jointly and converted during the period of the engagement. Only one person among them was unemployed at any time during the early months, and she had found a job by the time of the second interviews.

Saving and planning were core activities for these couples, both in the lead up to marriage and in the early months. The Fieldings are a good illustration. At the beginning of the first interview, having established with Ann (20), a secretary, how she had met Jim (25), an offshore works supervisor, I asked how the relationship had subsequently developed. She explained the process succinctly:

> Well we went together a year and then we got engaged. Yeah, we were going together a year and then we got engaged and then two years later we got married. So we'd planned it from the first year, got engaged and then planned to get married from the time we got engaged.

As Jim explained, after the engagement there followed a period of intense saving:

D.C.: What sort of amounts did you save?

Jim: We started off with £100 a month and we found we could save more than that and we opened out to £200 a month . . . we kept that up. Then we changed that and we just found that we could put in more than £200 a month, we had two different bank accounts . . . if I was offshore we'd use all that money and just put it straight into the bank or my overtime would go straight in.

They also looked forward expectantly to being married:

D.C.: Did you talk much between yourselves about what it would be like after you got married?

Jim: Towards, nearer towards the wedding we did. We didn't used to go out much then. Since we got the flat and that, speaking about how we'd get on and what we'd do . . . how life would change and everything. Just basically planning things, working things out.

Establishing the marriage took a slightly different form for those who had been married before, but with broadly similar underlying themes. Of the five remarried couples in this group, two were in local authority housing; the rest were buying their own homes. All of the spouses were in paid employment. Only one couple had a child from a former marriage living with them and this girl had no contacts with her natural father. In the case of Jim Rogers (32), a maintenance engineer, his two daughters by his first marriage visited them each weekend. But in general these couples had few parental legacies from the past which might interfere with the successful establishment of a new married life.

All five of the remarried couples were thinking about children. One man had a reversal of his vasectomy during the first six months; one woman became pregnant a few weeks before the marriage and another during the first six months; one couple by the time of the second interview were 'trying' to have a baby and another were considering it, despite a recent illness on her part. Among the first marrieds, although two women became pregnant during the period of the study, there was a general feeling that children should come after a planned period of further consolidation, as one man put it 'a two-year breathing space'.

It was noted on a number of occasions that this form of establishing the marriage could be a heavily gendered experience, illustrated in the following account from Julie Forsyth (23), a hospital clerical worker:

D.C.: How do you think that your life's going to change now that you're married?

Julie: Eh . . . I think it's a case of you've got to think less of yourself and more of a pair. You can't sort of . . . when you're single you go into a shop and you see a dress that you like and you think 'Oh, I'll budget for it next month.' You can't do that, you've got to think what's best for the pair of you, what you're needing for your house more than what you're needing for yourself. It'll probably change more drastically if we have family I would think, 'cos then I would have to give up work and I would lose quite a bit of independence, he's always said I'm far too independent. Well, I suppose I am really, but I like to have something that's mine (laughs) that I can do with what I want. That's the only thing about marriage that should change me, I'll have to watch that I don't try and be too independent. I realise that we are a couple, not just me and him that happen to live in the same house.

We can see from this that *establishing* could also be linked to notions of 'settling down' and the creation of some sort of domestic order, almost a family tradition in the making. The following passages from Thomas Foubister's (22) and Sarah Foubister's (21) second interview are remarkable in a couple who have only been married six months and present a startling vista of the instant establishment of a privatised and routinised domestic life. He is a draftsperson and she a nurse:

D.C.: What do you usually do on weekday evenings?
Thomas: Collapse.
Sarah: Watch television. In the summer . . .
Thomas: In the summer we do quite a lot really . . .
Sarah: We do odd jobs, there's gardening, I like to sit in the garden in an evening.
Thomas: We consider ourselves to be handy people.
Sarah: We were decorating all summer really weren't we, 'til it got too dark?
Thomas: And then in the winter we rest up until the warm nights and the light nights come in again, and we've got another hard six months next year. There's things we want to get done.

In a later passage, on the subject of the kinds of conversation which might take place between them, I asked when they were most likely to talk together:

Sarah: I think in summer when we're doing jobs together, that's when we talk most . . . whereas recently we've been sat in front of the television and he's got the newspaper and I think we've both been content to sit quietly, you know, I think we just feel lazy.
Thomas: I think as well we tend to find that sometimes it's not really worth speaking because you know what you are going to speak about and you know what you're going to talk about anyway.

Sarah: Don't say that Thomas, that makes it sound so boring.
Thomas: No, no . . . it's just as if Sarah knows what's going on in my mind half the time. . . .

Clearly this form of early marriage was dependent to a considerable degree upon an adequate level of material security. A few couples in this group were in high joint-income brackets (at or in excess of £20,000 per annum in 1980–82) and none were on particularly low incomes. Although one couple was having some difficulty in paying bills which were left over from the wedding, by the time of the second interview he was considering leaving his job as a recently qualified physiotherapist in order to take an offer of a better paid one as a medical sales representative. Keith Fowler's company paid all their domestic expenses in addition to a £25,000 salary; Alison Fowler thought they were 'the luckiest of all the people that we know, materially'. For those on more modest incomes, however, it was common to have anxieties about how they would maintain their current standard of living when children arrived and when, it was automatically assumed, the wife would give up her job. The Fenwicks are a good illustration of this dilemma and are worth describing at some length as an archetypal *establishing* couple.

Geoff Fenwick (29) was born and brought up in Glasgow; his parents separated when he was a year old, and though he kept in regular contact with his mother, he had not seen his father for fifteen years. He took an engineering diploma in his home city before going to work in England and first moved to Aberdeen in 1975. Dora Fenwick (19) was an Aberdonian and had lived in the city all her life, leaving school at sixteen with six O levels. Geoff and Dora met in 1978, whilst working for the same oil company, where he was a systems analyst and she a personal assistant. They were engaged in the autumn of 1979 and married in church in March 1981, going on to live in a semi-detached house, purchased on a mortgage shortly before the wedding.

This couple were clearly content with their house, situated in the country just outside Aberdeen; but Geoff also had plans for further moves, the reasons for which came together in a matrix of concerns about having children, improving their position in the housing market, and maintaining a comfortable way of life.

D.C.: Do you think you'll stay here?
Geoff: For . . . oh, five years at a guess. I don't know, it depends. With these sort of things you've got to keep increasing the mortgage that you've got until you get to the sort of age . . . 'til you get to about forty to make it . . . to keep the market going. So we might move to something bigger if we can afford it . . . if our salaries allow that. But it does mean

that I've got to earn considerably more because presumably in the next five years Dora'll have a child, or children and if she does, then I've got to earn my salary plus some more, in order to maintain the lifestyle.

At the time of the first interviews Geoff's net monthly income was £580 and Dora's was £270. I asked Dora if she had any financial worries, having just got married.

No . . . not really. We do have an overdraft but we could pay that off . . . y' know, tomorrow. We've got various amounts of money in different places and we really just keep our bank account . . . it goes up and down all the time, but if it starts going into, y' know if we start heavy overdrafts then we just tighten our belts, we don't actually transfer money, because we like to keep saving money . . . so we just tighten our belts with the cheques. (laughs)

By the time of the second interview, however, Dora was expecting a baby. Because of this, she had put aside thoughts about going to university and developing a career of her own. I asked Geoff in the joint interview how he thought his life would change with the baby and he replied: 'I don't really come into it, I'll be sent out every day to earn money.' They also acknowledged certain financial constraints upon their way of living during the early months of marriage, and had cut back a little on some of their hobbies, such as skiing. Geoff was concerned that they might have to move to more modest accommodation when Dora gave up her paid job to look after the baby. Once again, he elaborated their position in some detail:

We're very lucky in as much as though we have an overdraft and we have the windows on hire purchase, that's a fairly small amount compared with our assets. For example, the amount of money that we would get on this house. If we sold it, after paying the mortgage, it would be something in the region of £15,000 I would estimate, so compared to our assets what we owe to people is very limited, very small.

The Fenwicks are a good illustration of several of the 'forward planners' among the first marriages, and their relationship contained a number of typical gendered assumptions and constraining factors. Although they both worked in full-time employment, he was earning considerably more than her and it was his career development that took precedence over other factors, though this was constructed as a form of deferred gratification calculated to help them both in the longer term. This situation had perhaps been amplified by the bigger-than-usual age difference between them (he was ten years older than her).

Among most of these *establishing* couples, anxieties about coping with the financial burdens of having children were in general subjugated in the face of an overall positive view of what marriage could be like. The following two passages, taken from a remarriage and a first marriage, illustrate some of the possibilities for couples who were self-consciously establishing the marital and domestic world. Andy Robertson (32) is a foundry worker, his first marriage ended in divorce and he has no children; I asked him what he looked forward to most in marriage the second time around:

> Well, companionship for a start . . . I would just like us to have a good life together, aye a good social life as well as a private life. And then again it comes to, like family . . . bringing up children in a happy atmosphere, and I think that's what we've got to work for. The two's got to create a happy atmosphere like. Try and agree . . . mostly agree with each other . . . talk things over . . . I like to think Philippa would say to me like if she had something she was nae pleased about. I would like her to do the same . . . well I would do the same I would say . . . I'd like to be able to sit and talk it out.

The Farrs make a fitting ending to this section on *establishing* couples with their dual and gendered emphasis on communication and money. Geoffrey Farr (24) worked in a family-owned engineering company and Monica Farr (21) was an office clerk. Again I will quote them at some length, as they answered the final question in the joint interview.

> D.C.: What sort of things should a couple do to keep their marriage successful do you think?
> Monica: Keep talking to each other. Keep eh . . . communications going. The minute you drop communications you're stuck aren't you?
> Geoffrey: Aye, I think . . . there must be more things than that.
> Monica: Well, of course there is material things and everything, but as long as you can keep speaking to each other . . .
> Geoffrey: Aye, I suppose so, uh-uh.
> D.C.: What were you thinking of when you said there must be more to it than that Geoffrey?
> Geoffrey: Well, it seems too simple, doesn't it? I mean, just sitting talking to each other to keep a marriage going and keep it good.
> Monica: 'Ken, but the minute you stop speaking to each other you lose contact don't you? You drift apart and there's the start of it, you go your own separate ways.
> Geoffrey: But there is more, I mean the lack of money to start with.
> Monica: Money aye crops up . . .

Geoffrey: It is, but I mean it's just a thing that's got to be faced really. Lack of money just causes problems right, left and centre. No money, no house. No money, no kids. No money, no eat. Aye, I mean you're right enough in what you're saying, ehm . . . communications, talking things out instead of just flying off the handle and getting up and leaving . . . think about it first and talk it out . . . but as I say, money as well. Those two I would think.

Struggling (n = 15)

Among this group some combined set of factors had served to have a negative effect upon the couple in the period prior to marriage and/or in the early months. These could include: pregnancy, housing problems, employment and unemployment difficulties, psychological problems, continuing legacies of former relationships or a previous marriage. For these couples cohabitation was likely to have been precipitated by some set of problematic circumstances. Difficulties continued in the early months with the presence of a baby or small children, along with housing, employment and financial problems. Strained relations with parents were a source of further stress for some. These couples were in general pessimistic or unrealistic about possibilities of future change. They were likely to be disparaging when describing their lifestyle, claiming they did not have or were unable to establish one.

These struggling couples represent the most visible counterpoint to the *establishing* spouses we saw in the last section. Four key themes emerge in the lives of couples in this group, and sometimes they are found in combination: material hardship; pregnancy and the presence of small children; the influence of a former marriage; and other family influences. I shall briefly explore each of them in turn.

These were the low-earning couples among the fifty, those most likely to be unemployed, and the ones with most uncertainty of employment. For example, when, due to the vagaries of the fishing trade, Jennifer Finch (22) lost her job as a filleter, she and her husband found themselves in the poverty trap, earning '£5 a week too much' to be eligible for certain benefits. In the joint interview she described some of the consequences of this:

Jennifer: Well, we cannae just go out and buy what we used to buy. We had luxuries that we havenae got now.
D.C.: What sort of thing do you call luxuries?
Jennifer: Well, certain kinds of food and clothes for the bairns and for ourselves. Just say 'Right I'm needing shoes, right I'll get myself a pair

of shoes.' Things like that, 'ken? Steak and that. 'Ken, just get used to things? Now it's just down to bare minimums, you just buy what you have to buy and that's it.

D.C.: What sort of difference would it make to the sort of food you eat?

Jennifer: A big difference, doesn't it really? Like every week I used to buy chops and steak and things like that. Now it's mince and things, 'ken? It's right down, 'ken what I mean? He takes home fish [from his job] and we make out. Our budget lasts longer that way.

Five out of the six first married couples in this struggling group and three of the nine remarrieds were affected by unemployment. These couples, in stark contrast to those in the previous section, had been unable carefully to prepare for marriage and to embark upon a sustained programme of saving. Jean Finnie (16), unemployed, explained that they had not saved at all before marriage, but would now have to start doing so in order to be able to have a house of their own. One couple were already in considerable financial difficulties by the first month of marriage, and owed money on their rent. Another had money problems and were unable to pay the bills left over from their wedding; their difficulties led to an early period of separation, when she returned for some time to relatives in the south of Scotland. Three other couples had an air of middle-class poverty, unable to manage on their existing salaries and building up large overdrafts and pressure from their banks.

Housing problems were another facet of this material hardship. Only three of the couples owned their own homes; two were living in caravans; and a number complained of inadequate space, dampness, bad neighbours and a desire to move. A couple in this group had one of her illegitimate sons living with them in their tiny rented house, but with only one bedroom had to send him to sleep at the husband's parents' home; this had not been explained to the environmental health officer, however, in the hope that they might be rehoused more quickly due to overcrowding. A further two couples started marriage sharing accommodation with parents.

Pregnancy or the presence of a small baby could further compound these problems. Among the first marriages, in addition to the Finches, two teenage couples were expecting a baby at the time of marriage and a third, also teenagers, were expecting a baby by the end of the first six months. Three of the remarried couples already had a small baby of their own, prior to getting married.

For the nine remarried couples in this group a variety of legacies of former marriage could be seen to unhelpfully intrude upon the new relationship. In addition to a baby of their own, Alec Ross (30) and Ellen Ross (24) were suddenly given the responsibility for his three children by his first marriage, when their mother abandoned them (Ellen had no previous children and had not been married before). When Sally Ryan's (36) first marriage ended she went to live with her children in a house owned by her parents; after Harvey (34) began living with her and they were eventually married, this became an increasingly powerful symbol of their financial dependency and a source of arguments between them. In the Ramsays' case, she had great difficulty in living with any of his possessions from his former marriage, including everyday household objects; but there were also problems associated with his son's access visits at weekends and these led to arguments and in one case a night spent apart. In the first interview I asked Alan Ramsay (30), a development manager, how he felt about the accommodation:

> D.C.: How do you feel about the accommodation, are you happy with it?
> Alan: I'm becoming unhappy with it. I don't think it's conducive to a good marriage with the pair of us living here and my son at weekends, and we only have one bedroom.

Similarly, Margaret Robb (24), a housewife, found living in the former matrimonial home a constant reminder of her first marriage:

> Margaret: I'd like to start a new house somewhere fresh on our own.
> D.C.: Yeah, why is that?
> Margaret: I dinnae ken, I think we'd be much happier. Living in the same house with Dennis as with Mark, I dinnae ken. I often think about the things that me and Dennis used to do in the house, and I think about me and Mark and it's just different altogether. But I would like a new house. I think we would like just to start fresh on our own.

In another case Ann Riley (21), a shop assistant, had strong negative feelings about living in the same flat that David (26), an engineer, had shared with his first wife; but for him the problematic legacy was more psychological than material, as he struggled with echoes of his former wife's behaviour which he now projected onto Ann. Another case also showed a similar reflection process, with his pattern of behaviour in the first marriage reasserting itself in the second and making his new wife unhappy. In the case of Jane Rendall (29), a social worker, it was clear that she had still not managed to come to terms with why her first marriage had ended, and she frequently made unfavourable comparisons between her present and former circumstances. The Ritchies' struggles were with a complex web of material and emotional legacies from former marriages; although their relationship stretched back over many years, they had been separated for several months shortly before they married, and she complained at several points in the interview about his violent temper and drinking bouts, which she sardonically referred to as his 'wet seasons'.

In the case of the Runcies, they had moved to Aberdeen from a town on the Moray Firth, not only to escape the memories of his first marriage, but also to get away from a constant succession of rows with parents. These difficulties with parents were reported in a number of other cases. In one instance the couple's courtship and decision to marry were punctuated with a variety of such disagreements. One teenage wife was having problems living in the same house as her mother-in-law and the parents of another had at first been opposed to her marriage on the grounds that she was too young. Another was very disappointed that her mother did not come to her wedding; and I have just referred to Sally Ryan's feelings of financial dependency on her mother and father.

Couples like the Runcies embodied several of the hallmarks of this 'struggling' group. Their 'escape' to Aberdeen had clearly not succeeded as they had hoped. He had found no secure employment and they were both unemployed at the time of the study. Living in a 'hard to let' council flat after being rehoused with their baby from a caravan, they had fallen into arrears on the rent and had borrowed from a moneylender at a high rate of interest. When interviewed after six months their sexual relationship seemed to be petering out and Rhona (22) complained that she had no lifestyle whatsoever, 'just the same thing day in and day out . . . dead boring'. The Rosses struggled with a similar combination of material and emotional problems. In the second interview they seemed to quarrel a good deal, she complained about the lack of conversation and communication between them. They described their lifestyle as 'poor and struggling'.

Ben Rendall (32) and Jane Rendall (29), both social workers, also encountered a combination of emotional and material problems in the early period of marriage; towards the end of the second interview I asked them how they thought about the future.

D.C.: How do you see your marriage developing from here, do you think it will change?

Jane: Hope so . . . well, I wouldn't like to think that it would be this way forever . . .

Ben: In general terms life's a great big toil at the moment, it's just all toil.

D.C.: What about hopes and aspirations within marriage and your family?

Ben: It's difficult to see beyond the struggle, you know. If we can see our way out of that . . .

Jane: I tend not to look too far ahead, because I thought I was set the last time and I wasn't, so I don't. I mean I had no doubts the last time, full of doubts this time . . . .

This pessimism was a feature of many of the *struggling* couples, as they wrestled with complex impediments to the pursuit of married life together. Roddie and Jean Findlater were both aged eighteen at the time of marriage, she unemployed and he with an insecure job as a fish porter. I shall close with a quotation from one of the joint interviews in which they replied to my questions about the future.

D.C.: Do you ever think what life might be like in five or ten years time?
Jean: Often wonder where we'll be, where we'll be bidin' and what we'll be doing. We were watching a programme last week about old folks, all these stories and you think 'Christ, I'll be like that'.
D.C.: What was it you were watching?
Roddie: All these hard luck stories.
Jean: And you just wonder what you'll be like when you're their age.

CONCLUSIONS

In offering here a qualitative perspective on the social construction of the marriage relationship, I hope to have highlighted a number of key themes. The first of these turns around the interconnections between public and private dimensions of marriage in society. Despite powerful rhetorics which construct the marriage relationship as an intimate, personal domain, largely bounded by the wishes and motivations of the spouses, it is clear from this data that marriage is intruded upon at a variety of levels by the external, public world. Indeed, to talk in categorical terms of the division between the public and the private is called into question by the material I have presented here which points so often to a seamless relationship between the two. Couples are therefore seen moving back and forth between these inner and outer dimensions, in which personal choice, feelings and motivations constantly interplay with constraints, norms and structures.

This relationship between the public and the private in marriage is brought most clearly to our attention in the context of issues about gender. In many of the accounts which I have presented we can see the powerful role of gendered assumptions, norms and behaviours as they are brought to bear on the early period of marriage. These relate in particular to such issues as 'deciding' when to have children and the conflicts between the demands of paid work and domestic labour, as well as to more subtle and invisible notions of 'being a couple', planning 'joint' futures and creating a pattern of leisure and lifestyle. When seen from this viewpoint, husbands and wives, beneath a veneer of 'coupleness', are often not so much partners in a joint enterprise as competitors in a handicap race, rivalling each other for the prize of access to a variety of scarce resources: domestic servicing, material support, care, nurturing and affection.

My particular emphasis throughout this discussion has been upon some of the specific ways in which these public/private and gendered constellations are carried into the formation of a relationship and the process of getting married. I have referred to these on a number of occasions as the *legacies* of the past which are brought into the marriage. Whereas Jackie Burgoyne and I developed this notion in the particular context of second marriages, where both material and emotional legacies from former relationships could often be identified (Burgoyne and Clark 1984), it is also clear that these legacies are of crucial importance in first marriages, indeed all marriages. The couples in this study, although small in number, displayed a remarkable array of past legacies which served to influence why and in what circumstances they came to marry. Some spouses were clearly marrying to escape unhappy relationships – following years of conflict with parents, or a broken engagement, or a divorce. Some were embroiled in a constant struggle with the legacies of their material circumstances and position in the class structure, which denied them access to adequate housing and jobs. By contrast, others were enabled by their earlier circumstances to take some measure of control over their lives, having access to material resources and enjoying the practical and emotional support of other family members, particularly parents. These considerations could produce wide variations in the experience of just fifty couples marrying around the same time in one Scottish city. I have tried to show here how qualitative methods can be used to capture some of that variation and also the ways in which a qualitative analysis can allow diversity to be deconstructed to some more limited set of factors which shape the experiences of those who embark upon the process of constituting the marital world.

NOTE

1   All names are pseudonymous and a variety of details have been changed in order to preserve anonymity; those names beginning with the letter 'F' are first marriages and those beginning with the letter 'R' are remarriages. Ages of respondents are given in brackets. For full details on all aspects of the methodology of this study, see Clark 1989, Chapter 3.

REFERENCES

Askham, J. (1984) *Identity and Stability in Marriage*, Cambridge: Cambridge University Press.

Backett, K.C. (1982) *Mothers and Fathers. A Study of the Development and Negotiation of Parental Behaviour*, London: Macmillan.

Barrett, M. and McIntosh, M. (1982) *The Anti-social Family*, London: Verso.

Berger, P.L. and Kellner, H. (1964) 'Marriage and the construction of reality', *Diogenes*, 1–23.

—— and Luckmann, T. (1967) *The Social Construction of Reality*, London: Allen Lane.

Bernard, J. (1973) *The Future of Marriage*, New York: Yale University Press, second edition.

Brannen, J. and Collard, J. (1982) *Marriages in Trouble: The Process of Seeking Help*, London: Tavistock.

Burgoyne, J. and Clark, D. (1984) *Making a Go of It: A Study of Stepfamilies in Sheffield*, London: Routledge & Kegan Paul.

Clark, D. (1982a) 'Restarting a family: having children in second marriages', *International Journal of Sociology and Social Policy* 2(2): 55–68.

—— (1982b) 'Marriage and remarriage: new wine in old bottles', in S. Saunders (ed.) *Change in Marriage*, Rugby: National Marriage Guidance Council.

—— (1987) 'Changing partners: marriage and divorce across the life course', in G. Cohen (ed.) *Social Change and the Life Course*, London: Tavistock.

—— (1989) 'Constituting the marital world', unpublished PhD thesis, University of Aberdeen.

Clark, D. and Haldane, D. (1990) *Wedlocked? Intervention and Research in Marriage*, Cambridge, Polity Press.

Cunningham-Burley, S. (1987) 'The experience of grandfatherhood', in C. Lewis and M. O'Brien (eds) *Reassessing Fatherhood*, London: Sage.

Forster, N. (1987) 'Economic and social change in the 1980s: a study of the effects of redundancy on a group of South Yorkshire steel workers and their families', unpublished PhD thesis, Sheffield City Polytechnic.

Hart, N. (1976) *When Marriage Ends*, London: Tavistock.

Ineichen, B. (1977) 'Youthful marriage: the vortex of disadvantage', in R. Chester and J. Peel (eds) *Equalities and Inequalities in Family Life*, London: Academic Press.

Lasch, C. (1977) *Haven in a Heartless World. The Family Besieged*, New York: Basic Books.

Leonard, D. (1980) *Sex and Generation. A Study of Courtship and Weddings*, London: Tavistock.

Lewis, C. (1986) *Becoming a Father*, Milton Keynes: Open University Press.

Mansfield, P. and Collard, J. (1988) *The Beginning of the Rest of your Life? A Portrait of Newly-Wed Marriage*, London: Macmillan.

—— forthcoming, London: Macmillan.

Mason, J. (1987) 'A bed of roses? Women, marriage and inequality in later life', in P. Allatt, T. Keil, A. Bryman and B. Bytheway (eds) *Women and the Life Cycle*, London: Macmillan.

Morgan, D.H.J. (1981) *Berger and Kellner's Construction of Marriage*, University of Manchester: Department of Sociology, Occasional Paper No 7.

Schutz, A. (1964) *The Collected Papers*, 2 vols, The Hague: Nijhoff.

7 Making, breaking and remaking marriage

Christopher Clulow

Among the professional marriage watchers of the past forty years have been those offering therapeutic services to couples. In common with the couples they see, therapists (from the Greek θεραπεια, meaning 'attending') have tried to understand and alleviate marital problems on the premiss that they are symptoms of disorder or conflict in the personal relationship of marriage. On the whole they have paid little overt attention to the social institution of marriage but addressed themselves, rather as doctors or priests, to the 'cure' of conditions or to providing 'care' for couples in conflict.

Along the therapeutic continuum there have been many different approaches (see Dryden 1985). As socioeconomic conditions, cultural values and religious tolerance have changed to permit the greater private ordering of family life, those approaches which have explored private meanings (in preference to treating personal disorders) have matched a mood which has wanted to leave behind not only the view of divorce as socially deviant behaviour (enshrined in the concept of the 'matrimonial offence' which was at the centre of divorce legislation and judicial practice before 1971) but also that which regards marriage breakdown as the consequence of psychological illness or inadequacy. Therapy has developed its own theories about conflict in marriage which have found a place in the public consciousness alongside codes of morality and religious belief. While some might regard them as old sentiments dressed up in new clothes (in the same way that they have in the past been regarded as unacceptably new sentiments dressed up in traditional guise), they do represent an attempt to describe and explain what is happening in marriages in personal terms. Taking the *psychological* institution of marriage as their focus they tend to accentuate relatively unchanging aspects of human attachments.

As with all observers of family life, therapists describe what they see from a perspective that is neither wholly neutral nor objective. However much they strive to be outside what they are observing, their presence and particular objectives ensure they will, to some degree, be implicated with their subjects. Nevertheless, the therapist perspective contains essential pieces of the jigsaw which depicts the changing face of marriage in post-war Britain.

MAKING MARRIAGE

Within the therapist perspective, the psychodynamic model – or image (Sutherland 1980) – has offered particularly useful hypotheses about the substrata of human relationships. Based on psychoanalytical insights, the psychodynamic image gives form to unconscious motives in behaviour. Taking a developmental view, connections are made between a person's very earliest experiences of being in relation to others and patterns of relatedness in later life. The social and the personal are taken as inter-connected realities and interacting spheres of life, each influencing and being influenced by the other in their attempt to achieve congruence. The unformed inner-world images of young children develop through their relationships with significant people in their lives, always providing the images are sufficiently safe to be tested out with them. When they are not, they may be repressed from conscious awareness, relegated to a hinterland of the human psyche from where, like refugees, they constantly seek readmission to the homeland. Frozen in exile, such images remain un-formed because they are kept out of reach of the ordinary toings and froings of social intercourse. Instead, they exert from the backwoods strong pres-sure to reshape the outer world in the image of the world inside.

The psychodynamic image, then, portrays men and women as selective historians, unwittingly emphasising certain features and obscuring others as they interpret experience, but constantly challenged by the realities of everyday life (those that they venture out to meet or are unable to avoid) to broaden their perspectives. What they think is happening to them in the present, and therefore how they choose to behave in relation to events, is affected by past influences of which they may or may not be aware. These personal windows on life have been described as 'assumptive worlds' (Parkes 1971) and 'structures of meaning' (Marris 1974), each describing the personal maps assembled by people over their lifetime to make sense of their experiences. They define who we are as people and how we are likely to behave in different situations, and because they provide us with bearings in uncharted territory, they are not lightly to be discarded. Yet new territory always requires some revision of the existing map. There is, then, always a tension between inner and outer worlds which provides the impetus for change and development.

The capacity of people to manage this tension is significantly affected by the nature of the social environment. Marriage is an important part of that environment. As a social institution, and as 'the most direct heir of the intense primary relationships of childhood' (Thompson 1960), marriage has the potential not only to manage the present but also to recreate and rework the past within an intimate, present-day, adult partnership.

The psychodynamic image of marriage has been well-described in this country by writers like Pincus (1960), Dicks (1967), Lyons (1973), Skynner (1976) and Clulow and Mattinson (1989). Daniell summarises the contribution of clinical experience to understanding processes of interaction in marriage in these terms:

> First is the recognition that many of the problems of adulthood and many of the patterns of longings, fears and fantasies in marriage relationships stem from each partner's infantile and childhood experiences. Second, the motivations which underlie the choice of marital partner, sustain the relationship and give it a particular quality are as related to unconscious factors as to conscious ones. Third, there is a system of shared fantasies and shared defences which operate in a marital relationship. This leads to an unconscious as well as a conscious marriage contract in terms of what each spouse expects of the other. The overall crucial finding which emerges from an understanding of these mechanisms is that marriage has to be viewed as a psychic entity in itself – a system greater than the sum of the personalities of the two partners.
>
> (Daniel 1985: 171–2)

The unconscious factors in choice of and commitment to one's 'other half' (a colloquialism which captures a depth of psychological wisdom), and the concepts of shared fantasy and shared defence, speak to aspects of the unwritten contracts between couples which both bind them together and can be the source of much conflict.

To give one example: Mr Brooks was an only child of parents who gave him every educational advantage that money could buy. He was sent to boarding school at a tender age and earned their admiration, if not devotion, for his scholastic achievements. His upbringing provided him with few experiences of warm, intimate family relationships, and as a result he tended to keep people at a distance with his aloof manner.

He married a woman who, as the elder of two in her family, had taken more than her fair share of responsibility for bringing up a younger brother. She believed her parents favoured her brother, but rather than behave jealously towards him she devoted herself to his care in the hope that this would earn parental attention for herself.

Mr Brooks was drawn to his wife because she offered him the warmth and attention that he felt had been missing from his family. At an unconscious level he was also drawn to a woman who believed she was second best; she represented that part of his experience which he had not allowed to surface into conscious awareness: that he had been an unwanted child sent away from home to be brought up by others.

Mrs Brooks was flattered by the attention paid to her by such an intelligent man, and she was challenged by his aloofness which made her work all the harder to obtain a place in his eyes. When they married she felt she had become someone, and she lived vicariously through his work successes. Unconsciously he represented the competitive, achieving part of herself which she had sublimated in her relationship with her younger brother.

At its best, the shared defensive system allowed Mr Brooks to maintain himself as a success without having to forfeit the care and attention for which he craved. Mrs Brooks could bask in his reflected glory without having to know too much about her envious and destructive feelings – always provided that her contribution was sufficiently acknowledged. They maintained a comfortable distance in their marriage, and also from that part of themselves which was angry about the emotional neglect each feared they had experienced in childhood because they were essentially less loveable than others. This fear constituted part of their shared fantasy (Bannister and Pincus 1965): that each had to live a life prescribed by others (he to succeed, she to support his endeavours) in order to earn their place in the eyes of their loved ones.

The marriage ran into trouble when Mr Brooks' business interests collapsed and he started an affair. I shall return to the Brooks later, for now their situation is sufficient to illustrate some of the emotional ties which bind partners together in the psychological institution of marriage. Within this frame of reference, what distinguishes unsatisfactory marriages from satisfactory ones is not a fundamental difference in kind but the interplay of a complex web of factors of varying intensity at different points in time.

BREAKING MARRIAGE

Marriages are broken by death and divorce. Although not yet as common as losing a spouse through death, divorce is an experience which touches the lives of many people (without taking into account those who separate without untying the legal knot). In England and Wales there are around 160,000 divorces each year affecting nearly the same number of children. It is currently predicted that 37 per cent of marriages will end in divorce rather than death, and for those who marry very young, or who remarry, the risks are even higher (OPCS 1989). What is lost when a marriage breaks down?

This question can be answered at two levels. At a descriptive level there are many different strands to marriage which must be unravelled when the relationship comes to an end. They can be summarised under six headings:

1 *Ties as parents* are of crucial significance to both adults and children when a marriage breaks. Studies in this country and abroad have noted how frequently divorce results in children having to sustain the loss of one of their two parents, yet how important it is for children to know they have free access to two parents who continue to care for them despite the fact of divorce (Wallerstein and Kelly 1980, Walczak and Burns 1984, Lund 1984, Mitchell 1985, Wallerstein and Blakeslee 1989). Conflict between the parents, complexities introduced by new relationships which they may have entered into, and the inherent difficulties of sustaining the visiting relationship which freezes time frames, repeats the pain of parting and taxes ingenuity in trying to preserve a sense of normality, all conspire to defeat the best intentions of many non-resident parents (usually fathers).

For the adults, the daily reaffirmation of oneself as a parent can be an invaluable lifeline when personal identity feels shaky. Children provide a role and purpose in a crisis, and will help some adults to keep going where otherwise they may have broken down. Children may also provide some of the affection, support and even advice that is no longer available from the partner. Carried to extremes this can prove detrimental to adults and children alike, but especially to the children who then carry the burden of their parent's loss as well as their own (Wallerstein 1985).

2 *Ties of family and friends* may be weakened or broken by divorce. As these constitute the informal network of support for family members the losses involved can be considerable. Because, in our culture, women tend to be the ones to nurture family relationships and friendships, men may sustain the major loss in this area, finding themselves cut off from a network which previously had been taken for granted. For members of the wider family, strong feelings of loyalty may be stirred up by divorce which may make it impossible for them to contemplate maintaining their relationships with both parties. More commonly, and with friends too, a sense of uneasiness at being with only one partner, when previously the relationship had been with the couple, may introduce a barrier which can result in a process of distancing despite goodwill on both sides.

For children, the end of their parents' marriage may also signal the loss of one half of their wider family. If divorce is accompanied by unmitigated bitterness it may, for example, be almost impossible for parents to allow children to enjoy the company of a former spouse's parents. Relations between grandparents and grandchildren can become casualties of divorce. Because of the likelihood that marriage break-down will be followed by moving house and a change of area, the stability provided by continuing contacts with schoolfriends and neighbours may also be forfeited.

All this is in marked contrast to what is likely to happen if marriage is broken by the death of one partner. Then, family and friends are likely to gather round and increase the amount of support for the survivors. The bereaved parent will be more likely to welcome the contact with the partner's family, and will not feel they are there to censure or to steal.

3 *Economic ties* describe the financial basis of a marriage which may only become apparent when it ends. Divorce almost always leads to an erosion of material security, especially for women (Eekelaar and Maclean 1986), and is likely to precipitate changes in job-related behaviour. Figures prepared by the Office of Population and Censuses for the Lord Chancellor's Department (Law Commission 1988) indicate that the financial impact of marriage breakdown is greatest immediately after separation and following the decree. In this sample nearly two-thirds of divorcing women and one quarter of divorcing men had an income of less than £60 per week; the likelihood of claiming unemployment benefit and supplementary benefit (now income support) increased threefold and claims on state benefits such as Family Income Support doubled.

Divorce is likely to be financially more catastrophic than bereavement. When a partner dies the spouse stands to benefit from all worldly possessions, including life assurances and pensionable benefits where these have been provided for. Not so the divorcee. What previously was a joint income now has to support two households, and in an emotional climate where animosity may prevail over goodwill.

4 *Territorial ties*, while closely related to financial considerations, have practical and emotional associations which provide people with a sense of 'place'. It can be hard to give up a home which contains the results of past labours in a place where there are familiar landmarks. The sense of ownership and entitlement may make it difficult to decide what belongs to whom. And sometimes feelings of outrage will drive the partner who is left behind to damage the fabric, or to preserve damage earlier inflicted by their other half as some kind of memorial to injuries they feel they have sustained. Frequently the house will be sold, or the tenancy relinquished, to finance the setting up of two separate households. The same consequences are not as likely to follow the death of a partner.

5 *The legal ties* of marriage may appear to be no more than the formal contract holding a couple together, but they have immense significance for the experience of divorce because of what they represent (privately

and publicly) and because of the rules they establish for untying the knot.

Since the 1969 Divorce Reform Act became law in 1971, the only ground for divorce has been the 'irretrievable breakdown' of marriage. It is legitimate to ask who, other than the parties, is in a position to know whether a marriage has irretrievably broken down, a question recently considered in a judicial review of the ground for divorce (Law Commission 1988). As things stand, the old vestiges of the 'matrimonial offence' are still unearthed; 'adultery' and 'unreasonable behaviour' are offered as proof of irretrievable breakdown in marriage.

The problem is that when a marriage breaks, one partner commonly wants out while the other wants in. The experience of leaver and left is quite different, the leaver perhaps having ended the marriage while the couple were still together whereas the one left behind can still be struggling with disbelief even when they are living in separate places. Into this psychological system comes the judicial system with its own timescales and rules of conduct.

Much has been done in the past ten years to temper the worst effects of the adversarial means of settling disputes. Conciliation services have been introduced, the Solicitors Family Law Association has drawn up a non-litigious code of practice for its members, there has been an important review of matrimonial procedures (Booth 1985), and the recent Children Act aims to underpin and not undermine parents in discharging their responsibilities to children (Hoggett 1989). Moreover, the Lord Chancellor is shortly to propose changes which are expected to shift the emphasis of divorce law away from a preoccupation with establishing grounds for, and towards the business of addressing the consequences of, marriage breakdown. But there may be a personal investment in retaining the old system. The besieged psyche can be very adversarial, needing to blame others and secure a public vindication of the self in order to survive. In the nightmare world of monsters and villains to which divorcing parents may sometimes temporarily regress, the concept of the matrimonial offence is far more comprehensible than that of irretrievable breakdown. As one man said: 'I think adultery is a crime. Full stop. It's a terrible crime' (Clulow and Vincent 1987: 75), and he goes on to talk in terms of guilty and innocent partners, of crime and punishment. In cases like this the adversarial system, as well as inflaming conflict, can complement psychological needs by allowing for the construction and public exposition of a story which explains why the marriage has broken down and attributes blame elsewhere. A favourable court decision (over children, property, or financial issues) can be interpreted as both public vindication and an appropriate sentence for the offending party.

6 Interweaving all these connections are the *emotional ties* which bind a couple together and which can so powerfully influence reactions and behaviour in many different areas of life. The symptoms of their rupture can be violence, physical and psychological illness, abuse of children, absenteeism from work, unemployment, unremitting litigation and the other stress indicators which have been associated with marriage break-down. In turn, the stress reactions of parents set the scene for their children's experience of divorce which, in the short term at least, is likely to be one of receiving diminished parenting.

It is through considering the emotional ties which hold people together that one moves from the descriptive aspect of what is lost when a marriage breaks to a consideration of personal meanings in relation to that loss. This second-tier approach helps explain why the same traumatic event can be weathered so well by some people and so poorly by others. It is not so much what happens to people which determines their response as what they think is happening to them.

It is here that the psychodynamic image can assist understanding. In the example of Mr and Mrs Brooks' marriage, given earlier, the point was made that as well as being attached to each other as people in their own right, they were also unconsciously attached to a part of themselves which the other carried for them. Mr Brooks was drawn to someone who would not only reduce the risk of rejection for him by making all the running in the relationship, and who promised some of the warmth which had been lacking with his parents, but who would also represent that part of him which he feared was second best and did not qualify for attention. Mrs Brooks was not only flattered by the attention of a successful man but also drawn to someone who could express and contain her aggression and drive and make it work for them both through the life that he led.

A combination of circumstances surrounded the collapse of their marriage. With the advent of children, Mrs Brooks became less interested in and sustaining of her husband's work. A balance in their relationship was disturbed which each managed by withdrawing a little into their separate worlds. The crisis which precipitated the break-up was the collapse of a business venture, which Mr Brooks tried to keep from his wife, and her discovery of an affair he had started around the same time.

When they separated, each partner had to come to terms not only with the loss of each other and their marriage (including the rupture of many of the ties described earlier), but also a loss of self. This loss was the consequence not simply of there no longer being a habituated series of routines and relationships which gave life a predictable rhythm, but more specifically of the unwritten contract wherein each 'agreed' to carry and contain part of the other. The breakdown of marriage as a psychological container required both a fundamental reordering of other relationships to compensate for the loss and the assimilation of an image of self which previously had been carried by the spouse.

Loss, then, is defined by the meaning ascribed to personal circumstance. For some, the ending of marriage, far from being registered as a loss, will be seen as an unqualified gain. It makes a difference if the marriage is two years old or twenty years old, if you are the leaver or the left, if there are children or if there are not, but that difference cannot accurately be predicted by general statements. The mix of inner and outer worlds can produce many different outcomes.

What is more predictable is the sequence of reactions displayed by those who have sustained a loss. The reactions are more visible the greater the experience of loss, and there is no guarantee that the sequence will be satisfactorily completed; there are many Queen Victorias who build mausoleums for their departed Prince Alberts, some constructed in love and some in hate.

Building on the work of Bowlby (1969, 1975, 1980) and a study of bereavement, Parkes (1986) described mourning as the one psychiatric condition where the cause was known, the features were distinctive and the course was predictable. He identified four overlapping phases in the grieving process. First, there were initial reactions of shock and numbness, lasting anything from a few hours to a week or more. Defences of denial or, at the other extreme, euphoria acted like an anaesthetic to protect a person from the full import of what had happened to their world. This was followed by intense yearning and searching for the lost person, behaviour which could be acute in the first two weeks following the loss. Moments of anger and protest become increasingly evident, but directed towards recovering what has been lost rather than separating from it. A longer period of disorganisation and despair follows this; anger here may be in the service of letting go, and it may be directed towards the self as well as others. Finally, there is a phase of reintegration and recovery which enables people to pick up the threads of their lives again in new and meaningful ways.

Parkes estimated that in ordinary circumstances the work of mourning would be completed in two years. This contrasts with the three phases of divorce outlined by Wallerstein and Kelly (1980) which allowed between four and five years for recovery, an estimate Wallerstein and Blakeslee (1989) have revised upwardly for the not insubstantial group of people (mainly children) who emerged as chronic casualties of marriage breakdown in their sample. In this country there is also evidence of how long it can take some men to recover from divorce (Ambrose *et al.* 1983).

Why should it take longer to recover from divorce than from bereavement? Is the experience of bereavement an appropriate analogy for those who are divorcing or are there substantial differences?

Clinical observation (Mattinson 1988) suggests that conflicted or ambivalent relationships are the hardest to get over, whether they end as a result of death or divorce. For adults and children, marriage breakdown is preceded by a history in which individuals will have experienced rejection, animosity and personal hurt. The fact that one person has chosen to leave the family places a very different meaning on events than when Fate, or the Grim Reaper, intervenes. On a personal level, death can be easier to take than divorce. The often mixed and confusing feelings which accompany marriage breakdown can quickly polarise in the context of rejection. For the adults, particularly when one party becomes emotionally and sexually involved with another person, feelings of guilt or outrage may prohibit any contact which might enable both partners to understand and come to terms with what has changed in their lives. For the children, a sense of being to blame, or not being worth staying home for, may affect the success of future attempts made by the departing parent to keep in touch.

The fact of rejection, consciously known about and publicly recognised, accounts for much of the difference, in terms of personal meanings, between death and divorce. While this is obvious for the adults, it applies equally to children. The weakening of bonds between children and one (sometimes both) of their parents, with grandparents, other relatives and friends, has already been referred to as a possible, even probable, outcome of divorce. In contrast, family and friends are more likely to offer practical help and emotional support following bereavement, and the resident parent will be more trusting of such help than when it comes in the wake of marriage breakdown. There is not the problem of divided loyalties for either adults or children, and so the experience is more likely to be talked about and shared in a way which is mutually helpful.

Not so when one parent has chosen to leave. Then, children may have little hard information about what is going on, and they may feel no-one can be asked. So they fall back on supposition and fantasy in trying to understand what has happened and what may be about to happen. The consequence of that can be that they worry about their future security (if one parent leaves, why not both?), they blame themselves for the rift, or they become angry about their powerlessness in a situation which is not of their choosing and where their own wishes and feelings appear to have been disregarded by those who are supposed to care most for them. For in divorce, the wishes – and sometimes the interests – of parents and children are likely to diverge in a way which rarely happens following bereavement.

The experience of rejection may also explain why the two chief components of grief – sorrow and anger – are expressed differently according to whether a marriage ends through death or divorce. Sorrow is usually uppermost after a bereavement. The lost partner, or parent, can be idealised, as loving and affectionate memories flood back. Anger seems quite inappropriate to the occasion, and if it finds expression is most likely to be targeted on others, or come out in self-reproach. The opposite tends to be true of divorce. Anger and recrimination are uppermost, and the absent partner may well be degraded. Sorrow may be very hard to locate at all, at least in the early stages. Indeed, the anger may be necessary to achieve the break, as one man whose wife was wanting to leave said about his predicament: 'I'd have to hate her to go; I can be more civilised later on' (Clulow *et al.* 1986).

There is more sense of a 'later on' following divorce, and often an apprehensive sense. Partners are likely to meet each other again, and if they have children they must try to maintain contact as parents which on their own account they might far rather be without. Death involves a corpse from which leave is finally and irrevocably taken, at least in body if not in mind. The corpse must be buried or cremated. A social and religious ceremony caters for this necessity and, more importantly, allows for the loss to be registered publicly, actively encouraging a period of mourning.

No such social and psychological provision is made for those who divorce. The advice to delay important decisions frequently given following a bereavement is replaced by pressure to act now in order to gain a strategic advantage or to preserve a position in the hostile climate of divorce. Remarriage is more likely to follow divorce than bereavement and, at least until recently, it could be argued that for many divorcees there has been no other direction to take than into another marriage to resolve the uncertainty surrounding social status and individual identity.

Among the many factors which influence the time it takes to recover from divorce, seven can be highlighted as of particular importance: the significance of the loss, including the circumstances in which it is understood to have arisen, the number and the extent of other changes which must follow as a result; the practical and material worries to which these give rise; the availability and accessibility of social supports; the degree of forewarning received; how successfully past losses have been managed; and what is created to take over from what has been lost.

Some consideration has already been given to the first four of these seven factors. Of the remainder, the question of forewarning is a very important one. When a partner is dying slowly there is some opportunity to come to terms with the impending loss, to rehearse how life might be afterwards, and to provide some continuity by discussing together the arrangements which will follow the death. There is less shock, less sense of being helplessly upended than when a major loss comes unannounced, although the burden of grief will not be removed when death finally intercedes. One of the challenges in the field of divorce is how to make the experience more predictable, how to build in early warnings, or a moratorium, when partners are often feeling so mistrustful of each other that they believe the only way out is suddenly and without warning. Then there is little opportunity to understand why the break has occurred, and people are left alone to construct a story which explains why things have worked out as they have. Some stories, constructed in isolation and embellished with paranoid fantasies, can be extremely unserviceable – even damaging – guides for future behaviour.

Personal constructions of this kind will be coloured by history. Current losses are capable of reactivating past losses, especially when the past has not been laid properly to rest. The experience of the present day can be overlaid with meaning from times gone by. Some parents locked into combat over post-divorce arrangements for their children are motivated by past trauma. In some research about the work of divorce-court welfare officers (Clulow and Vincent 1987) one man was explicit about his reasons for fighting a child-custody case which he had very little hope of winning: as he saw it his first wife had succeeded in wresting their child from him when that marriage broke, and he was not going to let it happen again. A mother who behaved over-protectively towards her daughter remarked, in passing, that she had been the same age as her own little girl when her parents' marriage had broken down.

The impact of a broken marriage depends not only on what has been lost but also on what can be created to take its place. This is true for children as well as parents, and will be linked with the framework of social, emotional and material security which can be constructed in the place of the 'failed' marriage. Remarriage is one such construction.

REMAKING MARRIAGE

People have married more than once throughout history. Many have been those whose husbands or wives met untimely deaths in war, childbirth or epidemic. The ancient Jews insisted that a childless widow should be remarried to her husband's brother so children could be raised in the dead man's name. On the other hand, the Hindus required widows to follow their husbands into the funeral pyre. In Christian Europe there was more ambivalence: the mediaeval Roman church disapproved of remarriage but did not forbid it, and many accepted social penance as a price worth paying (Pengelley 1982).

In eighteenth-century Catholic France and Protestant England, remarriages accounted for around one-third of all marriages (Stone 1977), about the same proportion as today. Remarriage only fell into temporary decline in Britain for a relatively short period between the great advances in medicine and public health, which controlled premature mortality, and the advent of easier divorce in the 1970s. So what is new is not remarriage, but divorce as the precursor to remarriage.

What is also new is that divorce can be the sequel to remarriage. In statistical terms, second marriages are more vulnerable than first marriages (OPCS 1986). A divorced woman who remarries is twice as likely to divorce as a single woman who marries at the same age. The comparable likelihood for divorced men is one and a half times that of bachelors. One in five divorces involves a partner who has been divorced before. In these terms remarriage can be the 'meat' in the divorce 'sandwich', a sandwich that may sometimes be multilayered.

Why, then, is it that the process of remaking marriage appears to be more problematic than that of making marriage? Since it is the norm for couples to live together before they remarry (whereas only around one in four cohabit before a first marriage) why do they bother to marry in the first place, and why is it that being seasoned veterans of marriage they are more likely to fall in battle than their first-time counterparts? Two factors are relevant when considering these questions: first, remarriages are rooted in the experience of loss; second, remarriage is part of a hybrid family form when there are children from either partner's previous marriage, a hybrid with which neither society nor some of the individuals directly concerned have adequately come to terms.

Among the motives for marriage are the desire to make and be the object of a commitment, to belong to someone in a way which is recognised both publicly and privately, and to make good the past by planning a joint enterprise for the future. The immediate past can be very present in the minds of some who remarry, and it is true of all remarriages that they are founded in an environment which has been significantly created by a first marriage. Some second marriages will be founded upon the sense of loss that partners have in common; they will have been drawn together in adversity, and their partnership may even be on the rebound from a broken former attachment with which they have still to come to terms. Whether leaver or left, the temptation to turn to someone for the care, attention and love which has gone missing from the first marriage may be overwhelming.

The process of mourning, outlined earlier, can be interrupted at any stage. Some 'on the rebound' marriages can be indicative of the denial phase of mourning, a way of saying to someone (including oneself) that 'I don't need you' when the reverse is very much the case. Anger and protest may be displayed towards a former spouse or partner through becoming involved with someone else. Depression, and an absence of a reliable sense of oneself, may be relieved by a relationship which offers to restore self-esteem. But only when some recovery and reintegration has taken place will a person be really free to make a positive choice of another partner. Because mourning is painful, there is every temptation to bypass this taxing emotional work. The more bitter the feelings about the broken marriage, the greater the tendency to split affect between an all bad and depriving spouse and an all good and giving new partner who seems to offer a haven from the emotional storm. Some capacity to manage ambivalent feelings about a past marriage allows partners to be relatively free of historical distortion when making new relationships.

One of the casualties of a broken marriage can be the capacity to trust. This can lead to a wariness in subsequent relationships, and a self-enclosure which may interfere with communication. Mr and Mrs Brooks, whom we met earlier, sought help some years after they separated at a time when they were considering the possibility of getting back together again (something which eventually happened). Each felt so wounded by the breakdown of their past marriage (and they had gone to the extent of getting divorced) that neither could trust the other to appreciate sufficiently their hurt. Quite unconsciously they demonstrated their separate preoccupations. Mrs Brooks recounted an episode in which the two of them had been watching a Remembrance Day service at the Cenotaph on television. She had commented on the fact that the Princess Royal was there with her children but without her husband. She had been perplexed when Mr Brooks, apparently quite disconnectedly, had pointed to the presence on the edge of the screen of a visiting male Royal from overseas. In frustration, Mrs Brooks cited this as an example of their problem communicating with each other properly. Yet all the ingredients of their own predicament were represented on the screen: a woman on her own with her children, a man wanting to edge back into the picture, neither risking saying what they missed or wanted, and both coming together in a context redolent with past loss and injury.

Mourning what has been lost, and managing the ambivalence about what has gone before, is likely to be as important for those who have lost a partner through death as for those whose marriages have ended in divorce. The 'Rebecca Syndrome' is not unfamiliar. The story, *Rebecca*, Du Maurier's novel, describes the uphill struggle of the new Mrs De Winter to follow in the footsteps of her deceased predecessor at Manderley, a struggle conducted not only with the formidable Mrs Danvers, self-appointed guardian of an idealised image of the dead Rebecca, but also within herself and her own fantasies:

> Rebecca, always Rebecca. Whenever I walked in Manderley, wherever I sat, even in my thoughts and in my dreams, I met Rebecca. . . . Did she resent me and fear me as I resented her? Did she want Maxim alone in the house again! I could fight the living but I could not fight the dead. If there was some woman in London that Maxim loved, someone he wrote to, visited, dined with, slept with, I could fight with her. We could stand on common ground. I should not be afraid. Anger and jealousy were things that could be conquered. One day the woman would grow old, or tired, or different, and Maxim would not love her anymore. But Rebecca would never grow old. Rebecca would always be the same. And her I could not fight. She was too strong for me.
>
> (Du Maurier 1962: 231)

Behind the idealisation of Rebecca there emerges a thread of suspicion that Maxim might actually have murdered his first wife – not insignificant evidence of a failure to manage ambivalence after her death!

One explanation that has been offered for the vulnerability of second marriages is that some people are doomed to repeat their mistakes in close personal relationships. At its most pernicious, the argument runs that only the psychologically flawed divorce and have need of another marriage, and that they show little or no capacity to learn from experience. Since people often blame either themselves or their partner for the breakdown of marriage (that is, they interpret breakdown as a personal failure on someone's part) this explanation can be particularly unhelpful and disabling.

Franks (1988) says that hardly any of the remarried couples she interviewed saw a resemblance between their new and old partners. She is rightly concerned to present the positive face of remarriage and to avoid any suggestion that those who marry again are less able to sustain intimate relationships than those who marry only once or, indeed, those who choose to marry not at all. Yet it would be odd if the people with whom we have chosen to become intimately associated did not reflect certain aspects of the way we see ourselves or, in some way, conform with our assumptions about 'family relations'. Different people will be internally preoccupied with different issues. They will succeed in working out some of these with some people but not with others. Not only is it likely, but also evidence of the struggle to develop, that new partners are chosen, at least in part, on the basis of whether they are gauged capable of providing assistance with or protection from the kinds of relationships about which there is most ambivalence. The conscious attempt to preserve continuity in our assumptions about ourselves and others will be complemented by an unconscious drive to be hitched up to our own 'problem'; internal preoccupations thereby finding expression in an external relationship.

If the internal preoccupations are overwhelming, the result may be an attempt to obliterate part of the identity of the new spouse. The fact of death or divorce may be denied by choosing someone the same as the former partner (or closely identified with him or her). Conversely, the drive may be to find someone as different as possible. Thomas Hardy, whose novels often describe unhappy marriages and attempts (usually doomed) to escape from them, took the first route. He felt himself to be saddled with an unloving and unloved wife for much of his life, but when she died he was overwhelmed with remorse. In pilgrimages to the scenes of their once happy courtship, and in countless poems to her memory, he sought to make reparation. When he married again it was to the woman who had been literary assistant-cum-housekeeper to himself and his first wife – someone who was well acquainted with them both. When he died his ashes were deposited in Westminster Abbey, but on his order his heart was buried in his first wife's grave in the village of Stinsford.

Second marriages are rooted in loss not just for the adults but also for children. Indeed, any account of remarriage which is restricted to the adult partners is likely to be woefully inadequate, for if there is one fundamental difference between first and subsequent marriages it has to do with children. First marriages are usually entered into with an expectation of children; subsequent marriages usually begin with that expectation already having been fulfilled.

Stepfamilies are created when two adults:

> form a new household in which one or both brings a child or children from a previous relationship. Such families may be preceded by single parenthood, separation, divorce or bereavement, and may arise through cohabitation, marriage or remarriage. Stepchildren may be full-time or part-time members of the household.
>
> (De'ath 1988: 1)

In this situation children and adults have to manage different kinds of boundaries, each of which is capable of placing the hybrid family form of the stepfamily under pressure. The first boundary can be depicted as running along a horizontal axis and being concerned with degrees of inclusion and exclusion. The second can be seen as operating on a vertical axis. This one delineates between the generations and is concerned with authority, power and hierarchical differences.

For children, in particular, the first boundary raises questions about whether they can continue to have the same standing as before in their parents' eyes: 'If daddy's married someone else has he rejected me?' 'If mummy's living with someone else what happens to our special relationship?' 'If I'm no longer living under the same roof as mummy or daddy does that mean I don't belong anymore?' In the aftermath of divorce these questions can be very real, and the easy reassurance of adults may not necessarily allay anxieties about being shut out. In distress at feeling rejected, children may seek to protect themselves by turning the tables on parents who they feel have rejected them. Some determined statements about 'not wanting to see daddy now he's living with someone else' can mask a bitter disappointment and sense of loss. Remarriage marks the end of any lingering hope of reconciliation in the former marriage, and Wallerstein (1989) judged from her sample that, at best, it was a neutral event for children.

Within the newly formed household there may be jealousy of step-siblings and a preoccupation with being treated fairly. One ten-year-old girl complained bitterly about having to have tea on the settee while her father and stepmother's family sat up to the table. Whatever the reasons for this arrangement – and crass insensitivity on the part of the adults can be one – it represented perfectly how the child felt about her place in the re-formed family. The fact that children have no choice about their parents and siblings may take on new dimensions of meaning in stepfamilies. As well as feeling on the outside of the arrangements being made by others there can also be a determination not to belong. As Adrian Mole put it:

> My father has decided to go to Skegness on the 15th. He has booked a four berth caravan. He is taking Doreen and Maxwell with him! He expects me to go! If I go people will automatically assume that Doreen is my mother and Maxwell my brother! I am going to Scotland.
>
> (Townsend 1983: 110)

Add to these emotional realities the logistical complexities of servicing family life when the definition of 'family' transcends household boundaries, when the needs of adults and children are constantly changing, and when individual wishes and interests are frequently in conflict, and it is small wonder that the business of remaking marriage can be a difficult one for adults. Always there is an underlying tension over who is to come first, a tension that may be difficult to manage when loyalties are divided.

Hierarchical boundaries confer authority on certain family members over others. This can pose problems when children have three or more adults exercising parental responsibilities towards them. Stepparents have to guard against usurping the role of the natural parent, both in the eyes of the children and of their natural parents. There is more scope for children to play the game of 'divide and rule' when they sense that the adults in their world have not resolved the question of who has authority over them at different times and in relation to different areas of their lives.

Sexual confusion may result from children being part of a new situation in which the fact of their parents having a sexual life can no longer be avoided. When the children are older it can sometimes happen that there is very little age difference between the child and the parent's new partner. Stepsiblings may wonder about what kind of relationship they have with each other when they reach the age of sexual activity. And in extreme situations the incest taboo between stepparents and stepchildren may break down, resulting in sexual abuse.

These pressures on the children affect the adults as they try to build their new partnership together. Children come ready-made to stepfamilies and so the processes of getting married and becoming parents have to be managed simultaneously. This can be a shock for a partner who has, perhaps, not married before and had little experience of children. The hierarchy imposed by antecedent history may give priority to the relationship between a parent and his or her children, the marriage taking second place to parenthood. That may make it more difficult for a couple to feel they have the right to 'close the bedroom door' on the children and have a life of their own. Sometimes a new spouse may come to regard their partner's children as a threat, an envoy of the former spouse, and a continuing reminder that someone else has had – may even continue to have – an exclusive claim on their spouse.

Rooted in loss, vulnerable as is any hybrid, the tender plant of remarriage has to contend with an environment which is not always conducive to healthy growth. In what remains the major study of stepfamily life in the United Kingdom, Jacqueline Burgoyne and David Clark (1984) drew attention to how frequently remarried couples used the image of a first marriage to guide them through the labyrinth of subsequent partnerships. While this could work when there were no children from a previous marriage, or if the children were very young, it had limited usefulness as a working model for the very different demands on couples who were remaking marriage. Indeed, the image could contain in itself the seeds of destruction for stepfamilies.

As with individual images, so with collective images. It must be a remarkable tribute to the conservative principle in the human spirit that despite nearly two out of every five marriages ending in divorce, one in three marriages involving remarriage for at least one of the partners, more than one in four children born out of wedlock, one in seven children being brought up in single-parent households and at least six million people living in step-families, we perpetuate the cornflake-packet image of 'family' as consisting of two first-time married parents with their 2.2 children. While we do so it is very difficult for us to create the conditions, at public and personal levels, for families to thrive.

From the outset, the process of remaking marriage challenges people to come to terms with feelings of jealousy, envy and rivalry as they relinquish exclusive, proprietorial notions of relatedness. Time, money and energy flow from one household to another in attempts to maintain the ties of parenthood across a gulf which consists of more than geographical distance and physical absence. Remarried couples have to come to terms with more generous, complex and altruistic definitions of 'family' than those who marry for the first time. And they have to do all this when the attitudes and practices of society continue to be organised around a traditional view of marriage and assumptions of lifelong monogamy. They are swimming against a tide which is only slowly turning and, caught in the currents of past legacies, small wonder that some go under.

Nevertheless the tide *is* turning, bringing with it the possibility of change in attitudes to family and the tensions which are an inevitable part of the process of building family life. Social research has begun to map out the different forms of family life, breaking down any notion of there being one model. Therapists and counsellors have explored the personal meanings of the different choices that people make, and there is less stigma attached to seeking help in finding a personal solution than in days gone by. Released from the traps of an old institution, couples have more scope to tailor their relationships to a form which suits them. This may create its own problems, since people crave for a norm as well as feel trapped by convention, and the burden of choice can be every bit as onerous as that of an imposed commitment. But the conditions are created in which couples can take responsibility for the decisions they make.

As a psychological institution marriage, however it may be defined in years to come, will continue to be a very important forum for the development of self and society. Inner and outer realities will continue to be mediated through the intimate associations people choose to have and make, and from that process will come the course couples set for themselves and others in the future. It remains to be seen what form, or forms, the social institution of marriage will take. But the success of couples in 'making a go of it' – a phrase now associated with Jackie Burgoyne's contribution – will in no short measure be affected by those other 'marriages' contracted in the inner world of the psyche and in the many different circumstances where men and women come together to undertake a common enterprise.

186   *Christopher Clulow*

REFERENCES

Ambrose, P., Harper, T. and Pemberton, R. (1983) *Surviving Divorce: Men Beyond Marriage*, Brighton: Wheatsheaf Books.
Bannister, K. and Pincus, L. (1965) *Shared Phantasy in Marital Problems*, London: Institute of Marital Studies.
Booth, The Hon. Mrs Justice (1985) *Report of the Matrimonial Proceedings Committee*, London: HMSO.
Bowlby, J. (1969) *Attachment. (Attachment and Loss vol. 1)*, London: Hogarth Press/Institute of Psycho-analysis.
—— (1975) *Separation, Anxiety and Anger. (Attachment and Loss vol. 2)*, London: Hogarth Press/Institute of Psycho-analysis.
—— (1980) *Loss: Sadness and Depression. (Attachment and Loss vol. 3)*, London: Hogarth Press/Institute of Psycho-analysis.
Burgoyne, J. and Clark, D. (1984) *Making a Go of It: A Study of Stepfamilies in Sheffield*, London: Routledge & Kegan Paul.
Clulow, C., Dearnley, B. and Balfour, F. (1986) 'Shared phantasy and therapeutic structure in a brief marital psychotherapy', *British Journal of Psychotherapy* 3(2): 124–32.
Clulow, C. and Mattinson, J. (1989) *Marriage Inside Out. Understanding Problems of Intimacy*, Harmondsworth: Pelican Books.
Clulow, C. and Vincent, C. (1987) *In the Child's Best Interests? Divorce Court Welfare and the Search for a Settlement*, London: Tavistock.
Daniell, D. (1985) 'Marital therapy: the psychodynamic approach', in W. Dryden (ed.) *Marital Therapy In Britain, vol. 1*, London: Harper & Row.
De'ath, E. (1988) 'What is a stepfamily?' in *Working With Stepfamilies*, Proceedings of a Conference held in London 30 November, National Stepfamily Association.
Dicks, H.V. (1967) *Marital Tensions*, London: Routledge & Kegan Paul.
Dryden, W. (ed.) (1985) *Marital Therapy in Britain*, vols 1 and 2, London: Harper & Row.
Eekelaar, J. and Maclean, M. (1986) *Maintenance After Divorce*, New York: Oxford University Press.
Franks, H. (1988) *Remarriage*, London: Bodley Head.
Hoggett, B. (1989) 'The Children Bill: the Aim', *Family Law* 15: 217–26.
Law Commission (1988) *Facing the Future: A Discussion Paper on the Grounds for Divorce*, Lord Chancellor's Division, Document 170, London: HMSO.
Lyons, A. (1973) 'Therapeutic intervention in relation to the institution of marriage', in R. Gosling (ed.) *Support, Innovation and Autonomy*, London: Tavistock.
Lund, M. (1984) 'Research on divorce and children', *Family Law* 14(7): 198–201.
Marris, P. (1974) *Loss and Change*, London: Routledge & Kegan Paul.
Mattinson, J. (1988) *Work, Love and Marriage*, London: Duckworth.
Mitchell, A. (1985) *Children in the Middle*, London: Tavistock.
Office of Population and Censuses (OPCS) (1986) *Fact Sheet on Divorce and Remarriage*, London: HMSO.
—— (1989) *Population Trends*, 55, London: HMSO.
Parkes, C.M. (1971) 'Psycho-social transitions: a field for study', *Social Science and Medicine* 5: 101–15.

—— (1986) *Bereavement: Studies of Grief in Adult Life*, Harmondsworth: Penguin, second edition.

Pengelley, P. (1982) 'Second marriage', Paper given at a conference entitled 'A Natural History of Marriage', 21 May, London.

Pincus, L. (1960) *Marriage: Studies in Emotional Conflict and Growth*, London: Methuen.

Stone, L. (1977) *The Family, Sex and Marriage in England, 1500–1800*, Harmondsworth: Penguin.

Sutherland, J.D. (1980) *The Psychodynamic Image of Man: A Philosophy for the Caring Professions*, Aberdeen: Aberdeen University Press.

Skynner, A.C.R. (1976) *One Flesh, Separate Persons*, London: Constable.

Thompson, A.G. (1960) 'Introduction', in L. Pincus (ed.) *Marriage: Studies in Emotional Conflict and Growth*, London: Methuen.

Townsend, S. (1983) *The Secret Diary of Adrian Mole Aged 13³/₄*, London: Methuen.

Walczak, Y. and Burns, S. (1984) *Divorce: The Child's Point Of View*, London: Harper & Row.

Wallerstein, J. (1985) 'The overburdened child: some long-term consequences of divorce', *American Journal of Social Work*, March/April: 116–23.

Wallerstein, J. and Blakeslee, S. (1989) *Second Chances. Men, Women and Children a Decade after Divorce*, London: Bantam.

Wallerstein, J. and Kelly, J. (1980) *Surviving the Break-up. How Children and Parents Cope with Divorce*, London: Grant McIntyre.

8 Interventions in families

Janet Walker

The purpose of social work is to help individuals or families with various problems, and to overcome or lessen these so that they may achieve a better personal, family or social adjustment.

(Younghusband 1959: 21)

For at least two hundred years there have been concerns that 'the family' is in a state of crisis and disintegration. Whilst pre-industrial family life is characterised as offering stable, supportive networks within caring communities, the modern family is viewed as small, private and insular, living in an environment devoid of 'community spirit'. There have been far-reaching social, political, and economic transitions since industrialisation, all of which have had a major impact on family life, but descriptions of earlier supportive family networks and caring communities have been grossly overstated. Expectations of what the *ideal* family should be are based on long-held assumptions about the roles, status and behaviour considered appropriate for men, women, and children not only within family relationships, but in society generally (Gittins 1985). Notions of equality between men and women during the twentieth century severely challenge the more traditional roles (Finch and Summerfield, Chapter 1, this volume).

Delinquency, domestic violence, child abuse, mental illness, illegitimacy, and family instability are not products of the twentieth century. They have all existed over centuries and in many cultures. They have emerged, however, as the moral panics and social problems of post-war Britain and this emergence has coincided with fundamental shifts in family relationships. It has become fashionable and somewhat convenient to place the blame for these problems on the family, thereby highlighting the dangers associated with its apparent demise as the cornerstone of a stable society, and justifying the need to find ways of preventing further deterioration. The response has been to design an ever-increasing range of social interventions with the aim of buttressing and supporting families, thus legitimising almost any intrusion into family life under the guise of 'prevention' or 'protection'. Almost anyone is a potential recipient of social-welfare services, to the extent that Gittins (1985) asks how far the state is now creator or destroyer of family solidarity. In this chapter I shall explore this question by examining the development and the implications of professional intervention in families in post-war Britain, drawing attention to some of the central dilemmas and contradictions in current social-work practice.

LEGACIES FROM THE PAST

The state has a long history of involvement in the definition of what constitutes a family, the legal relationships of its members, and the rights of individuals. Such definitions almost always imply what is considered to be 'normal' and 'good' in family life (Morgan 1985). This history has had a fundamental influence on recent developments in social welfare and provides an important backcloth to the discussion.

Whilst notions of prevention and protection are more characteristic of recent social policies, recognition that the state should take some responsibility for its marginal, less-fortunate members has been a feature of legislation since the Poor Laws of Elizabethan England. Local parishes assumed responsibility for distinguishing between the needy and the idle, punishing the latter, but providing relief for the former – the able-bodied poor, the impotent poor and dependent children. Rapid industrialisation was accompanied by dramatic changes in the economic and social order. Victorian England faced escalating social problems – bad health, bad housing, and poverty. Victorian concepts of relief were hugely inadequate, promoting a plethora of policies and legislation which were designed to 'tidy up' society. The emphasis was on the control and the removal of individuals who could not be adequately cared for within families and communities. Thus workhouses, prisons, asylums, infirmaries, reformatories, and orphanages categorised and contained the mad, the bad, the sick and the destitute, all of whom were seen as a threat to economic progress and stability. Such people became 'more and more subject to surveillance and interference by state agencies' (Gittins 1985: 146). Social welfare was informed by the belief in patriarchal authority and a patriarchal household imbued with a puritanical work ethic. Anyone living outside such a family environment was considered a social threat. The vision was one of social order, respectability and authority.

Victorian institutions did not, however, stem the cumulative effects of the industrial revolution and by 1909 the Royal Commission on Poor Laws and the Unemployed was stressing the need for more curative treatment and rehabilitation, and the need to exercise compulsion in the 'best interests' of individuals and communities. Here was the public shift from repression to prevention (Fink 1978), from a negative approach to social problems to a positive approach reflected in the acceptance of an interdependence between the individual and the state and the value of maximising human potential. The introduction of insurance, pensions and unemployment assistance established a national minimum of services which, just as the Poor Laws, were aimed at the most vulnerable members of society.

Although state provision had been developing for 300 years, voluntary help for the disadvantaged and destitute had been provided, principally by religious groups, for much longer. Money for the poor, shelter for the homeless, and care for the sick were a central part of religious training and religious life. Within local communities voluntary self-help had long been encouraged and was promoted by the later development of the Co-operative movement. Throughout the Victorian era Christian and humanitarian principles influenced many people to become actively involved in welfare work. Octavia Hill has been referred to as the grandmother of modern social work because of her pioneering training of voluntary helpers (Young and Ashton 1956). Dr Barnado, Elizabeth Fry, Mary Carpenter, Lord Shaftesbury, and John Howard, amongst others, paved the way for a network of voluntary services. By 1869 the Charity Organization Society was formed to develop a machinery to co-ordinate these services in order that they might offer more effective intervention. By the end of the nineteenth century, state services were developing alongside this flourishing voluntary, charitable sector, and this duality of provision has continued through to the present day.

POST-WAR DEVELOPMENTS IN SOCIAL WELFARE

It is during the past forty years that Britain has witnessed the most dramatic changes in social welfare provision. The most significant landmark was, undoubtedly, the Beveridge Report of 1942. The report was based on the principle that it was the duty of the state to provide protection against want, disease, ignorance, squalor and idleness, and contained a vision of a post-war Britain which offered a framework of welfare 'from the cradle to the grave'. The late 1940s saw this vision come to reality through the introduction of policies for social security, health, education, employment, housing and personal social services.

By the end of the Second World War the government had:

assumed and developed a measure of direct concern with the health and well-being of the population which . . . was very little short of remarkable. No longer did concern rest on the belief that . . . it was proper to intervene only to assist the poor and those who were unable to pay for services. . . . Instead, it increasingly regarded as a proper function or even obligation of government to ward off distress . . . among all classes of society.

(Titmuss 1950)

Here was the turning point which legalised state intervention in the life of every family. Services were no longer aimed solely at a minority group, but were to be universally available. Building on the legacies of earlier philosophies and agencies, the concept of universality opened the floodgates for welfare interventions, often with unclear objectives, blurred boundaries, and uncertainty about who the clients were and how their needs should be prioritised.

One of the key elements in this package of reforms was the emergence of a new kind of social welfare to be provided by local authorities. 'Specialists' were appointed to work with specific client groups – child care officers, mental welfare officers, probation officers and almoners had designated roles backed by statutory authority. It was not unusual for a family with multiple problems to have several of these 'experts' dealing with one or more family members. A mood of optimism that social problems could be effectively tackled and eradicated, characterised the new welfare state.

Institutions from a previous era continued, new institutions developed and some changed their names. Reform schools became approved schools, orphanages became children's homes and asylums became mental hospitals. Alongside the state welfare services, charitable institutions proliferated. By the mid-1970s Fink commented that 'there is hardly a public social service for which there is not one or more like services offered under voluntary auspice' (Fink 1978: 37). The Nathan Report (1952) had observed that 'historically, state action is voluntary action crystallized and made universal'. New agencies, such as Family Service Units developed in the 1940s with a strong commitment to family work, a focus on the provision of practical help and friendship, and a pervasive informality (Miller and Cook 1981). This agency and many others have continued to make a vital contribution to welfare provision. The co-operation of statutory and voluntary services has become the cornerstone of the modern welfare state, yet although they share a mutual concern for families, differing policies and practices have frequently resulted in minimal co-ordination which in turn has created additional stresses and strains for some of the most vulnerable families (Parker 1982).

This was exacerbated within the statutory sector where child care and welfare services were provided by different departments. There emerged four outstanding issues:

1 the problem of co-ordination;
2 increased delinquency and an identified need for family policy;
3 the emergence of community care as a key policy goal; and
4 the need for consolidation of social work as a discrete profession.

The dismantling of the Poor Law had split services between health and welfare resulting in a 'multiplication of enquiries and visitations, causing annoyance and waste of time and money' (Hall 1976).

From specialism to generic social work

Social services have been described as 'people-changing institutions' (Romanyshyn 1971) whose employees are invested with authority derived from legislation, professional knowledge and expertise. During the 1960s the belief emerged that there was a body of skills, methods and knowledge common to a wide range of professionals and hence specialism was re-considered. Transferability became the new buzzword as steps were taken to unify the fragmented services. The Seebohm Committee was appointed in 1965 'to review the organisation and responsibilities of the local author-ity personal social services in England and Wales, and to consider what changes are desirable to secure an effective family service' (Seebohm Report 1968: para. 1). The Kilbrandon Committee (1964) had a similar remit regarding Scotland. The recommendations of these committees con-firmed the desirability of a unified social-work profession. Embodied into the Local Authority Social Services Act (1970) and the Social Work (Scotland) Act (1968) their recommendations ensured that by the 1970s only specialist work with offenders in England and Wales remained a discrete activity under the continued auspices of the probation services which maintained a separate structure, organization and identity. The new social services departments were to provide a community-based and family-oriented service, available to all, and enshrining the notion of reci-procity for the wellbeing of the community. Alternatives to institutional care were to be found wherever possible, and those institutions which remained were to be humanised and used only as a last resort. Seebohm (1965) was keen to see total institutional care provided by the state dis-mantled and replaced by variable support services designed to keep people within their communities.

The recommendations received a mixed response and, in particular, were criticised for failing to take the clients' perceptions into account, for minimising unmet need and for failing to develop a clear philosophy for the personal social services (Townsend 1970). There was general enthusiasm, however, for the affirmation of generic social work practice. Within this an individual or family was to be the responsibility of a single worker who would co-ordinate specialist help as appropriate. The hope was that a continuum of service could be provided for every client group. Embodied within this was a desire to undertake preventative work with families *before* crisis situations arose. Thus, people who had never before been involved with social welfare might now receive advice and support regardless of the existence of any difficulties or problems. Such an objective substantially challenged the stigmatisation associated with the Poor Law inheritance, and sought to encourage help-seeking with commonplace life events such as bereavement, child-rearing, and old age. Such changes demanded increased professionalism and a move away from the vocational nature of social work which had hitherto relied heavily on committed, but untrained staff. The establishment in 1971 of the Central Council for Education and Training in Social Work (CCETSW) was a step towards professionalisation, and the introduction of a single qualification – the Certificate of Qualification in Social Work (CQSW) did much to ensure uniformity of training and the maintenance of practice standards.

From genericism to specialism

Social work became a boom industry in the 1970s. New legislation gave increased powers to social workers. Three pieces of legislation were particularly influential: the Health Services and Public Health Act (1968); the Children and Young Persons Act (1969); and The Chronically Sick and Disabled Persons Act (1970). New responsibilities demanded the development of new skills. Social welfare interventions had a psychosocial orientation, centred on theories of individual pathology and the one-to-one casework approach. With a shift towards a model of social causation in many everyday problems, the focus turned to the family and the community. Social casework became somewhat outmoded as social workers learned new skills – group work, community work, advocacy and welfare-rights work, and family therapy. Area field teams of social workers have been at the centre of the new integrated services, with other groups of workers – domiciliary, residential, and care assistants – providing specialist facilities and help (Webb and Wistow 1987). This vision of integration did not, however, create the efficient, comprehensive service which had been sought. It became increasingly unrealistic to expect every social worker to be able to offer such diverse skills and thus the trend in the 1980s was to encourage specialism. Social work now tackles three main groups of problems:

1 those associated with life events – childbirth, old age, illness, death, marital breakdown and so on;
2 those related to inadequate care and socialisation in families – child abuse, learning difficulties, domestic violence, fostering and adoption; and
3 those which result from social and economic disadvantage – unemployment, poverty, and homelessness.

At the same time, social workers are expected to control those whose behaviour is unacceptable – offenders, alcoholics, and drug abusers (Webb and Wistow 1987). Such diverse client groups and tasks have promoted the creation of a sophisticated bureaucracy with an increasing trend towards centralisation for the control of scarce resources.

The expectation that social-welfare intervention could provide for the needs of all groups in society has not been met and, inevitably, the focus has remained on addressing the needs of the more vulnerable and marginal groups. 'Those who are, and have been, most susceptible to state legislation and interference are the poor. For it is the poor who pose a serious financial risk to the government' (Gittins 1985: 153). Social work intervention still carries a stigma associated with the Poor Laws, unacceptable to the majority of families who would much prefer to keep their family life private.

Although generic training and practice were attractive goals, they failed to recognise the variety of roles and tasks comprehensive welfare provision would entail. Widespread claims about the 'failure' of social work led to a detailed examination of its roles, tasks and skills. Reporting in 1982, the Barclay Committee called for a reorientation of social work, and placed emphasis on the importance of using and supporting informal caring networks within the community, thus reaffirming some of the central ideals of Seebohm who had advocated that the community should define its own needs and then contribute to the services designed to meet them. Barclay argued that 'social services departments need to discover and bring into play the potential self-help, volunteer help, community organizations, voluntary, and private facilities that exist' (Barclay 1982: 198). The vision of the 1980s was of citizens and social workers as partners in the provision of social care. The ideal was an *enabling* model of intervention.

The post-Barclay years have seen a re-emergence of specialist workers within the generic model. While the statutory sector services have progressed full circle from specialism to genericism and back to specialism, the voluntary sector services maintained their specialist functions throughout, often with a clearer remit for their work. Not surprising then that social work has been described as experiencing an identity crisis. Over several hundreds of years there has emerged 'a large and still flourishing range of functions that compose society's response to a variety of problems posed by marginal individuals of many kinds' (Davis 1981: 3). The struggle to respond to the many social and economic changes in family life as well as to cope with society's inadequate and disadvantaged groups has constantly escalated the role of the state in both maintaining social order and promoting a higher quality of life. A variety of concerns about when to intervene, how to intervene, who to work with, and who should take responsibility have emerged in recent years as crucial issues in social work policy and practice. Rooted in differing philosophies and beliefs, many interventions appear confused and contradictory as social workers attempt to combine surveillance, treatment, support and compulsion in a tangled web of care and control. It is possible to look more closely at the nature of these confusions and contradictions by examining two of the current social issues – the protection of children, and the changing structure of households.

CHILDREN IN TROUBLE

Towards the end of the nineteenth century, government concern began to focus on the problem of children. Working-class families were judged to lack appropriate discipline – creating breeding grounds for criminality. The rise in crime, particularly juvenile delinquency, has caused concern ever since but particularly in the post-war years. This has been associated with the apparent failure of families, the courts and social workers to effectively tackle the problem. By the beginning of this century, the juvenile court was established to separate juvenile from adult offenders. A feature of this jurisdiction was its civil remit to deal with the needy, deprived child. It provided the basis for a confusion and tension which has existed ever since and has fuelled the care/control debate. The theoretical foundation was enshrined in the belief that 'pauperism and crime too often act simultaneously as cause and effect . . . poverty, in numberless instances, leads to the perpetration of offences . . . ' (Day 1858: 30). The contradiction was a long-held principle that the young should be deemed responsible for their actions confused still further by the idea that kindness might promote reformation. Harris and Webb (1987) have argued that blurring the boundaries between the deprived and the depraved has resulted in the expansion of state control over both.

By the beginning of the post-war period, juvenile justice and child-care systems were intertwined. It was the Report of the Curtis Committee (1946) and the subsequent Children Act (1948) which created local authority children's departments to both provide care in the community and to receive children into care. The Ingleby Committee in 1960 reiterated the close, causal relationship between neglect and delinquency and advocated that preventive intervention in family life was, therefore, justified. However, as crime rates soared, new theories emerged which indicated that the courts were not the best places to deal with young people and family councils might be more appropriate. In Scotland, the Social Work (Scotland) Act (1968) embodied this belief as juvenile courts were replaced by a welfare-oriented children's panel system designed to divert offenders wherever possible, and to focus on their needs when intervention was inevitable. Although such a radical step was not taken in England and Wales, the Children and Young Persons Act (1969) was based on the principle that juvenile crime was a normal part of growing up, and only when it was symptomatic of personal distress should be a wide range of *help* be available. In reality, the result was a compromise. The court retained the power to commit juveniles to custody, it provided for supervision by social workers in the community, and in between the two alternatives created an opportunity for 'intermediate treatment'. The Act gave considerable power and authority to the new social workers who in the name of offering help to families with children in trouble could intervene in almost any way they saw fit. The unintended consequence was a dramatic increase in the use of custodial sentences and a decrease in the use of supervision in the community, yet social workers were criticised for being too permissive and too soft with young criminals. The 'care order' was at the centre of the struggle – children returned to their families only to get into more trouble. Shortages of specialist workers to work with these families had resulted from the move to genericism. By the late 1970s there appeared to be a serious crisis in juvenile justice as crime rates continued to rise and more and more children were removed from their families to be placed in the care of the local authorities. The autonomy of these authorities to assess the 'best interests' of these children caused increased dissatisfaction (Colvin 1984).

The loss of direction in social work with children in trouble was attributed by sociologists to the process of 'labelling' (Becker 1963; Lemert 1967). Interaction theories stressed the process of stigmatisation which attached deviant labels to the clients of social services. Individuals and families became labelled as deviant, as problems, and so became the target for increased surveillance. Increased emphasis on the social workers' assessments of children in trouble led to diagnoses which formed the bases of future interventions. This promoted stereopathy and problem amplification. Seeing clients not as people but as problems authorised interventions 'for the clients' own good' which were, in fact, coercive and controlling, and which could remove children from their parents 'in the child's best interests'.

The doctrine of 'best interests' is a long-established principle but one which clearly puts social workers in a position of considerable power. Taylor and colleagues (1979) mounted a scathing critique of the systems for child care and juvenile justice, as hypocritical and denying human rights. They pointed to the fact that most of the large number of children in England and Wales in the 'care' of local authorities were there not as a result of committing offences but as a result of social deprivation. Rather than providing the financial and practical resources to counter deprivation, children were being removed from their parents. Social workers, doctors, psychologists all defined what was good for the child. Parents experiencing all types of social disadvantage were measured against some notional 'ideal type' in a comprehensive process of assessment. Such assessments were powerful determinants of a child's future and the means by which labels gained credence (Thorpe 1979). Concern about the number of children 'in care' might have been less if the benefits were easily discernible. There is an obligation on social services departments to provide 'good parenting' but this seems hard to achieve. 'In terms of health, educational improvement, social skills, employment prospects, psychological and social well-being, those long in care present as a particularly disadvantaged group' (Millham and colleagues 1989). Residential institutions have had a remarkably poor record in preventing further delinquency; children frequently abscond and, perhaps worst of all, some children have continued to be abused. Children returned to their parents under supervision did not do much better, largely because the supervision offered was unable to tackle basic family and social problems. The experience of care was not particularly enriching or caring, and the reforming ethos tended to take precedence over the rehabilitation and caring ethos (Tutt 1976).

One of the dilemmas for professionals is that the best interests of the child may not always match the needs of the parents, or vice versa, and pressure may well be exerted on families with 'problem' children to have them removed to institutional care. Taylor and colleagues (1979) argued that removal from home should occur only when it is deemed to be the least detrimental alternative to the child, whatever the circumstances and referred problem.

CHILDREN AT RISK

In many ways, children 'at risk' present a different challenge to the state. Whereas social workers have been criticised for their over-zealous intrusion into the lives of families with children in trouble, with an over-emphasis on control and removal, they have been equally criticised for their failure to take action and their inadequate surveillance of families with children 'at risk'. Whereas crime and delinquency have long been recognised as social problems requiring a solution, child abuse has only recently emerged as a public issue. It emerged as a result of the tragic deaths of a number of young children. The first was Dennis O'Neill who, in 1945, died in a foster home. Here the failure was in the system of substitute care, but at a time when there were no child-care services and no qualified social workers. The Monckton Inquiry (Monckton Report 1945) pointed to the complicated division of responsibility between departments and the resultant confusion in the care of Dennis. The Seebohm reorganisation addressed that issue directly (Seebohm Report 1968) but, sadly, there followed a number of similar tragedies – including Maria Colwell, Lisa Godfrey, Lester Chapman, Wayne Brewer, Maria Mehmedagi, Carly Taylor, and most recently, Jasmine Beckford. Committees of Inquiry have repeatedly pointed to the inadequate co-ordination of welfare services when children are known to be 'at risk', and their failure to intervene and remove children, despite obvious anxieties about their safety. The most important general issue raised by the reports is the growing commitment by social workers to 'the family', sometimes it seems, at the expense of the child within it. Strenuous efforts to preserve family ties have blurred the requirement to protect children (Packman 1981). Nevertheless, there are now carefully documented procedures for consultation and collaboration, and a central feature of this is the 'at risk' register.

Child protection is a high-cost, high-risk area of responsibility for social workers, yet within the generic local authority social services departments it is competing for resources with all the other problems they tackle (Dingwall *et al.* 1983). Pressure of work has consistently rendered social workers reactive rather than proactive. Community health service practitioners are the most likely to detect suspected child abuse, but a range of other agencies – schools, the police, probation services, the National Society for the Prevention of Cruelty to Children (NSPCC) as well as statutory social workers all have a role in dealing with the problem, and most become involved in one way or another in the assessment process. Some social workers have expressed concern that so much effort has been concentrated on refining procedures between agencies, but not enough in helping them to work *with* families at risk. Not surprisingly, many families view social workers as powerful professionals able to remove their children from them, and hence are often reluctant to seek or accept help. Many of the tragedies indicate how successful the families were at deceiving and avoiding contact with social workers.

No-one likes to believe that parents abuse their children but it is probably easier to 'understand' in families who are clearly socially and economically deprived. Yet disorganisation and disadvantage in these families may well be the focus of intervention, thereby masking identification of child abuse. In middle-class families there seems to be a long search by professionals for alternative explanations of injuries to children and a reluctance to accept that they are non-accidental. Dingwall and colleagues (1983) describe a rule of optimism which protects upper-class, middle-class and 'respectable' working-class parents but makes more vulnerable the 'rough', indigenous, working-class group. Families higher up the socioeconomic spectrum receive greater respect for their privacy. This probably reflects the delicate balance social work aims to achieve between welfare paternalism and liberal guardianism. Donzelot has talked about the 'policing of families' (1979) in which he distinguished two types of family problem requiring intervention: the abuse of paternal power and the abuse of parental power. But we still live in a patriarchal society where parents have rights as well as responsibilities. In Packman's view:

> Child care practice . . . seems to have reached an uneasy stage where there is increased awareness of the most extreme forms of harm to which children can be subjected and a determination to understand, prevent or compensate; but where knowledge and skills are not yet sufficiently developed to guarantee a consistently helpful response.
>
> (Packman 1981: 186)

One controversial way in which local authorities have avoided having to *prove* mistreatment of children has been the use of wardship proceedings under the Guardianship of Minors Act 1971. Such proceedings have allowed more discretion in the grounds for intervention and the rules of evidence are less strict. The result is to vest all parental power in the court which, in practice, transfers responsibility to the local authority. There has been mounting concern about the disadvantaged position this creates for parents who become locked in conflict with local authorities – the very agency set up to help them.

One consequence of children being removed from their families is the poor links they maintain with their parents. Millham *et al.* (1989) have described these children as 'lost in care'. Where parents are accused of abusing a child the decision about access is a difficult one, but we do know that absence from their families can adversely affect the psychological and social functioning of children. Since 1984 parents have had the right to question access decisions, although extended family members have not. Barclay's notion (1982) of a partnership between parents and social workers has not yet been realised and parents are rarely actively involved in planning for their children's future once the local authority has assumed parental rights. Balancing protection with family support has proved to be a real dilemma for social workers.

Perhaps the issue which has confused it the most is that of child sexual abuse. Just as physical abuse was a moral panic of the 1960s and 1970s, so child sexual abuse became the moral panic of the 1980s. It involves exposure, molestation, sexual intercourse and rape. It is normally a family secret and other family members may collude to protect the perpetrator. It is now widely recognised that the extent of child sexual abuse is probably much greater than has yet been revealed. Evidence of the scale of the problem was reflected in the diagnoses (during five months in 1987) of the sexual abuse of 121 children from fifty-seven families living in Cleveland. These diagnoses and the subsequent removal of whole families of children, as ostensibly preventative interventions, caused a public outcry and the establishment of a judicial inquiry. One of the issues identified by that was the tendency for professionals to consider children as 'objects' of abuse rather than as 'persons' within a family and social context. This led to precipitant removal of children 'on suspicion' with little attempt at family assessment, and often in a somewhat draconian way. The reality of abuse is that it usually occurs within the family and is perpetrated by adults who are normally loved and trusted by the children. The concern to protect these children has sometimes prevented professionals from considering the wider emotional and family bonds. The Butler Sloss Report (1988) pointed to a sorry lack of inter-agency communication and recommended the establishment of Specialist Assessment Teams. Social workers can rarely 'get it right', it seems. Either they are criticised for being over-zealous or for failing to take effective action.

CHANGING FAMILY LIFE

One of the dominant features of post-war Britain, as B. Jane Elliott shows in Chapter 4 of this volume, has been the rapid increase in family breakdown. The divorce rate rose sixfold between 1960 and 1980 and by 1985 one and a quarter million children lived in households containing only one parent. Poverty, poor housing, unemployment, and ill health all contribute to the pressures which predispose and precipitate divorce. Some 75 per cent of lone-parent households rely on state income support and many have long-term housing and financial difficulties. Divorce is one of the most stressful life events families ever experience and the consequences may well be felt for many years. Some 24,000 'homeless' persons in 1986 were said to be so as a result of divorce.

There is now abundant research evidence confirming that children of divorce are more vulnerable than those in conflict-free, two-parent families. They are more likely to get into trouble, particularly at school, they are more likely to experience stress-related illness, and they are more likely to get divorced themselves (Emery 1988). Divorced adults also increase their risk of serious physical and mental illness and fatal car accidents. We also know that divorce in itself is not the main problem, rather it is the social, economic and emotional consequences for families.

The changes in family life occasioned by the end of a marriage are not new. Prior to this century, death usually ended the marriage, but at a much earlier age than it does now. Remarriage was common as were stepfamily relationships (Burgoyne *et al.* 1987). The choice to terminate a marriage is, however, a modern phenomenon in our society, and as such continues to raise moral, ethical and religious considerations all of which impact on the state's response. Marital problems are still contained in the private sphere of life and marriage breakdown is an intensely personal experience. However, the rapid rise in divorce has focused increased public attention on the negative consequences and a wide range of social problems have been blamed on 'broken homes'. Not surprisingly, then, state interventions have proliferated.

The Divorce Reform Act of 1969 had two main objectives: first to support and buttress marriages which might be saved, and second to end those which could not with the minimum of bitterness and humiliation. They implied two discrete modes of intervention. Marriage-saving activities, or reconciliation, began and have remained in the voluntary social work sector. The Harris Committee of 1948 recommended that marriage guidance was best left to voluntary agencies (Harris Report 1948). With an initial emphasis on marriage saving, the move towards marital counselling has reflected a more therapeutic and less advice-laden approach in recent years. Marital intervention has relied on psychodynamic, behavioural, and systems theories:

> Ways of helping husband and wife to understand each other, to express themselves more effectively to each other, to resolve problems jointly . . . these are central to each of the models, though the methods and processes of achieving them are very different.
>
> (Clark and Haldane 1990: 68)

Clients attend on a voluntary basis and the process is confidential. Marriage Guidance/Relate counsellors are volunteers and most work part-time. Over the years the moral overtones of seeing only married couples have diminished and a wide range of relationship difficulties have been tackled. Such agencies offer a 'private' service, far removed from the glare of statutory agencies where marital work has remained a low priority. In the statutory sector, however, the emphasis on crisis intervention has over-looked the value of marital therapy or counselling as a focus for intervention (Clark and Haldane 1990).

By contrast, the process of marital dissolution contains various statutory interventions designed to protect children. The welfare principle in law can be traced from 1857, and the 'best interests of the child' remains the paramount consideration in post-divorce arrangements. A decree of divorce cannot be made absolute unless the court is satisfied with the proposed arrangements for the children. Such state intervention is based on the premise that all children of divorce are potentially at risk. The purpose of the Children's Appointment is to screen and identify children at risk, but the ability of the court to do so effectively is in considerable doubt. Unless detailed 'policing' takes place, courts, by and large, have to accept that what parents decide is in fact in the child's best interests.

However, divorce is a stressful process for most families and conflict, hostility and bitterness are often characteristic features. Professionals have, in recent years, become more concerned about the detrimental effects of conflict in the family, particularly between parents and in relation to the children. Whilst most parents agree between themselves where the children will live and how they will retain contact with absent children, some fight. Following the report of the Denning Committee in 1947 probation officers were attached to divorce courts as welfare officers as an extension of their long-standing work in voluntary marriage counselling. They have since become key figures in assisting courts to reach decisions in contested custody and access cases, by undertaking investigations to assess the best future arrangements for children. In 'exceptional circumstances' this investigatory function may be extended to the provision of supervision which could last until the child attains the age of 16.

As probation officers are commonly associated with the supervision of criminals, one criticism of the civil work remit is its stigmatising effect on families and the construction of divorce as a 'deviant' activity in which social control is authorised. Sutton (1981) has also argued that probation officers have been set up as experts in child care able to make far-reaching recommendations about the future. Since the early 1970s, despite their separate administrative structures, probation officers have been trained generically as social workers but most training includes very little, if any, skills for marital and divorce-related work.

The traditional role of the probation service in civil work has been considerably extended in the past fifteen years to include con-ciliation/mediation with divorcing couples in dispute. A growing concern about the negative effects of parental conflict and the tendency of the legal process to inflame it led to the search for an alternative dispute-resolution mechanism. Family conciliation had gained credibility in North America and Australasia as a 'better way' and social workers and lawyers in Britain were motivated to develop conciliation services. Of all social work interventions, conciliation is the most recent to challenge the privacy of family life.

The essential features of family conciliation are its belief in parental autonomy, informality and the notion of voluntarism. Its main aim is to enable couples to negotiate a mutually acceptable settlement to their disputes and, in so doing, to reduce conflict in the family. As such it was not to be contaminated by legal structures and statutory processes. Enthusiasm for this new approach led to an unco-ordinated growth in services, some of which were operated by divorce-court welfare officers in the courts, and others which grew in the voluntary sector, often funded by children's charities. Pressure on government to fund conciliation on a national basis led to the commission by the Lord Chancellor in 1985 of a major piece of research into its costs and effectiveness. That research (Conciliation Project Unit Report 1989) highlighted yet again the tensions inherent in family intervention. Whilst the rhetoric of conciliation has universal appeal, the reality falls far short. Divorce-court welfare officers are identified by families as authority figures who are inclined to take control of the process, thus undermining parental responsibility. Many parents in the study felt under strong pressure to attend conciliation often in very unsuitable surroundings, and then to settle their disputes as quickly as possible, preferably with socially acceptable solutions. Conciliation in the voluntary independent services was the most effective in resolving disputes, where the intervention was more client-focused and client-led. This is hardly surprising since the ideology of conciliation is pro-family and anti-interventionist. Indeed, Parkinson described it as 'an organizational system which mediates between the private family system and the powerful system of state control, reinforcing the former against the threatened intrusion of the latter' (Parkinson 1985: 245). If it is to retain such a role, conciliation must be located outside the statutory welfare agencies, with clear boundaries and objectives. Although some proponents argue for it to be a mandatory intervention for couples in dispute, this would clearly defy the rhetoric and raise even more questions about the legitimacy of state intervention in the private lives of families. Roberts accuses conciliation of providing 'a cover for value-laden tampering with family life' (Roberts 1983: 537) in which guidance and support really mean direction and control by experts. Conciliators struggle to be neutral but their backgrounds in marital and social work purvey values and ideologies which largely support the existing social order and reflect the public concerns about the effects of divorce. Conciliators play a powerful role as advocates for children in their capacity as 'experts'. The rhetoric provides for minimal state intervention in favour of private ordering, but conciliators, like most social work professionals, find it hard to relinquish control to families. If the aim is to provide a forum for non-coercive, non-judgmental mediation, one might question the need for social work professionals to be involved at all. A major concern has been the desire of professionals to keep disputes out of court at all costs. Due process is compromised and there is little legal protection for these couples. There is a real danger that access to justice is impeded by the requirement of some courts that conciliation *must* precede litigation. Couples find that they have to jump through innumerable 'hoops' on the way.

The Report of the Conciliation Project Unit (1989) also revealed the paucity of comprehensive services for separating and divorcing families. It recommended the establishment of a co-ordinated network of support, ranging from advice, personal counselling for parents and for children, family therapy and conciliation, to the provision of access centres. No one agency currently takes primary responsibility for work with families in transition, so a myriad of agencies may become involved, blurring boundaries and confusing objectives.

SOCIAL WELFARE – A PARTNERSHIP WITH FAMILIES

The research on conciliation strengthens the arguments in favour of parental responsibility and autonomy as guiding principles in the provision of social care. Enabling families to find their own solutions to their problems is an attractive ideology for many professionals. The move away from individual pathology opened the way for family-focused interventions, and a conceptual shift in the application of systems theory to family life. Research in psychiatry on interaction patterns in the families of schizophrenics (Lidz 1963; Wynne 1965) gave new insights into the maintenance of schizophrenic behaviour, and promoted therapeutic interventions with family members and the identified patient.

The basic belief in *family therapy* is that within the family can be found both the source and the solution for a wider range of problems of individual maladjustment (Fink 1978). Individual problems are reframed as family problems and the therapist then joins the family in order to facilitate change within it. The focus is on the present and the future and the intervention is normally much briefer than casework. Whereas in North America family therapy has developed as a professional discipline in its own right, in Britain it has been social workers, psychologists and psychiatrists who have developed family therapy as one of a range of methods of intervention. As an approach it has gained popularity and has been used to deal with a wide range of problems, but particularly those centred on children. The danger in the early years of family therapy was the 'bandwagon' effect which heralds any new intervention as a panacea, promoting its use sometimes to the detriment of other treatment approaches with proven value. Family therapy is now maturing and most social workers, whilst continuing to work primarily with individuals, are able to adopt a family-therapy orientation as appropriate. One of the positive spin-offs has been the improvement in skills in communicating and working with children. This has been particularly beneficial in the assessment and treatment of child abuse, but has raised difficult ethical issues about working within a family group when victim and perpetrator are both present. Those who have advocated the use of family therapy in violent families have argued that violence is itself an issue for society and that the family should face the consequences (Bentovim and Kinston 1987). But others have argued that the social worker's primary responsibility is to protect the child from abuse and that nearly always implies removal from the family of the child, the perpetrator or both (Margolin 1982). The dilemma, however, centres around the belief that children should not feel responsible for the abuse and therefore must not be 'punished' by removal into care, nor should they shoulder the responsibility for the removal or arrest of a parent which may destroy the whole family unit and cause considerable damage to all family relationships. The Great Ormond Street Sexual Abuse Project (Bentovim and Jacobs 1988) has dealt with the conflict by offering therapy to such families whilst another agency, the social services or the NSPCC, retain statutory responsibility for the protection of the child. 'Therapeutic work is thus lodged at the interface between the individual, the family and the agencies of society whose task it is to protect children whose development is being impaired' (Bentovim and Jacobs 1988: 225). Such an approach clearly demands effective inter-agency and interprofessional co-operation and co-ordination, together with a clear structure and safe setting for the family facing the problem. An integrative treatment approach requires more than offering protection, it demands partnerships at many levels, and requires the acceptance that 'children and their needs be seen as part of an inter-acting family context' (Bentovim and Jacobs 1988: 237). If social-welfare professionals agree with Younghusband's definition of social work at the beginning of this chapter, then family therapy would appear to be a commendable model of intervention since it aims primarily to increase the opportunities for 'healthy' family functioning.

One of the weaknesses of family therapy, as, indeed, of all social work practice is the lack of comprehensive research. Most interventions have proceeded on some blind faith that it must be 'good'. Whilst research in medicine is accepted and expected, research in social work has often been regarded as unnecessary and of little practical value. Polemic has substituted for scientific data. Research is, without a doubt, difficult to do; rigorous experimentation is less acceptable in family welfare provision than in medicine and measures of effectiveness remain elusive. Many studies fall down on methodological grounds, and 'improvements' may not be easily attributed to the interventions. Nevertheless, research has challenged the claims made for the effectiveness of much social work practice and Fischer (1976) has criticised the reliance on talk as the main therapeutic medium for clients.

Research which takes into account the consumer view of intervention provides salutary reading. Over the years, studies by Mayer and Timms (1970), Timms (1973), Sainsbury (1975), Sainsbury *et al.* (1982) and Howe (1989) have all exposed the gap between the perceptions of clients and those of professionals in relation to the purpose and outcome of various interventions. Social workers are particularly poor at giving concise, clear information to families who, on the whole, do not understand legislation, welfare and legal processes or the roles of the 'experts'. If clients are confused about the services, then there is potential for frustration and 'failure'. Social workers have considerable power and authority but have tended to minimise this in the search for a friendly and informal relationship with their clients, to the extent that intimacy becomes collusion. Clients may derive personal benefit and pleasure from these relationships, but they may not be conducive to effective change in perceived problem areas. Clients primarily value attempts to meet practical needs as well as emotional needs. Talking and listening are usually not enough and 'talking therapies' can be criticised for their inability to 'get things done'. The clients of social work are frequently disturbed and unhappy, but they have some ideas about what help is needed, and do not take kindly to therapeutic interventions which appear to be unrelated to their immediate difficulties. Change can be painful and resistance to it from families is not unreasonable. Some of the verdicts on 'treatment' have been harsh, particularly where it involves the 'medicalisation' of problems. Family therapy has tended to do this since it is often practised in clinical settings. These have been criticised for their 'mystique', particularly when one-way screens and observer/consultants are part of the team. Howe (1989) in his study of a social services team found that most families did not like family therapy as a method of help, and 71 per cent did not complete the treatment. The use of 'anonymous' observers was cited as one of the dislikes. Families also felt that they had little choice about 'going for family therapy' – they had to 'play the game'. Indeed, many clients of social services are 'well experienced' in telling and retelling their stories, knowing what the social worker would want to hear, or would act on. Some become 'expert' clients.

Social workers, doctors, psychologists and psychiatrists are also experts. They use specialist knowledge in order to 'help' people with problems in everyday living. Their ideologies are highly significant. Social welfare incorporates policing, paternalism and participation: the surveillance of families in danger or out of control; the provision of kindly help and advice to those in trouble; and a desire to work *with* families, facilitating their ability to determine their own destinies. 'Surveillance and regulation, diagnosis and treatment, proscription and prescription form the subtle, chimerical world of the social worker' (Howe 1989). Donzelot (1979) saw the family as 'invaded' and colonised. Lasch (1977) described it as 'besieged'. Cohen (1985) used the terms 'penetrated' and 'occupied' by a series of experts. Certainly, those in a position of power can determine the meaning of any referred problem, circumscribe its definition and therefore decide what knowledge and skills will be brought to bear on it. Barbara Wootton (1980) accused social workers of professional arrogance, pointing to the image of 'Daddy knows best' to describe the overbearing stance of social work intervention. Her criticism was that social workers imposed their own conceptions of problems and needs on clients and failed to listen to their clients (Mayer and Timms 1970).

Knowledge also reflects prevailing ideologies and the expectations of society. As family life has changed so, too, have the roles of family members. One of the key features has been the increasing emancipation of women. Traditionally, husbands have been responsible for providing for the family and for making the decisions, wives have taken responsibility for homemaking and child care. Such gender roles were being challenged from the turn of the century, but the increase in divorce in the last twenty years has revealed starkly the extent to which women are now heading up households with a declining dependence on their husbands. Feminist critics of the Beveridge reforms were concerned that the benefit system denied the married woman 'rich or poor, housewife or paid worker, an independent status. From this error springs a crop of injustices, complications and difficulties' (Price 1979). Social policies continue to perpetuate traditional gender roles within traditional household units. Beveridge himself exemplified this with the words: 'In the next thirty years housewives as mothers have vital work to do in ensuring the adequate continuance of the British race and of British ideals in the world' (Beveridge Report 1942: 53). Inadequate assumptions about marriage and divorce, and about women's role in the workforce led to services which have treated women rather badly (Pascall 1983). Whilst today's policy makers are prepared to accept that many fathers play an important and sharing role in child care, there has been a reluctance to recognise this in intervention. Family therapists are criticised for facilitating adjustments in families which conform to traditional role expectations; probation officers and conciliators have been criticised for assuming that in post-divorce family structures the mothers will have custody of the children. Few fathers obtain physical custody, particularly of young children, and usually only if the mother is somehow 'unfit'. Any mother preferring that her children should live with their father is considered deviant and irresponsible. Mothers who choose careers rather than full-time child care meet with professional disapproval. Interventions, then, reinforce a particular kind of family life and a particular view of femininity (Wilson 1977). The emphasis in social work on protecting the needs of children has neglected the needs of women despite a family orientation. In fact, very little support and protection has been afforded to women inside the family. Domestic violence, principally wife abuse, only surfaced as a public issue in the 1970s despite evidence of serious harm inflicted by husbands. Despite the Domestic Violence Act of 1976, the police have remained reluctant to intervene in 'domestic disputes' even when injuries are life-threatening. The only sanctuary for women has been within women's refuges, run in the voluntary sector, but these provide only short-term respite and few long-term solutions. The statutory services have declined to show much interest in physical abuse between adults and yet it serves to undermine the stability of many families and is a major factor in divorce.

The traditional role of women in the home is reinforced also in notions of community care. Barclay's (1982) vision of social workers drawing on informal networks in the provision of care is consistent with the emphasis on community care particularly in relation to the elderly and the mentally ill. Care in and by the community has an alluring rhetoric, but in reality means care by women. We have a growing elderly population, as a result of advances in health care, at a time when there are fewer adult children to care for elderly parents because of reduction in family size since the Second World War. It is normally only daughters who provide the care. Local authority services for the elderly are subject to wide variations. Carers complain of minimal help from professionals who rarely have any structure for offering support.

In contrast to interventions in family life to protect children, few interventions are aimed at the protection and care of adults. Indeed, it is no accident that in a chapter which considers interventions in family life, the focus is on child saving, for that indeed has been the preoccupation in social welfare in the past forty years.

The probation service is one of the few agencies to work primarily with adults. It has retained the remit to undertake social work with offenders. The probation service developed from humanitarian, charitable ideals towards the end of the last century, and its task 'to advise, assist and befriend' offenders has remained – in theory. In practice, the post-war years have seen continuous moves towards the control and regulation of criminals. Willis (1981) described this as a shift from 'therapeutic optimism' to 'correctional nihilism'. One of the key changes of the 1970s was the extension of the probation service into the penal system, and with a critical need to reduce the ever-growing prison population, new developments in the 1970s and 1980s have emphasised the focus on 'supervision' in the community. Rehabilitation is no longer a credible unifying ideology for the probation service (Raynor 1985). Crime is viewed as a pernicious social problem and little public sympathy is evoked for offenders, thus increasing the demand for punishment and control whilst effectively dismissing a treatment orientation as 'soft'. Bryant *et al.* (1978) coined the phrase 'sentenced to social work' to illustrate the point. It is significant that the majority of clients of the probation service come from the most deprived sectors of society. Most probation officers cling to their belief in the respect for human beings regardless of their misdemeanours, and are concerned to offer counselling and therapeutic support to offenders and their families. They have staunchly advocated community alternatives to imprisonment as being in everyone's best interests, but they are being rapidly catapulted into taking responsibility for the community policy of offenders. Raynor asks how far the task of social work is to 'concentrate on providing help for offenders' (Raynor 1985: 184) and to what extent it will become merely a form of corrective coercion by the state.

TOWARDS THE FUTURE

'Social work is a human activity in which certain members of society, paid or voluntary, intervene in the lives of others in order to produce change . . . through caring and concern' (Haines 1975: 1–3). Social work remains difficult to define. It is a political activity with political consequences, yet it is rarely acknowledged as such. Its development was prompted by concern about the poverty and deprivation in society, pressure to contain and eliminate social problems and a concern to sustain a stable social order. These provide for different ideologies and therefore different methods of intervention. The conflict is about whether social work is treating symptoms or causes (Day 1981). Looking back over the post-war years the extension to social workers' roles, powers, and responsibilities has been considerable. The vocational aspect of social welfare has been subsumed in a panoply of professional expertise designed to deal with almost every social problem. Some commentators have argued that 'generic' means 'muddled' (Wilkes 1981) – a way of reducing competence to deal with problems only superficially. A gradual return to specialisation has become inevitable.

A recurring theme in this chapter has been that of defining the limits of state intervention in family life. Although the privacy of family life has been held as a fundamental principle for many centuries, absolute privacy can only survive if the state takes no responsibility to protect its members and promote their wellbeing. Most people would agree that the state must exert some responsibility in respect of its citizens; thus the question becomes 'at what point should the state intervene and in what manner?' To date, the answer has been confused as well as complex. In its attempts to buttress rapidly changing structures in family life, the state has persistently undermined the autonomy of the family, but the experience of intervention is not universal. Just as in the past, particular categories of people with particular problems are targeted. Most clients of social services are poor, deprived and in the lower socioeconomic groups. When reacting to moral panics, intervention is more indiscriminate and more intrusive.

Dingwall and colleagues have argued that we need 'much more sophisticated conceptions of law, medicine and social welfare if we are to understand their complex, and sometimes contradictory roles in advanced societies' (Dingwall *et al.* 1983: 210). It is easy but not constructive to attack social welfare professionals for failing to achieve clarity, equality and justice. It is more pertinent to consider the societal context, its values and ideologies, in which they operate. Clearly there needs to be a flexible definition of the family, a recognition of change in family life and a re-examination of moral values. A number of serious ethical issues must be addressed.

There are signs that a new approach is on the horizon. The Children Act (1989) which will be implemented in 1991 marks an important change in the legislation and policies in relation to children. Codifying and simplifying previous legislation, it specifically attempts to strike a new balance between family autonomy and the protection of children. It rests on the belief that children are generally best looked after within their families, that parents should retain responsibility for their care and that social workers have a duty to support both children and families. Children are to be protected from harm from within the family, and from harm which can be caused by unwarranted intervention in their family life. Whilst protective powers are widened, so too are the regulations governing the use of those powers. Orders must only be made where not to do so would put the child at greater risk. In order to protect children 'in need', services may be provided to the family and not just to the child (Department of Health 1989).

The new legislation may enable closer partnership between families and social work agencies; it may redress the balance of power and ensure due process. More effort will be needed to change traditional views of family life, to acknowledge greater equality, both between men and women, and for minority groups. Ethnic issues have received scant attention despite our multiculturalism. There will continue to be concerns, dilemmas and conflicts as the helping professions struggle with the extent to which interventions are imposed on, provided for or shared with families. As Dingwall and colleagues put it: 'Practitioners are asked to solve problems every day that philosophers have argued about for the last 200 years and will probably debate for the next 2000' (Dingwall *et al.* 1983: 244).

REFERENCES

Barclay, P. (1982) *Social Workers, their Role and Tasks*, report of a Working Party set up by the National Institute of Social Work, London: Bedford Square Press.

Becker, H.S. (1963) *Outsiders*, Glencoe: Free Press.

Bentovim, A. and Jacobs, B. (1988) 'Children's needs and family therapy: the case of abuse', in E. Street and W. Dryden (eds) *Family Therapy in Britain*, Milton Keynes: Open University Press.

Bentovim, A. and Kinston, W. (1987) 'Focal family therapy', in A. Gurman and D.P. Kinshern (eds) *Handbook of Family Therapy*, New York: Brunner/Mazel.

Beveridge Report (1942) *Report on Social Insurance and Allied Services*, Cmnd 6404, London: HMSO.

Bryant, M., Coker, J., Estlea, B., Himmel, S. and Knapp, T. (1978) 'Sentenced to social work', *Probation Journal* 25: 4.

Burgoyne, J., Ormrod, R. and Richards, M. (1987) *Divorce Matters*, Harmondsworth: Penguin.

Butler Sloss Report (1988) *Report of the Inquiry into Child Abuse in Cleveland*, Cmnd 412, London: HMSO.

Clark, D. and Haldane, D. (1990) *Wedlocked? Intervention and Research in Marriage*, Cambridge: Polity Press.

Cohen, S. (1985) *Visions of Social Control*, Cambridge: Polity Press.

Colvin, M. (1984) 'Care and the local state', in M.D.A. Freeman (ed.) *State, Law and the Family*, London: Tavistock.

Conciliation Project Unit, University of Newcastle upon Tyne (1989) *Report to the Lord Chancellor on the Costs and Effectiveness of Conciliation in England and Wales*, London: Lord Chancellor's Department.

Curtis Report (1946) *Report of the Care of Children Committee*, Cmnd 6922, London: HMSO.

Davis, A. (1981) *The Residential Solution: State Alternatives to Family Care*, London: Tavistock.

Day, P.R. (1981) *Social Work and Social Control*, London: Tavistock.

Day, S. (1858) *Juvenile Crime, its Causes, Character and Cure*, London: J.F. Hope.

Denning Report (1947) *Report of the Committee on Procedure in Matrimonial Causes*, Cmnd 7024, London: HMSO.

Department of Health (1989) *Introduction* to the Children Act 1989, London: HMSO.

Dingwall, R., Eekelaar, J. and Murray, T. (1983) *The Protection of Children: State Intervention and Family Life*, Oxford: Blackwell.

Donzelot, J. (1979) *The Policing of Families: Welfare Versus the State*, London: Hutchinson.

Emery, R.E. (1988) *Marriage, Divorce and Children's Adjustment*, Beverly Hills: Sage.

Fink, A.E. (1978) *The Field of Social Work*, New York: Holt, Rinehart & Winston.

Fischer, J. (1976) *The Effectiveness of Social Casework*, Springfield, Ill.: Charles Thomas.

Gittins, D. (1985) *The Family in Question: Changing Households and Family Ideologies*, Basingstoke: Macmillan.

Haines, J. (1975) *Skills and Method in Social Work*, London: Constable.

Hall, P. (1976) *Reforming the Welfare*, London: Heinemann.

Harris, R. and Webb, D. (1987) *Welfare, Power and Juvenile Justice*, London: Tavistock.

Harris Report (1948) *Report of the Departmental Committee on Grants for the Development of Marriage Guidance*, Cmnd 7566, London: HMSO.

Howe, D. (1989) *The Consumer's View of Family Therapy*, Aldershot: Gower.

Ingleby Report (1960) *Report of the Committee on Children and Young Persons*, Cmnd 1191, London: HMSO.

Kilbrandon Committee (1964) *Children and Young Persons* (Scotland), Cmnd 2306, London: HMSO.

Lasch, C. (1977) *Haven in a Heartless World. The Family Besieged*, New York: Basic Books.

Lemert, E. (1967) *Human Deviance, Social Problems and Social Control*, London: Prentice-Hall.

Lidz, T. (1963) *The Family and Human Adaptation*, New York: International Universities Press.

Margolin, G. (1982) 'Ethical and legal considerations in marital and family therapy', *American Psychologist* 37: 788–801.

Mayer, J.E. and Timms, N. (1970) *The Client Speaks*, London: Bedford Square Press.

Miller, J. and Cook, T. (1981) *Direct Work with Families*, London: Bedford Square Press.

Millham, S., Bullock, R., Hosie, K. and Little, M. (1989) *Access Disputes in Child-care*, Aldershot: Gower.

Monckton Report (1945) *Report on the Circumstances Which Led to the Boarding out of Dennis and Terence O'Neill*, Cmnd 6636, London: HMSO.

Morgan, D.H.J. (1985) *The Family, Politics and Social Theory*, London: Routledge & Kegan Paul.

Nathan Report (1952) *Report of the Committee on the Law and Practice Relating to Charitable Trusts*, Cmnd 8710, London: HMSO.

Packman, J. (1981) *The Child's Generation*, Oxford: Blackwell and Martin Robertson.

Parker, R. (1982) 'Family and social policy: an overview', in R.N. Rapoport, M.P. Fogarty and R. Rapoport (eds) *Families in Britain*, London: Routledge & Kegan Paul.

Parkinson, L. (1985) 'Conciliation in separation and divorce', in W. Dryden (ed.) *Marital Therapy in Britain*, vol. 2, London: Harper & Row.

Pascall, G. (1983) 'Women and social welfare', in P. Bean and S. Macpherson (eds) *Approaches to Welfare*, London: Routledge & Kegan Paul.

Price, S. (1979) 'Ideologies of female dependence on the welfare state – women's response to the Beveridge Report', British Sociological Conference, mimeo.

Raynor, P. (1985) *Social Work, Justice and Control*, Oxford: Blackwell.

Roberts, S. (1983) 'Mediation in family disputes', *Modern Law Review* 46(5): 537–57.

Romanyshyn, J. (1971) *Social Welfare*, New York: Random House.

Sainsbury, E. (1975) *Social Work with Families*, London: Routledge & Kegan Paul.

Sainsbury, E., Nixon, S. and Phillips, D. (1982) *Social Work in Focus*, London: Routledge & Kegan Paul.

Seebohm Report (1968) *Report of the Committee on Local Authority and Allied Personal Social Services*, Cmnd 3703, London: HMSO.

Sutton, A. (1981) 'Science in court', in M. King (ed.) *Childhood, Welfare and Justice*, London: Batsford.

Taylor, L., Lacey, R. and Bracken, D. (1979) *In Whose Best Interests?* London: The Cobden Trust.

Timms, N. (1973) *The Receiving End*, London: Routledge & Kegan Paul.

Thorpe, J. (1979) 'Social enquiry reports: a survey', *Home Office Research Study*, no. 48, London: HMSO.

Titmuss, R.M. (1950) *Problems of Social Policy*, London: Longman.

Townsend, P. (1970) 'The re-organisation of social policy', *New Society* 22, October.

Tutt, N. (1976) 'Recommittals of juvenile offenders', *British Journal of Criminology* 16: 4.

Webb, A. and Wistow, G. (1987) *Social Work, Social Care and Social Planning: The Personal Social Services since Seebohm*, London: Longman.

Wilkes, R. (1981) *Social Work with Undervalued Groups*, London: Tavistock.

Willis, A. (1981) 'Effective criminal supervision towards new standards and goals', lecture to NAPO Conference, Dartington, unpublished.

Wilson E. (1977) *Women and the Welfare State*, London: Tavistock.

Wootton, B. (1980) *Social Science and Social Pathology*, London: Allen & Unwin.

Wynne, L. (1965) 'Some indications and contra-indications for exploratory family therapy', in I. Boszormenyi-Nagy and J. Franco (eds) *Intensive Family Therapy*, New York: Harper & Row.

Young, A.F. and Ashton, E.T. (1956) *British Social Work in the Nineteenth Century*, London: Routledge & Kegan Paul.

Younghusband, E. (1959) *Report of the Working Party on Social Workers in the Local Authority Health and Welfare Services*, London: HMSO.

9 Pretended family relationships

Jeffrey Weeks

We live in a culture which is suffused with familial values (Barrett and McIntosh 1982) and where the language of alternatives is feeble and etiolated. Yet, of course, large numbers of people live in unconventional families or in no families at all. Alternatives exist. The real problem lies not in discovering them, but in evaluating and validating them.

Most of the time the various unorthodox patterns of intimate relationships and domesticity develop quietly under the surface of social life, leading an often subterranean existence. Occasionally, a particular way of life breaks surface and becomes a *locus classicus* of moral anxiety. It could be the alleged dysfunction of single-parent black families as a factor in the deprivation of inner cities. Or there might be a flurry about young girls getting pregnant in order to obtain social welfare benefits. Or it might be outrage at the alleged 'promiscuity' of gay lifestyles as the harbinger of plague. At such moments, the borders of the private and the public become blurred, and the contours of the social are redefined – often, perhaps usually, at the expense of what is unconventional and different.

In this chapter I want to explore the place of the unconventional or the alternative in the debates on the family. It is an exploration of the limits of otherness in a moral and political climate which gives powerful obeisance to 'the family', even as social trends and political decisions made or not made contribute to its continual transformation. The argument begins with an incident which while ostensibly about homosexuality is extremely revealing about the standing of the family. Then I explore the somewhat inconclusive discussions about 'alternatives to the family' and 'alternative families' which have punctuated the wider debate about the family over the past few decades. Finally, I shall return to the 'subterranean social order' where diverse patterns of life are shaped, and new moral communities develop. It is here, and not in the heads of theorists, that genuine 'alternatives' are created.

For reasons that will become clear, the chapter is dedicated to 'pretended family relationships'.

CLAUSE 28

Certain social events become, in Jacqueline Rose's useful phrase, 'flashpoints of the social' (Rose 1988: 20). In a heightened moral climate underlying social shifts and the sense of anxiety to which they give rise are crystallised in what one can only call an ideological seizure, a symbolic moment which casts light not only on a murky past but illumines the present in a new way.

One such moment occurred towards the end of 1987 with the introduction of a backbench amendment to the Local Government Bill, then trundling quietly, if not entirely innocently, through the House of Commons. The declared aim of this new clause was to prevent the 'promotion' of homosexuality by local authorities, and although its introduction, and subsequent acceptance by the government, was unexpected it was the culmination of a sustained campaign by a group of Conservative MPs over the previous year. Eventually passed into law as Section 28 of the Local Government Act 1988, Clause 28, as it became known during the sharp campaign preceding its enactment, offered a revealing snapshot of the balance of political and moral power in the Britain of the late 1980s.

The terms of this amendment were important in themselves and for what they revealed about current attitudes towards homosexuality. But even more significant was the light that this episode cast on prevailing attitudes to the family and sexuality, and to the new social identities that were an increasingly visible part of the social and political geography of the industrial nations.

Like all such symbolic moments, this one was heavily overdetermined. The moral enthusiasts of the New Right had long been concerned with 'the family', and in particular with the threats posed to its stability by 'permissiveness', the weakening of traditional gender demarcations posed by feminism, and the threat of sexual diversity posed by the modern lesbian and gay movement. These anxieties had focused on the issue of 'sex education': its tendency towards explaining the choices that might actually confront the child, rather than the adumbration of firm moral positions, seen as a critical element in the weakening of traditional values.

In the previous year Conservative MPs had already secured significant concessions with the placing of responsibility for sex education in the hands of school governors, with the assumption that these would be parent-dominated (and with the implication that this would mean a more 'traditional' curriculum). As it turned out, this early victory was in the end to vitiate the effectiveness of Clause 28. Local authorities had very little power to promote any alternative way of life.

But that lay in the future. What gave a particular saliency to the issue in 1987 were the controversies generated by the efforts of several Labour-controlled local authorities to encourage the development of 'positive images' of homosexuality. In the run-up to the 1987 general election this issue had been particularly effective in marking out the 'loony-left councils', and almost certainly in further helping to detach working-class support from its traditional Labour allegiance. The confused reaction of the Labour opposition in the immediate aftermath of the introduction of the new clause provided graphic testimony to the success of this ideological mobilisation (Weeks 1989). Despite formal endorsement by the Labour Party of support for the rights of lesbians and gay men, the uncertain response of some of its leading members following the introduction of the clause suggested that this policy was far from being instinct on the part of the main party of opposition.

In fact, the government was almost certainly taken aback by the eventual opposition that Clause 28 did produce. There was an unprecedented mobilisation of lesbian and gay political energies, supported in the end by important sections of liberal opinion. Although this did not prevent the amendment becoming law, significant concessions were extracted during the course of its passage through Parliament, and even before it was safely on the statute book, it became clear that its effects were likely to be less draconian than first anticipated, or intended (Robinson 1988). Yet more significant was its impact on the main target: far from diminishing the public presence of lesbians and gay men, it greatly contributed to an enhanced sense of identity and community. After many years of fissiparous divisions, lesbians and gay men of various social and political positions found it possible to work together in a common cause. Like many such moral eruptions in the past, the unintended consequences of this episode were as important as the intended.

Nevertheless, the whole *demarche* was extremely revealing, as a closer examination of the terms of Clause 28 illustrates. As finally passed, the clause stated that:

A local authority shall not –
(a) intentionally promote homosexuality or publish material with the intention of promoting homosexuality;
(b) promote the teaching in any maintained school of the acceptability of homosexuality as a pretended family relationship.

The two key phrases 'promoting homosexuality' and 'pretended family relationship' are clearly closely related. The first is a direct reference to the attempts of several local authorities to support 'positive images' of homosexuality, which by implication advanced the argument that homosexuality should be regarded as of equal validity with heterosexuality. The belief that 'heterosexism', that is compulsive heterosexuality, was at the heart of the denigration of homosexuality was central to the positive-images campaigns (see GLC 1985; Cant and Hemmings 1988). Whether or not positive images could in any real sense 'promote' the practice of homosexuality was a highly debated issue during the passage of Clause 28, and subsequently (Marshall 1989). It was undoubtedly the case that the diminution of hostility towards homosexuality would inevitably encourage a climate where homosexuality could indeed be seen as a valid sexual choice.

But as the phrase 'pretended family relationships' suggested, it was more than simply sexual preference that was at stake. Much more threatening, apparently, was the affirmation of alternative patterns of relationships that this implied. As David Wilshire, the Conservative MP who originally introduced the amendment, put it: 'Homosexuality is being promoted at the ratepayers' expense, and the traditional family as we know it is under attack' (Letter to the *Guardian*, 12 December 1987). This is the key to the whole episode.

It may well be true that 'homosexuality is much less anti-family than families are anti-homosexual' as Muller (1987: 140) has suggested. Nevertheless, it is also undoubtedly the case that the significant growth in the lesbian and gay community over the previous two decades had posed an implicit challenge to the hegemony of family values, or at least family values as endorsed by leading exponents of the New Right, the strongest advocates of Clause 28 (Weeks 1985, 1989). There is no reason to doubt the statements of those supporters of the clause who argued that they were not actually in favour of recriminalising homosexuality; their stated objective was to restore the 'compromise' embodied in the 1967 Sexual Offences Act, whereby (male) homosexuality had been decriminalised under certain limited circumstances.

As a number of judicial statements made clear following reform, this did not mean that homosexuality was either fully legal, morally acceptable or to be regarded as on a par with heterosexuality (Weeks 1990).

The problem was that in the succeeding twenty years, as a result of the impact of the lesbian and gay movement and the associated massive expansion of the gay community, homosexuals had acted as if their full social rights were there for the asking, as if homosexuality could legitimately be regarded as on a par with heterosexuality, as if lesbian and gay relationships were as valid as traditional family relationships. Clause 28, in this light, can be seen as a great halt sign: thus far, and no further.

In adopting this position, the supporters of Clause 28 appeared to be swimming with the tide of public opinion. The British Social Attitudes Survey for 1987 (Jowell *et al.* 1988) found that the British public had apparently become marginally less discriminatory in attitudes towards homosexuality since 1983, with a greater reluctance to see homosexuals banned from certain professions, such as teaching, simply on the basis of a person's sexual preference. (This was markedly the case with social classes 4 and 5.) At the same time, when asked if they approved of 'homosexual relationships', there was evidence of a sharp increase of hostility over 1983: in 1983, 62 per cent had censured such relationships; in 1985, 60 per cent; and in 1987, 74 per cent.

The drift of public opinion was even clearer when people were asked their opinions about recognising the rights of homosexuals to adopt children on the same grounds as heterosexuals. In 1987, 86 per cent would forbid lesbians adopting children, while an overwhelming 93 per cent would prevent gay men.

This survey suggests that while the slowly developing liberalisation of attitudes towards sex was continuing, and still influencing attitudes to the rights of individual homosexuals, when confronted by homosexuality as the focus for alternative forms of relationships, the public drew back. The British Social Attitudes Survey findings were confirmed by a subsequent Gallup poll (*Sunday Telegraph* 5 June 1988) which found that 60 per cent thought that homosexuality should not be considered an accepted lifestyle, compared to 34 per cent who did (though interestingly, 50 per cent of those under 25 were accepting).

Many factors can be adduced to explain this situation, not least the impact of AIDS in generating hostility towards homosexuality (Watney 1987; Sontag 1989). But perhaps there is a more deep-seated reason, hinted at by other statistics in the British Social Attitudes Survey. These indicated that public hostility to extramarital sex of any sort had increased significantly during the decade, from 83 per cent in 1983 to 88 per cent in 1987, and this was at a time when acceptance of premarital sex had become widespread. Such evidence suggests that while the long-term growth of more liberal values was continuing, it was very much in the context of the general acceptance of monogamous heterosexual coupledom as the basis for intimate relationships and domestic life. Alternative patterns, whether heterosexual or homosexual, might receive more tolerance than they did in, say, the 1960s, despite that decade's much reviled leaning towards 'permissiveness' (see Weeks 1989). But there could be no doubt about the strength of the norm, which appeared to be increasing rather than diminishing as the 1980s wore on. If this is the case, however, it becomes all the more interesting and revealing that it was at this particular time that there was a political intervention against homosexuality.

FAMILY VALUES

To understand this we must look at the wider context of political concern about the family. Clause 28 can be seen as a crystallisation of anxieties about the stability of the family which had been growing over the previous decades, not only in Britain but throughout the advanced industrial countries. In the late 1970s Demos (1979: 43) observed a 'diffuse sense of "crisis" ' about domestic arrangements generally, reflected in a flowering of commissions, task forces, conferences and publications on various aspects of family life. The family became increasingly defined as a problem area in social arrangements, and this was the prelude to the emergence of 'the family' as a charged political talisman, engaging the energies of politicians on left and right (Pankhurst and Houseknecht 1983: Weeks 1986a).

On the surface this new preoccupation with the family was paradoxical, for despite all the usual indices usually cited for 'decline' – increasing divorce rates, growing cohabitation, the number of one-parent families, the impact of feminism – familial values remained sturdily entrenched. The number of marriages in Britain, which had dipped in the late 1970s, increased again in the 1980s, rising to 400,000 by 1986 (compared to a peak of 480,000 in 1972). Some 21 per cent of live births were outside marriage, but half of these were registered by both parents, suggesting the growth of stable non-married relationships. Even the high divorce rates, with a third of marriages likely to end in divorce courts, could be seen in an optimistic light, for the majority remarried, seeking presumably the fulfilments of family life not found in the first attempt (Clark 1987).

This has led commentators to talk of the rise of the 'neo-conventional' family (Chester 1985, 1986). As Fletcher, an ardent defender of the family, has put it: 'there is no doubt whatever that *the family* is not only what the great majority of the people of Britain *want*, it is also what, in fact, they actually *have*' (Fletcher 1988a: 81, emphasis in original). But to state this is not to resolve the issue, for apparent continuity can obscure crucial changes taking place under the patina of stability, and an emphasis on normative affirmation may hide a genuine crisis of subjective meanings. As the liberal journalist Melanie Phillips has suggested, the family 'is now suffering from a chronic crisis of identity and self-confidence' (Phillips 1988). This was underlined by the wave of moral anxiety induced by the Cleveland child-abuse crisis in 1988 (see Campbell 1988). Here was a situation where two apparently stable and complementary discourses (about the needs of children and the rights of parents) became entangled and apparently contradictory as medical evidence suggested that child sex abuse within families was widespread.

In the resulting moral panic, contradictory messages about family life emerged from the miasma of rumour, suspicion and political ambition. Many of those who previously had been most vociferous in the search for child sex abuse found themselves unable to believe that so many (middle- as well as working-class) respectable parents (i.e. fathers) might be involved, whilst those who had long disputed any medical hegemony over sexual issues found themselves supporting the controversial evidence of doctors using largely unproven methods of detecting abuse. But what it revealed above all was that the family could not be seen as unproblematic haven of harmony. As the director of Newcastle's social services said: 'Belief in the sanctity of the family must not blind us to the fact that the family is a hotbed of violence' (quoted in Phillips 1988). Whether or not this generalisation is true, the very fact that it could be made is suggestive.

I want to suggest that a widespread anxiety about the family has three interrelated focuses. The first concerns the contradictory demands made upon the family in a period of rapid social change. As Deakin and Wicks (1989) point out, these demands bear particularly strongly on women: a greater reliance in social policy on care in the community places an ever-increasing burden on women (see also Finch 1987). At the same time, demographic changes and the changing patterns of employment pull women increasingly into the workforce. Such contradictory pulls not only impose growing burdens on women; they also, inevitably, underline the potentially contradictory interests of women and men in domestic life.

These pressures are being experienced – and this is the second potential focus – at the same time as other forces are working to emphasise the value of family life. Barbara Laslett has argued that: 'changes in household composition, in the demography of kinship, and in the relationship between the family and other institutions have contributed to the increased emotional significance of the family (Laslett 1979: 234). But the very intensity of emotions that the family generates and which is in turn reinvested in the family is potentially both unsettling and dangerous. It can offer the possibility of support and a sense of belonging. It can also act as the fulcrum for the generation of violence, against women and against children.

Problems occur within families; but there are many types of families, and this is a third potential focus of anxiety. As Rayner Rapp put it: 'People are recruited and kept in households by families in all classes, yet the families they have (or don't have) are not the same' (Rapp 1982: 170).

The existence of a diversity of family and household forms is, as these quotations suggest, perhaps the most challenging issue of all, because it poses in an acute fashion the question of value: not only the empirically verifiable issue of what is changing in the family, or families, but the more critical question of what ought to change, and what are the most appropriate means of satisfying individual and collective needs.

It is in this context that we must try to understand the ways in which the family has entered political discourse. It is an issue which cuts across traditional political boundaries, but it is nevertheless the case that over the past decade, in the USA and Britain, it has become an issue *par excellence* of the political right (see David 1986; Weeks 1989). A reassertion of what were conceived of as traditional family and sexual values was at the moral centre of the New Right's agenda from the 1970s onwards. In practice, the political regimes associated with the New Right, such as those of Reagan in the USA and Thatcher in Britain, were much less energetic or successful in pursuing this cultural reversion than in achieving other strategic goals. Despite Mrs Thatcher's espousal of 'Victorian values' there was no sustained effort to turn back the clock in Britain, even beyond the much attacked 1960s. Nevertheless, just as the 'permissive' reforms of the 1960s were shaped by the brief emergence of the 'liberal moment', so the new moralism of the 1980s, represented by Clause 28, depended upon the initiative being seized by the New Right.

The attraction of the reassertion of traditional values concerning family and sexual life is that it offers a symbolic focus for the resolution of personal and social problems that might otherwise seem intractable. The reality might actually be quite different as affluence, social dislocation and social policy continue to undermine those values. But 'the family', with its powerful myth of harmony and personal integration and fulfilment, retains a powerful appeal.

This is all the more significant because of the absence of any alternative patterns of relating that had widespread acceptance. The language of non-family life remains feeble compared to the power of the familial, despite the heat and fury generated by earlier debates. An examination of these attempts to define alternatives to the family will help to reveal why.

ALTERNATIVES TO THE FAMILY

There is a long history of critiques of the family, and of the offering of alternatives to it. But for both practical and ideological reasons we must start with the 1960s. This is the period which has been most starkly pinpointed as the source and origin of attacks on the family, the period, in Margaret Thatcher's graphic phrase, which taught the citizenry never to say No (speech reported in the *Guardian*, 20 March 1989).

Fletcher (1988b), within a more academic if scarcely less polemical mode, has identified the 1960s as the period of a new, and much sharper assault on the family than ever before. He has described five types of attack: (a) that associated with the anthropologist Edmund Leach, which identifies the family as the 'source of all our discontents'; (b) the critiques of psychologists such as Laing, Cooper and Esterson which see the family as the 'destroyer' of its members' sanity; (c) revived Marxist interest in the family which identifies it as a material and ideological prop of capitalism, and an 'ideological state apparatus'; (d) the developing feminist critique, which sees the family as a 'prison', a site of oppressive socialisation, gender stereotyping and sexual exploitation; and (e) the commune movement, with its proffered, if somewhat amorphous, alternative to the family.

Despite Fletcher's pulling of all these together under the label of 'abolitionists', clearly these critiques have different theoretical origins and are attached to differing and sometimes conflicting political agendas. Leach in his famous Reith lectures of 1967 might lament the dominance of the family, 'with its narrow privacy and tawdry secrets' (Leach 1968), but it was difficult to see what the programmatic implications of this were. Feminist critiques of women's subordination within the family do not necessarily involve a radical call for abolition, as later writings made clear (for example, Friedan 1983). Nor did the Marxist interventions against the family inevitably imply a radical challenge to existing gender and sexual relations.

Nevertheless, it is possible to link these critiques together in a loose but vital way. In the first place they were able to draw on a long, if often buried tradition of critical explorations of family life and the search for alternatives going back at least to the earliest days of industrialisation. The commune movement in particular could look back to a real history of attempts to build alternative communities as the basis of new ways of life, either within the hostile environment of capitalist society (Taylor 1982), or as far away from its heartlands as possible (Muncy 1974).

Second, despite their disparate origins and implications, the critics of the family in the 1960s were reflecting a widespread feeling, echoing the critical findings of sociologists, anthropologists and psychologists that the family as it existed was becoming increasingly dysfunctional (Morgan 1975, 1985). It was not surprising that these findings were readily incorporated into the more amorphous aspirations of what became known as the 'counter-culture' (Abrams and McCulloch 1976). At the heart of the 1960s challenge to the family was a strong libertarian belief that the traditional family was a bulwark of hierarchical, class society (Segal 1983). It followed that it was necessary to build freer alternatives: hence the revived interest in communal ways of living.

As Abrams and McCulloch noted: 'the positive qualities of communes are perceived with overwhelming frequency in contra-distinction to the negative qualities of the nuclear family' (Abrams and McCulloch 1976: 248). Hostility to the nuclear family was the strongest element in giving a sense of common purpose to the commune movement.

The sociological research on communes confirms this. Rigby (1974a) developed a sixfold typology to consider the communes: (1) self-actualising communes, seen by their members as contributing to a new social order; (2) communes for mutual support, whose members sought individual self-realisation in a supportive framework; (3) activist communes, providing a base for 'outside' social and political activities; (4) practical communes, defined primarily in terms of the economic and practical material advantages to be obtained; (5) therapeutic communes, having the prime purpose of therapy; and (6) religious communes, where the goals are defined primarily in religious terms.

Despite his great enthusiasm for the movement Rigby (1974b) was able to find little common ground either within or across these, whether in forms of leadership, attitudes to relationships, patterns of money distribution or work, decision making and types of accommodation. What most of them did have in common, however, was a desire to challenge the taken-for-granted naturalness of family life. As the movement's newsletter observed: 'we have no uniting ethic apart from a belief in communal life as a possibly happier alternative to the normal family unit' (quoted in Abrams and McCulloch 1976: 248).

The real limits of this challenge can be observed if we look a little more closely at the heart of Rigby's case. The following quotation is representative:

> If our aim is not merely to change the system of ownership and control of wealth and property in society, but to transform all areas of life and in the process create a world where everyone is his own master, where we care for each other in a spirit of love and fraternity . . . then it can only be achieved through means which embody these ideals in the here and now, through people in all walks of life working to put these ideals into practice in their daily living. This is the message of the communes.
>
> (Rigby 1974b: 148)

Two points are striking: the aspiration towards (and expectation of?) total transformation ('not merely to change'), which provided the sharp counter-cultural energy; and the frankly masculinist terms in which these are expressed ('his own master', 'spirit of love and fraternity'). No doubt such verbal lapses are typical of the period, but they reveal a more fundamental hesitation. In spite of the commitment to total change, and the genuflection to the then new feminist and gay movements, there is no real integration of their critiques into the analysis of communes. As Abrams and McCulloch

(1976: 246) comment, in their noticeably more jaded examination of the commune movement, there is an impression of 'the virtual irrelevance of communes as a solution to the problem of sexual inequality'.

Both the women's liberation movement and the gay movement, in their heroic period of the early 1970s, flirted with the idea of collective living, embracing much of the ideology of the commune movement whilst attempting to go beyond it in relation to gender and sexual relations. But sexual enlightenment did not necessarily prevent other problems in collective living. Birch (1988), for example, describes life in the gay commune he lived in in the early 1970s as one of constant meetings, incessant self-questioning and a commitment to openness to such an extent that 'to be honest, perhaps we were never honest': 'At times the tension was so great, especially around the formal sessions themselves, that everyone dreaded the house meetings. The commitment to the ideal prevented us from asking whether we really liked or understood one another' (Birch 1988: 55).

Nava (1983), while examining feminist attitudes to collective living in the early 1970s, has pinpointed more fundamental problems: the domination of a moralism and voluntarism concerning alternative living styles that limited their appeal to very narrow circles, and led to the censure of those who did not share the vision. This was accompanied by an optimistic failure to recognise the power structures in the outside world that shaped the relations of men and women with regard to domestic responsibilities, child care and paid employment.

By the mid-1970s the commune movement had lost its elan, at precisely the time when the first sociological surveys were appearing, though the movement still claimed 50 functioning communes in Britain in 1989 (Ansell *et al.* 1989). Even at its height the movement was relatively small (it is noticeable how commentators like Rigby and Abrams and McCulloch tend to home in on the same examples). Neither its rise nor demise had a major effect on the way most people lived.

Yet it is worthy of an extended note precisely because it did represent an 'alternative to the family', on paper at least, of the most uncompromising sort. Like others that have been mooted over this century, such as the kibbutz (Irvine 1980), the hopes proved more extensive than the realities. Nevertheless, its theory, if not its practice, did offer a different type of model for organising domestic life from that offered in the traditional nuclear family of the movement's mythology. As such its traces can be found both in the personalism of the 'lifestyle politics' that were to develop in the later 1970s and early 1980s, and in the revived critiques of the family that were to re-emerge during the 1980s. Which is why, no doubt, the shadow of *its* myth continues to dog that of the family.

ALTERNATIVE FAMILIES

The demise of the radical critique of the family permitted the emergence of a more pluralist perspective. Its hallmark was a concentration on the variety of family forms, and an attempt to recognise and do justice to 'alternative families'. More than the commune movement, its starting point was an awareness of social diversity. The problem, as ever, was what to do with it.

The spirit of this new emphasis is captured in this statement in the first annual report of the Australian Institute of Family Studies:

> The family is the most basic unit. . . . 'The family', however, is not and never has been, of one uniform type or structure. . . . Moreover, the family changes both its function and composition over the life cycle. Thus any arbitrary definition of 'the family' is unhelpful and misleading in that it defines out of existence many family forms that are a reality, and which social policy and social arrangements must take into account.
>
> (IFS 1981)

This new emphasis during the late 1970s and early 1980s, was interestingly signalled at the highest official level by President Carter's convening of a White House conference on *Families* in 1980 (Berger and Berger 1983: 63). Underlying it is a clear attempt to affirm the values of family life whilst attempting to come to terms with the fact of change and variety.

The dual aim is reflected in the book sponsored by the British Family Research Committee in 1982, with the significant title, *Families in Britain* (Rapoport *et al.* 1982). In his introduction, the distinguished family historian, Peter Laslett, denied the existence of a single British family (Laslett 1982). In the book itself five types of diversity are postulated:

1 Organizational, dependent on the internal division of labour and relations to the external world.
2 Cultural, as a result of different ethnic, religious, class, political and child-rearing traditions.
3 Class, as a result of differential resources and social access.
4 Life course, resulting from change over time. And
5 Cohort, resulting from historical changes, in patterns of work, marriage, divorce, the ratio of young to old people, etc.

(Rapoport and Rapoport 1982: 479ff)

These are variations within something which can still recognisably be defined as 'a family'. The problem becomes more difficult if you attempt to broaden your definition. Macklin (1980) lists a range of what she calls 'non-traditional' families. These include: never-married singlehood, non-marital singlehood, voluntary childlessness, the 'bi-nuclear family', involving joint custody and co-parenting, the stepfamily, open marriages/ open families, extramarital sexual relations, same-sex intimate relations and multi-adult households.

Such 'non-traditional' forms have been seen as essentially alternative lifestyles, 'relational patterns around which individuals organize their living arrangements' (Zinn and Eitzen, 1987: 370), a 'smorgasbord' from which individuals must select the options they prefer, with all the opportunities and risks that suggests (Blumstein and Schwartz 1983: 46). The assumption is, however, that they offer, in their different ways, viable ways of organizing personal life, both at the level of domestic living arrangements and in intimate relations.

According to Zinn and Eitzen: 'These alternatives exist together with traditional family forms and in this way contribute to the diversity and flexibility of the family' (Zinn and Eitzen 1987: 387). It is, however, difficult to see what, apart from their assumed viability, all these forms have in common. Some are the result of contingent factors (such as changing patterns of divorce and remarriage); others are clearly a matter of personal choice, and perhaps favourable circumstances or social possibilities. Some are obvious variations on traditional patterns, such as the 'commuter marriages', heterosexual cohabitation or 'singlehood' described by Zinn and Eitzen. Such patterns can involve quite large numbers of people. 'Commuter marriages', where the partners live in different parts of the country and commute to be together at weekends or holidays, are estimated to involve a million people in the USA (Zinn and Eitzen 1987: 394).

Other relationships, however, while they may have a long historical lineage, have not hitherto been seen as family forms at all. Lesbian and gay relationships fall most clearly into this category. Can or should they all be easily assimilated under the rubric of the family?

To deploy the term 'families' instead of family is still, as Morgan (1985: 274) argues, 'to maintain some, perhaps changed or expanded, notion of what "family" is, of what all the different varieties have in common'. If the key elements of the family are seen in classic terms as socialisation of the young and reproduction (in the broad sense of social reproduction as well as biological); intensity of interaction between members and continuity over time; domestic arrangements with a sustained degree of cohabitation; and the ordering of gender and sexual relations, then, clearly not all 'non-traditional' patterns or lifestyles fit in. Lesbian and gay relationships might when they involve parenting (Bozett 1987), but not when they involve complex patterns of 'non-exclusive' relationships (Weeks 1988).

The broadening of the term 'family' to embrace a variety of both domestic arrangements and types of relationships (and it is important to stress that these are not necessarily the same) must be seen as a political response to diversity rather than a useful sociological categorisation. In effect it takes for granted the discourse of family life, and simply incorporates every other form of workable lifestyle into it. Against this, it is important to stress that not all household patterns can be called families, whatever their 'family-like' qualities. On the contrary there exist a plurality of relational forms which are regarded by many as both legitimate and desirable which are different from any recognisably familial pattern.

For some, this diversity is a welcome sign of the growth of personal choice and freedom; for others, it is a sign of potential societal breakdown. Fletcher (1988a: 186–218), for example, wonders whether conditions in the modern world are leading to a 'de-moralization' of society as a result of a disturbance of the 'natural–social' sequence of socialisation, rearing and caring. Lasch (1985) attacks the advocates of 'choice' and an easy plural-ism as a surrender to the culture of consumerism. Berger and Berger fear for the breakdown of stable identity formation through the unthinking acceptance of diverse patterns. They in particular deplore the way in which the empirical fact of diversity is quietly turned into a norm of diversity, where 'demography is translated into a new morality' (Berger and Berger 1983: 63).

These challenges cannot be answered simply by reiterating the merits of choice. If diversity is to become a new norm, then its contours need to be more clearly defined. This is the challenge facing those who want to continue to offer critiques of the family.

THE SUBTERRANEAN SOCIAL ORDER

Social diversity is a fundamental given of modern life, a product of ever-increasing social complexity (Lash and Urry 1988). The patterns of life and domestic organization that currently exist are therefore the result of a complex play of determination and contingency, historical legacy and rapid social change. In such a situation it is tempting to search for the security of what we know, or believe, to be secure and stable, a haven, in Lasch's famous diatribe, where those who feel besieged may find protection (Lasch 1977).

This has always been the classic attraction of the family as myth, cer-tainly since the early nineteenth century (Weeks 1989) and is a powerful element in the rhetoric of today's defenders of the family. But more significantly, perhaps, as we have seen, the family is a potent trope even in the hands of those whose adherence to a traditional model is dubious. The language of the family pervades our thinking about private life.

That is another way of saying that there is a poverty of thought, and of language, concerning non-family forms. A classic example of this can be found in the rhetoric of fraternity (and to a lesser extent, sorority) which echoes through the language of the movements of the left over the past hundred years, and was replicated in the conventional terms of the feminist and gay movements of the 1970s at the very time when their critiques of the family were most pointed (Phillips 1984). It seems that we can only find the terms to describe even our most passionate loyalties within the language of family relationships.

This is only symptomatic of a wider inability to forge a generally recognisable and acceptable language of belonging which can describe at both the intimate and the public level the complex patterns of relationships that actually bind people to one another.

Yet there is much evidence of the richness and depth of other, non-family relations, some forged across the boundaries of family life, some entirely outside the field of family relations altogether. Recent historical work has powerfully challenged the belief that the family is a natural, unitary organism, subversive of all states, hierarchies, churches and ideologies as the conservative polemicist Ferdinand Mount would have it (Mount 1982). On the contrary, the family most usefully can be seen as a variable set of relationships, between men and women, adults and children, shaped and structured by uneven power relations, whose unity is historical and ideological rather than natural.

Taking this rather abstract formulation as a starting point, it becomes possible to explore the strength of other loyalties that strain against family ties. Some are loyalties that affirm the existing hierarchies of power, ensuring male dominance and female subordination, such as the affiliations of clubs and pubs, business and trade union cultures, senior common rooms and working-class subcultures, that work to preserve and assert the bonds between men. Others, on the contrary, are cultures of obligation, support and resistance, such as the bonds of kin, neighbourhood and friendship forged by women within and across their broad family commitments. Still others are transparently outside the cultures of families altogether, such as those of all-female institutions and of the subcultures of lesbians and gay men that have become increasingly apparent over the past 100 years.

These are just examples of what Peter Willmott (1986) has described as a 'subterranean social order' which incorporates relationships with friends, relations, neighbours and work colleagues. Such relationships are mediating structures which connect the public and the private, provide sociable human contact, value systems and socialisation and act as major sources of support and practical help.

Relationships like these have no necessary essential meaning, any more than being a member of a family magically conveys the promise of happiness or fulfilment. They have a different weight in the lives of people at different times and places. The meanings of neighbourhood are different for a white middle-class family in a leafy suburb from those of black youth in the embattled inner city, where the temples, churches, clubs and cafes can provide the focus of powerful cultural and political identities (Gilroy 1987).

Similarly, the neighbourhoods organised around sexual preferences (such as San Francisco's gay Castro district) or religious enthusiasm (Fitzgerald 1987) may provide the continuity over time and the 'generalized reciprocity', in which people give gifts and perform services for each other unconditionally in the general expectation that similar gifts and services will be at some time be returned (Jordan 1989: 43), normally associated with family and kin relationships.

It is potentially misleading, therefore, always to see sharp breaks between family or kin relations and other patterns (which is not to deny the unique weight given to kin relationships). This becomes clearer if we look at the deployment of two other key terms, friendship and community. Peter Willmott (1986: 71), following Abrams, has argued that family relationships are entirely different from friendships, and generally weaker than ties of kin or neighbourhood for primary social support.

But for many, whether organized into households or not, non-family relationships do act as the primary source of social belonging. Parker Rossman, for example, has described the growth of 'network families', groups of people ('friends') bonded together for mutual support (quoted in Zinn and Eitzen 1987: 383). These have been a marked characteristic of the new urban gay communities of the past 20 years (see, for example, Voeller 1980; also Raymond 1986). The language used is still unavoidably familial, but the social relationships are different: based on choice rather than ascription, although carrying many of the characteristics of family-type obligations.

The situation is yet more complex with regard to the idea of community. Willmott (1986: 85) has distinguished three types of community: of territory, of interest and of attachment. All can give rise to intense loyalties, and clearly the categories can overlap to a considerable degree. But it is the last category, the 'community of attachment' that is most interesting. It is equivalent to the 'expressive cultures' identified by Gilroy (1987) in relationship to the experience of black people in Britain, or the 'community of affect' described by Hebdige (1989) around inter-racial music and efforts of international solidarity such as Band Aid, or the communities of identity so characteristic of the lesbian and gay networks of the 1980s (Weeks 1988).

Such attachments give rise to what can best be termed 'moral communities', in which solidarities of mutual support and need give rise to value systems in which the community itself becomes the focus of attachment and the location for the growth of intimate relationships. One powerful example of this derives from the experience of HIV disease or AIDS. Here is a disease and illness where both the people with AIDS and the syndrome itself are highly stigmatised because of the linkage of the disease with socially unpopular or execrated groups (drug users, male homosexuals). Yet the experience of stigma and pain and death has given rise to a sophisticated culture of survival, particularly among gay men in which 'buddying' (the informal but carefully structured system of individual support for the sick or dying) has become symbolic of new ties of solidarity (Nungesser 1986; Plummer 1988).

Attachments such as these are, like kin relationships, often dispersed communities, and provide the context of relationships rather than the primary focus. But their role in the formation and sustenance of personal and social identities can be crucial. If, as Berger and Berger (1983) lament, the family as the source of strong social identities is now under challenge, it is in these moral communities that alternative sources of identification and value are emerging.

Communities like these affirm simultaneously identity and difference: what we have in common and what divides us (Cohen 1986). In the contemporary world, the differences can often be antagonistic, as different world views contest. The attempt to reassert the values of traditional family relations in embattled Asian communities in Britain against the forces of assimilation and secularistion sit uneasily side by side with the frankly sexual–political ties that bind homosexual people in the gay community. At the same time, it would be wrong to believe that even within the self-designated communities of identity there are universal patterns of domestic life. The point is that these communities reflect the increasing complexity and diversity of the modern world and in their very existence challenge the idea that there can possibly be a single pattern of relationships universally applicable to all. In practice, there never has been in the past; there is highly unlikely to be such a pattern in the future.

This suggests that the real challenge lies not in attempting to find alternatives to the family, nor in attempting to make the term family so elastic that it embraces everything, and comes to mean nothing. On the contrary, the more dangerous and difficult task lies in the attempt to forge a moral language which is able to come to terms in a reasoned way with the variety of social possibilities that exist in the modern world, to shape a pluralistic set of values which is able to respect difference (Weeks 1990).

An ethical pluralism need not mean an easy acceptance of everything that exists. On the contrary, it should challenge us to work through the principles that make a pluralistic society possible: a common acceptance of the value of diversity and choice; a sensitivity to the power relations that hinder and inhibit the fulfilment of individual needs; and above all, an avoidance of the proselytising zeal of those who believe that they have the key to the good life. It does not mean that 'the family' is redundant or that it can contribute nothing to individual or social wellbeing. But a true pluralism must begin with the assumption that happiness and personal fulfilment are not the privileged prerogative of family life.

CONCLUSION

We have moved a little way from the political manoeuvrings of 1987, but not perhaps so far from the underlying issues. At stake in the debate about Clause 28 was the degree to which the state through parliamentary fiat had the right to intervene in the dense world of civil society to declare what was right or wrong, appropriate or inappropriate in personal moral and sexual choices. This is not an easy issue to deal with, because it raises profound questions about the desirable balance between individual rights and social needs. There can be no single boundary drawn, saying this far and no further.

But that is precisely what the British Parliament and Government sought to do at the end of 1987 in introducing Clause 28. In its actions both were in effect insisting that one way of life was preferable to another. This essay has attempted to adopt a less imperialistic stance, by offering a modest defence of those much maligned 'pretended family relationships'.

REFERENCES

Abrams, P. and McCulloch, A. (1976) 'Men, women, and communes', in D.L. Barker and S. Allen (eds) *Sexual Divisions and Society. Process and Change*, London: Tavistock.

Ansell, V. *et al.* (1989) *Diggers and Dreamers. The 1990/1 Guide to Communal Living*, Sheffield: A Communes Network Publication.

Barrett, M. and McIntosh, M. (1982) *The Anti-social Family*, London: Verso.

Berger, B. and Berger, P. (1983) *The War over the Family. Capturing the Middle Ground*, London: Hutchinson.

Birch, K. (1988) 'A community of interests', in C. Cant and S. Hemmings (eds) *Radical Records. Thirty Years of Lesbian and Gay History*, London and New York: Routledge.

Blumstein, P. and Schwartz, P. (1983) *American Couples: Money, Work, Sex*, New York: William Morrow.

Bozett, F.W. (1987) *Gay and Lesbian Parents*, New York: Praeger.

Campbell, B. (1988) *Unofficial Secrets: Child Sexual Abuse – the Cleveland Case*, London: Virago.

Cant, C. and Hemmings, S. (eds) (1988) *Radical Records. Thirty Years of Lesbian and Gay History*, London and New York: Routledge.

Chester, R. (1985) 'The rise of the neo-conventional family', *New Society* 19 May.

—— (1986) 'The conventional family is alive and living in Britain', in J. Weeks (ed.) *The Family Directory*, London: The British Library.

Clark, D. (1987) 'Wedlocked Britain', *New Society* 13 March.

Cohen, A.P. (1986) *The Symbolic Construction of Community*, Chichester: Ellis Horwood; London: Tavistock.

David, M. (1986) 'Moral and maternal: the family in the right', in R. Levitas (ed.) *The Ideology of the New Right*, Cambridge Polity Press.

Deakin, N. and Wicks, M. (1989) *Families and the State*, London: Family Policy Studies Centre.

Demos, J. (1979) 'Images of the American family, then and now', in V. Tufte and B. Myerhoff (eds) *Changing Images of the Family*, New Haven and London: Yale University Press.

Finch, J. (1987) 'Whose responsibility? Women and the future of family care', in I. Allen *et al.* (eds) *Informal Care Tomorrow*, London: Policy Studies Institute.

Fitzgerald, F. (1987) *Cities on a Hill. A Journey through Contemporary American Culture*, London: Picador.

Fletcher, R. (1988a) *The Shaking of the Foundations*, London and New York: Routledge.

—— (1988b) *The Abolitionists: Family and Marriage under Attack*, London and New York: Routledge.

Friedan, B. (1983) *The Second Stage*, London: Abacus.

Gilroy, P. (1987) *There Ain't No Black in the Union Jack: The Cultural Politics of Race and Nation*, London: Hutchinson.

GLC (1985) *Changing the World. A London Charter for Gay and Lesbian Rights*, London, Greater London Council.

Hebdige, D. (1989) 'After the masses', *Marxism Today* January: 48–53.

IFS (1981) *Annual Report 1980–1*, Melbourne: Australian Institute of Family Studies.

Irvine, E. (1980) *The Family in the Kibbutz*, London: Study Commission on the Family.

Jordan, B. (1989) *The Common Good: Citizenship, Morality and Self Interest*, Oxford: Blackwell.

Jowell, R., Witherspoon, S. and Brook, L. (eds) (1988) *British Social Attitudes. The Fifth Report*, SCPR, Aldershot, Gower.

Lasch, C. (1977) *Haven in a Heartless World. The Family Besieged*, New York: Basic Books.

—— (1985) *The Minimal Self. Psychic Survival in Troubled Times*, London: Pan Books.

Lash, S. and Urry, J. (1988) *The End of Organized Capitalism*, Cambridge: Polity Press.

Laslett, B. (1979) 'The significance of family membership', in V. Tufte and B. Myerhoff (eds) *Changing Images of the Family*, New Haven and London: Yale University Press.

Laslett, P. (1982) 'Foreword', in R.N. Rapoport, M. Fogarty and R. Rapoport (eds) *Families in Britain*, London and Boston: Routledge & Kegan Paul.

Leach, E. (1968) *A Runaway World? The Reith Lectures 1987*, London: BBC Publications.

Macklin, E. (1980) 'Non-traditional family forms: a decade of research', *Journal of Marriage and the Family* 42(4): 905–22, November.

Marshall, J. (1989) 'Flaunting it: the challenge of the 1990s', *Gay Times* 124: 12–14, January.

Morgan, D.H.J. (1975) *Social Theory and the Family*, London and Boston: Routledge & Kegan Paul.

—— (1985) *The Family, Politics and Social Theory*, London and Boston: Routledge & Kegan Paul.

Mount, F. (1982) *The Subversive Family: An Alternative History of Love and Marriage*, London: Jonathan Cape.

Muller, A. (1987) *Parents Matter. Parents' Relationships with Lesbian Daughters and Gay Sons*, New York: The Naiad Press.

Muncy, R. (1974) *Sex and Marriage in Utopian Communities*, Baltimore: Penguin.

Nava, M. (1983) 'From utopian to scientific feminism? Early feminist critiques of the family', in L. Segal (ed.) *What Is to Be Done about the Family?* Harmondsworth: Penguin.

Nungesser, L.G. (1986) *Epidemic of Courage. Facing AIDS in America*, New York: St Martin's Press.

Pankhurst, J.G. and Houseknecht, S.K. (1983) 'The family, politics and religion in the 1980s', *Journal of Family Issues* 4(1): 5–34, March.

Phillips, A. (1984) 'Fraternity', in B. Pimlott (ed.) *Fabian Essays in Socialist Thought*, London: Heinemann.

Phillips, M. (1988) 'Pity the battered family', *Guardian* 15 July.

Plummer, K. (1988) 'Organizing AIDS', in P. Aggleton and H. Homans (eds) *Social Aspects of AIDS*, Lewes: The Falmer Press.

Rapoport, R.N., Fogarty, M.P. and Rapoport, R. (1982) *Families in Britain*, London and Boston: Routledge & Kegan Paul.

Rapoport, R.N. and Rapoport, R. (1982) 'British families in transition', in R.N. Rapoport, M.P. Fogarty and R. Rapoport (eds) *Families in Britain*, London and Boston: Routledge & Kegan Paul.

Rapp, R. (1982) 'Family and class in contemporary America', in B. Thorne and M. Yalom (eds) *Rethinking the Family: Some Feminist Questions*, New York and London: Longman.

Raymond, J. (1986) *A Passion for Friends. Towards a Philosophy of Female Affection*, London: The Women's Press.

Rigby, A. (1974a) *Alternative Realities*, London and Boston: Routledge & Kegan Paul.

—— (1974b) *Communes in Britain*, London and Boston: Routledge & Kegan Paul.

Robinson, G. 'Fear not Clause 28, only the prejudice behind it', *Guardian* 1 June.

Rose, J. (1988) 'Margaret Thatcher and Ruth Ellis', *New Formations* 6: 3–29.

Segal, L. (ed.) (1983) *What Is to Be Done about the Family?* Harmondsworth: Penguin.

Sontag, S. (1989) *AIDS and its Metaphors*, London: Allen Lane.

Taylor, B. (1982) *Eve and the New Jerusalem*, London: Virago.

Voeller, B. (1980) 'Society and the gay movement', in J. Marmor (ed.) *Homosexual Behavior. A Modern Reappraisal*, New York: Basic Books.

Watney, S. (1987) *Policing Desire. Pornography, AIDS and the Media*, London: Methuen.

Weeks, J. (1985) *Sexuality and its Discontents. Meanings, Myths and Modern Sexualities*, London and New York: Routledge & Kegan Paul.

—— (1986a) *Sexuality*, Chichester: Ellis Horwood; London: Tavistock.

—— (1986b) *The Family Directory*, London: The British Library.

—— (1988) 'Male homosexuality: cultural perspectives' in M. Adler (ed.) *Diseases in the Homosexual Male*, London and Berlin: Springer Verlag.

—— (1989) *Sex, Politics and Society. The Regulation of Sexuality since 1800*, 2nd edn, Harlow: Longman.

—— (1990) *Coming Out*. Homosexual Police in Britain from the Nineteenth Century to the Present, 2nd edn, London: Quartet.

Willmott, P. (1986) *Social Networks, Informal Care and Public Policy*, London: Policy Studies Institute.

Zinn, M.B. and Eitzen, D.S. (1987) *Diversity in American Families*, New York: Harper & Row.

10 Afterword

Does the ring make any difference?
Couples and the private face of a public
relationship in post-war Britain

Jacqueline Burgoyne

Although most commentators and social historians charting the changes which have taken place in marriage and domestic life since the end of the Second World War emphasise the importance of marriage as a now almost universal experience, there is much less agreement about the direction and significance of change within marriage itself. Such uncertainties and potential disagreements do of course have many origins. On the one hand, beliefs safeguarding the privacy of domestic life, and couple relationships in particular, make it very difficult to know what actually goes on in families and households from day to day. This is in turn compounded by our often uncritical acceptance of social arrangements within society to the extent that family circumstances may be seen to be determined by the 'facts' of human nature, requiring no explanation or interpretation. Also, and somewhat paradoxically, despite this bedrock of taken-for-granted beliefs about the naturalness of our own family patterns, episodes of media-generated public concern about the apparent erosion of commitment to conventional patterns of marriage in the post-war period, particularly among women, have periodically transformed marriage into what C. Wright Mills describes as a 'public issue', when 'some value cherished by publics is felt to be threatened' (Wright Mills 1959: 15). Thus members of the generation that in their twenties married immediately after the Second World War have not only witnessed the increasing popularity of marriage among younger generations, but have also had to come to terms with the way increases in divorce, remarriage, and unmarried cohabitation seem to have undermined these 'cherished values'.

Although the divorce rate had been rising since the 1920s, the increase in the years following the implementation of the Divorce Reform Act 1969 meant that an ever-greater proportion of those who married in the post-war period, though relatively unlikely to divorce themselves, were affected at secondhand by the personal distress, the 'private troubles' (Wright Mills 1959) endemic to marriage breakup (Burgoyne *et al.* 1987). During the

1960s and 1970s they watched friends, members of their families, work colleagues or even (through media accounts) prominent public figures, including a member of the royal family pass through the legal, economic, social and personal transitions associated with divorce. Inevitably, the cumulative effect of such changes was to raise questions, expressed both publicly and privately, about the future of marriage in an institutional sense.

During the same period, public discussion of such matters was also fuelled by an increasingly visible 'divorce industry' – members of a variety of legal and therapeutic occupations whose clientele sought various kinds of help to end their marriages. Not only did members of such occupations, as well as social researchers, seek to draw attention to the scale and importance of their work in order to increase their available resources, but their deliberations in conferences and public gatherings (see Morgan 1985: 21–32) demonstrated their own disagreements and divisions of opinion. In these same years this was also matched by a growth in the media coverage of issues relating to marriage and divorce. Newspaper, magazine and broadcasting documentary features dealing with topical issues and debates (the changing roles of men and women; the extent and significance of marital violence; divorce law reform and the debates about maintenance, 'alimony drones' and lifelong 'meal tickets') were all matched by fictional treatments of the same problems in soap operas, film and drama. As a result, media representations of contemporary marriage presented a similar picture of confusion and uncertainty, so that as Wright Mills observed, it is hard to define with any precision either the values which are held to be under threat or the mechanisms by which they are being undermined. As I have argued elsewhere, public discussion of alterations in patterns of domestic life in the post-war period resulting from the increases in divorce, remarriage and women's employment outside the home is permeated by considerable uncertainty and disagreement about both the real extent and the significance of such change (Burgoyne 1987).

In part this is because those who enter such public debates, whether as politician, expert or moral entrepreneur frequently base their arguments on an appeal to the 'naturalness' and obvious normality of the domestic arrangements of those closest to home for them, those inhabiting the same micro-worlds as themselves (Berger and Kellner 1964). These are then contrasted with their perceptions of the private worlds of their patients or clients, as revealed when they seek help with problems in marital relationships. Indeed the legitimacy of the experts is based, at least in part, on having access to knowledge about those 'private' aspects of other people's marriages which are normally hidden from the public gaze. Whilst doctors, lawyers and clergymen have been the traditional recipients of such confidences, they are now joined by a new therapeutic elite of marital counsellors whose conceptualisations of marriage and its attendant difficulties are, as David Morgan suggests, often based on a medical model (Morgan 1985, Chapter 2).

However, if we consider the range of individuals and sectional interest groups, both formal and informal, who would expect to form part of the constituency of a 'marriage' or 'family' lobby and who contribute to media debates on anxieties about changing patterns of marriage, the hegemony of this therapeutic elite does not go unchallenged. Church leaders, representatives of one-parent family groups, and pressure groups for divorced fathers, as well as, of course, apparently neutral social scientists with a research interest in the area, all play their parts. As a result, the orchestration of a 'balanced' broadcast, in the sense beloved by the BBC, has become an increasingly complex matter. It is, however, very significant that such lay experts and pundits have also begun to act as if the legitimacy of their own expertise lies in their access to 'backstage' secrets of married life. Consequently, they attempt to strengthen their arguments by commissioning surveys of the problems of their particular constituency, as well as referring to 'cases' on their files and couples helped – even healed – by their interventions. Such strategies inevitably reinforce the polarisations implicit in medical models of marriage. A sharp contrast is drawn between a needy, pathological 'client' group with unsatisfactory marriages (or in some instances, divorces) and those whose expertise gives them access to the secrets of a happy, healthy marriage or trouble-free divorce. This polarisation even affects representatives of interest groups whose political analysis of marriage as a public issue generates antagonism to the institution itself. On occasion their contributions to such debates seem to imply, somewhat smugly, that the whole problem would be solved if others followed their example and avoided matrimony altogether.

Thus whenever marriage surfaces as a public issue, contributors of many different ideological persuasions and professional backgrounds, including of course social scientists, each make reference to their privileged access to a knowledge and understanding of the interior of couple relationships conventionally safeguarded by the norms of privacy surrounding married life.

The origins and development of the ideological division between the public and the private domains have a complex and controversial history. This chapter is offered as a specific case study of the normative context of marriage and partnership in the post-war period. It casts doubt on some conventional and influential conceptualisations of marriage as an increasingly 'private' matter and also raises important methodological questions about the investigation of the so-called 'private sphere' of couple relationships.

My interest, along with that of David Clark, in the study of marriage and partnership began in 1977 when we began working together on a study of stepfamilies in Sheffield (Burgoyne and Clark 1984). It led us, separately and together, to various pieces of research and writing on marriage. In the second half of this chapter, considerable use will be made of material collected in a later study of unmarried couples in Sheffield[1]. For many of these couples prevailing beliefs in the essential privacy surrounding their sexual relationships and domestic arrangements meant that they did not see any real point in getting married. Further, a minority who were committed consciously to remaining unmarried portrayed their positive decision to do so as a way of avoiding the potentially stereotyped roles and coercive scripts attached to conventional marriage.

PRIVACY, PRIVATISATION AND SYMMETRY

Many different kinds of evidence are used to support the view that the significant changes in patterns of marriage and domestic life which have taken place in the post-war period have generated qualitatively different expectations and experiences of marriage. Some of the problems which occur when we attempt to distinguish myth from reality and theory from practice in this debate arise precisely because the supporting evidence, except in the most obvious and general sense, does not necessarily refer to the same kinds of social phenomena. As a result it is important to delineate some of the most significant types of change referred to by sociological, therapeutic and other commentators.

Rimmer and others have drawn attention to the increasing popularity of marriage in the post-war period. It is now an almost universal experience and over 90 per cent of the population will be legally married at least once for some period in their lives (Rimmer 1981). Furthermore, despite the very significant increase in divorce and remarriage in the same period, Haskey calculates that if present trends continue, between two-thirds and three-quarters of today's newly-weds will remain together until their marriage is ended by the death of one partner (Haskey 1982).

In the immediate post-war period considerable emphasis was placed on building up a stock of housing, both privately and publicly owned, which would enable young couples to have a 'place of their own', if not at the time they married, at least when they 'started their own family'. Such phrases do themselves illustrate some of the tacit, taken-for-granted beliefs about what had begun to constitute the norms of post-war domestic arrangements. The family unit implied when a couple married, for childbearing was seen to flow naturally and obviously from the decision to marry (Busfield and Paddon 1977), should ideally be independently housed. Several ethnographic studies carried out in the 1950s and 1960s illustrate how parents from different social classes used their economic and interpersonal resources to help their adult children to achieve this goal. Thus parents would variously attempt to influence landlords and rent collectors to obtain accommodation for their children (Young and Willmott 1957); offer their services in decorating and repairing an engaged daughter's or son's future home (Leonard 1980); transfer or lend capital to their adult children to facilitate house purchase (Firth 1956; Bell 1968). With the exception of a minority of young adults who 'leave home', at least in some senses, to enter some form of higher education or to follow an occupation which offers independent accommodation or takes them away from home, marriage remains a significant rite of passage, symbolised as much by the transfer of their personal belongings from one household to another as by the ritual elements of the wedding itself (Kiernan 1985).

One of the most persistent and potentially difficult legacies of the influential research and social commentary undertaken by the Institute of Community Studies in the 1950s and 1960s (Young and Willmott 1957; Townsend 1957; Young and Willmott 1973) has been a widespread belief in the 'decline' of the importance of the extended family. A parallel inference was also made that 'isolated' conjugal couples with or without children now represent both a statistical and social norm. This work has justly been subject to criticism on methodological grounds (Platt 1976); but if the case for a decline in the significance of extended family networks remains unproven, there is little more reliable research data on the subject with which to replace it. Comparison of the evidence about patterns of residence among non-resident kin in more recent studies confirms the impression of considerable diversity, which I have also observed through my own empirical work. For the purposes of this chapter I would wish to argue that recent cohorts of newly-married or cohabiting couples have a greater likelihood of beginning their domestic partnership at some distance socially, geographically or emotionally from non-resident kin, especially parents; but that it is impossible to assess accurately the magnitude of that change. Although it is possible to point to the influence of class-related factors, their effects are likely to be much more subtle and complex than much traditional class analysis allows.

Those most likely to fit into the flawed but suggestive ideal–typical 'modern' marriage, described by Berger and Kellner (1964), who meet and marry as 'strangers', unaffected by parental preferences or membership of a pre-existing close-knit network of friends, neighbours and kin, are those who leave home *before* they marry. Additionally, we might include those who experience significant social and/or geographical mobility in the early years of partnership, who have little to gain psychologically or materially from remaining close to one or both families of origin or who, as a result of family feud or conflict, have deliberately severed ties. Such couples are amongst those who are most consciously aware that they are creating a partnership *de novo* with minimal reliance on familial or cultural continuities. Furthermore, their belief in the unique and individual character of their partnership is reinforced in the privacy of their domestic arrangements. Not only have they achieved the goal of a 'place of their own' but the foundations of the rituals of domesticity, described somewhat romantically by Tolstoy as 'the poetry of the trivia of married life', are laid without reference to the expectations and conventions of their immediate families.

The appraisal of the longer-term consequences of post-war reconstruction was an important item on the research agendas of academic social scientists in the late 1950s and early 1960s and is clearly illustrated in several highly influential pieces of writing published during this period. Moving beyond analyses of demographic and social trends or specific pieces of empirical research, attempts were made to capture the 'spirit of the age' and, significantly, to use these to make predictions about the future. Underpinned by a preoccupation with class analysis which characterised much post-war British sociology (Giddens 1973), there was a marked tendency to isolate examples of change taking place within particular social strata or subcultures which, as they permeated downwards, might signal the shape of things to come in a more general sense. Two specific examples are particularly relevant to this argument. In exploring them further I should point out that I am less concerned with the extent to which the changes described actually took place than with the contribution such studies made to a prevailing mythology of change.

Even before the findings of the *affluent worker* studies were published (Goldthorpe *et al.* 1969), discussions of class differences in patterns of domestic life had begun to focus on the potential for change amongst some sections of the working class (see *par excellence* Klein 1965, Chapter 6). As a result of the kinds of changes summarised in the previous section, which were matched by evidence of the growth in domestic and home-centred patterns of consumption, it became common to refer to a trend towards *privatisation* (Lockwood 1966) which was explicitly investigated in the affluent-worker studies. Although chiefly concerned with the political consequences of finding that affluent, male manual workers as heads of nuclear-family households were now expending more of their time, money and energies on their homes and families, and that as a result, many traditional workplace ties were being undermined, the *privatisation thesis* also began to raise questions about the meanings attached to family and domestic life.

The answers to such questions were provided by parallel research, mainly emanating from the Institute of Community Studies. These findings were used to argue that greater affluence, privacy and autonomy experienced by such manual-worker households was indeed giving domestic life a new meaning and significance. Building on their earlier research, Young and Willmott's study of 'work and leisure in the London region' bore testimony to the emergence of a new type of 'symmetrical' family, affected in turn by trends towards privatisation, the increased isolation of nuclear-family households, and especially significant for my argument here, a reduction in the role segregation within marriage (Young and Willmott 1973: 29, 30). Although this study has been subject to very considerable criticism among sociologists (Oakley 1974: 164), it remains a very influential book, frequently appearing on the reading lists of, for example, student teachers and social workers. Along with the Rapoports' study of dual career couples (Rapoport and Rapoport 1976) it has also been widely used by commentators and journalists (Green 1984) as evidence of a sea-change in marital norms and behaviour. The reasons why such studies have acquired an influence way beyond their merits are complex. On the one hand, their findings present a comforting picture of harmony and adaptability to the changed economic circumstances of the late 1950s and early 1960s, which had resulted in a marked increase in *part-time* employment opportunities for women. More significantly, their portrayal of contemporary marriage was very optimistic, conveying a move towards the kind of marital partnership portrayed as an ideal in the contemporary therapeutic literature. Together such writings made a significant mythology of marriage as a partnership of equals.

PRIVACY AND NEW NORMS OF SEXUAL SATISFACTION

By today's standards, levels of divorce in the 1950s might not have been expected to generate much public concern, but church leaders in particular expressed considerable alarm about the rising divorce rates. Then as now it was widely suggested that an erosion in commitment to marriage would inexorably lead to a 'breakdown' in family life, eventually affecting the stability of society as a whole. From the 1950s onwards the range of public responses to moral panics about divorce bore testimony to the increasing influence of the new social–therapeutic expertise, in which social scientists and therapeutic experts joined hands in support of 'permissive' trends and new patterns of marital partnership. On the one hand, commentators like McGregor (1957) and Fletcher (1966) argued that increases in divorce were best understood as evidence of raised expectations and an increased social investment in the institution of marriage; whilst influential members of the therapeutic elite, as described, for example, by Lasch (1977), spoke publicly of the importance of mutual compatability and sexual fulfilment in marriage. This unconscious alliance has been a powerful force in the creation and maintenance of contemporary public images and ideals of marriage, which emphasise the essentially individual, personal and above all *private* and ungendered character of contemporary couple relationships, both inside and outside of marriage.

One of the most influential factors contributing to the enhanced sense of privacy surrounding couple relationships has been, paradoxically, increases in both the frequency and the candour of public discussion about the meaning and purpose of sexuality. As Weeks demonstrates, although the 1920s and 1930s were characterised by a relaxation in the norms surrounding discussion of sex, it remained strictly within the confines of marriage (Weeks 1981: 206). However, by the 1950s survey evidence, alongside the confessional disclosures of patients and clients, bore testimony to the prevalence of extramarital sexual encounters and relationships. Once again, social–therapeutic experts argued that such 'experimentation', as it was often described, was in the long run more likely to enhance than to undermine the marriages of those who indulged in such practices (Weeks 1981: 238). Commenting on that period generally Jeffrey Weeks concludes:

> Official sexual morality was in a curious state of tension. A fear of decline of standards had to confront a considerable degree of stability in actual behaviour, while the perceived dangers were to be curiously resolved by an ideology that encouraged sexuality to flourish, but strictly within the confines of monogamous marriage. It was as if the age had developed a growing fear of the effects of sex unconfined, so the chrysalis had to be firmly locked in its cocoon.
>
> (Weeks 1981: 239)

One obvious and highly significant consequence of the dissemination of images of the 'ideal marriage' as having a strong sexual component was to legitimate and encourage couples' desire for the privacy normally thought necessary to turn myth into reality. This was demonstrated not simply in the growth of a belief that newly-married couples 'should' start their married life in their own place but, in some communities and social circles at least, created new norms which probably gave young couples considerably greater autonomy and privacy. Recent ethnographic accounts of the working and domestic lives of young working-class men and women hint at the sense of isolation which surrounds their transition into marriage (Willis 1977; Pollert 1981; Westwood 1984). Although their older workmates often tried to prepare them for the mundane realities of married life, for example, through the ritualised joking about sex which accompanied their wedding preparations, once the formal celebrations were over they were left on their own. It is probably important, in this respect, that public recognition and acceptance that most couples have already become sexual partners *before* they marry does not seem to have diminished the power of traditional honeymoon jokes and pranks. Such rituals continue to suggest that marriages are defined, as in legal terms they are consummated, through participation in sexual intercourse; and as such the significance of the couple's sexual encounters changes when they marry. This transformation helps us to understand some of the origins of the kinds of sexual problems reported by therapists, which only surface *after* couples actually marry.

Marriage locates the partners' sexuality within a particular contemporary discourse, controlled not through prohibitions but through the generation of diffuse sets of 'oughts' or expectations (Foucault 1979) in which privacy looms large. Thus while the 'private' inner core of couple relationships may protect many secrets – facts about each other and their relationship not disclosed to others – sex is, as Foucault suggests, likely to be regarded as *the* secret, the most 'private' element of their relationship. Such beliefs regarding the centrality of the sexual relationship in contemporary partnership have also generated new orthodoxies which challenge traditional assumptions about the differences – biological, psychological and social – between men and women. From Marie Stopes onwards medical and therapeutic expertise emphasised the importance of sexual fulfilment to women; the ideal marriage was symbolised by mutual and simultaneous orgasm (see Mace 1948, Chapter 18). Debates about women's physiological capacity for sexual pleasure, fuelled by survey evidence indicating its absence for the majority of, particularly working-class, married women (Slater and Woodside 1951; Chesser 1956) were transformed into moral imperatives about married women's right to a satisfactory sexual life. Popular sex manuals began to stress the importance of husbands – still the senior partners in this joint endeavour – learning to give their wives pleasure. However, evidence based on the experience of clinicians and correspondence to newspaper and magazine 'agony' columns suggests that couples who fail to achieve this ideal are often locked in a cage of misery based on *mutual* self-blame. For some at least, their difficulties in achieving the publicly defined goal of a satisfactory sexual relationship within marriage may be compounded by uncertainties about gender roles and differences both inside the bedroom and beyond. The strength of taken-for-granted assumptions and beliefs about the 'naturalness' and implied superiority of heterosexual partnership is derived from a wealth of diffuse, often unconscious imagery about the complementary or 'interlocking' physical and psychological characteristics of each sex.

However, as traditional gender divisions and stereotypes have been

challenged and undermined in recent decades, prevailing expert orthodoxies of marriage as a partnership of equals offering the same satisfactions
and fulfilment to *both* sexes also seemed to imply that men and women
attach similar meanings to their sexual life and inhabit their own sexuality
in an identical manner. Such assumptions do of course run parallel with
both the common-sense 'theories' about gender differences and relationships between the sexes now held by many members of the new therapeutic
elite, and perhaps to a lesser extent, with their own domestic and sexual
practices (the Posy Simmonds cartoons being a useful example). None the
less, the overwhelming conclusion to be drawn from the available evidence
about the effects of gender through the life course is that the *divisions*
between the personal and social worlds, the investments and preoccupations of the majority of women and men, have not been undermined
in the post-war period. However, it is most frequently within the private
confines of heterosexual couple relationships that individual uncertainties
about gendered aspects of the identity of both partners are acted out. In this
respect *both* the elements of the Scottish common-law definition of cohabitation as a partnership of 'bed and board' are equally significant. To
that extent contemporary ideologies of sexual liberation are as much concerned with the politics of the kitchen as with the secrets of the bedroom.

Changing sexual norms and the growing influence of the new social–
therapeutic expertise in shaping couple relationships have also been significant in creating a climate of opinion in which cohabitation became more
popular and more widely accepted. As long as official sexual moralities had
continued to proscribe extramarital sexual relationships, men and women
who 'lived together' and were assumed through their implied or proven
occupancy of the same bed, to be enjoying a sexual relationship, found it
necessary to portray themselves as 'really' married.

Recognition that many 'stable' and 'respectable' couples of long
standing were forced to live in unregistered relationships because of one
partner's difficulties in obtaining a divorce was an important catalyst for
divorce reform in the 1960s. During that decade, the influence of what was
labelled 'educated' liberal opinion on sexual matters increased considerably. Although the availability of oral contraceptives for women was
significant in reducing adult concern – whether as parents, teachers or
college residential authorities – about protecting young women from the
consequences of premarital sex, the influence of new social–therapeutic
orthodoxies was also very important. The contention, derived from an
increasingly popular subFreudian view of human nature, that adults,
whether married or not, needed to be able to express their sexuality, was
translated into a belief in satisfying sexual relationships as a form of
personal growth, even a basic human right.

This change in values may be illustrated by considering shifts in the policy and practice of the National Marriage Guidance Council (NMGC) [now RELATE – ed.]. As the name implies, its origins were as a 'marriage mending' movement, which in the immediate post-war period was *inter alia* concerned with the preservation of the traditional Christian views about premarital sex. However, by the mid-1960s the NMGC's counselling service was being offered without discrimination to all couples, whether married or not. By this stage indeed the liberalism of key texts recommended to counsellors in training contrasted sharply with writers like Mace's earlier insistence on the desirability and morality of monogamy.

Data from General Household Surveys point to a marked increase in the number of couples who at any one time live together in unmarried partnership. Although the majority of these include at least one formerly married partner who is not yet legally free to marry or who may be reluctant to do so as a result of earlier experiences of being married, an increasing proportion of couples marrying for the first time have begun to live together before their wedding day [see B. Jane Elliott's chapter, this volume – ed.]. These data also provide some indirect evidence of likely educational, and by implication, class differences in cohabitation. The largest proportion of women under the age of twenty-five who were cohabiting in the early 1980s were either separated or divorced already, having married relatively early. They were therefore more likely to be part of a group of early-marrying working-class women, particularly associated with a high incidence of divorce (Thornes and Collard 1979; Ineichen 1977). By contrast, over half the women aged between 25 and 34 were still single. As there is a clear association between fathers' class position, the age at which they completed full-time education, their own occupational position and age at marriage (Reid 1981; Martin and Roberts 1984) it is safe to infer that *pre*marital cohabitation is more likely to involve women with higher-than-average educational achievements, working in occupations which offer the prospect of a career. Given prevailing patterns of mate selection (Macrae 1986) their partners are also likely to enjoy similar or even greater educational and occupational advantages. Thus it would appear that it is the children of earlier generations of middle-class, liberal 'progressives', whose own advocacy of greater tolerance and the importance of sexual fulfilment helped to create new ideals of partnership, who have been the principal beneficiaries of the changing moral climate their parents helped to create. As I will suggest, for such couples at least it is possible for them to argue, albeit with some reservations, that marriage as a legal institution is now irrelevant and that for them the ring no longer makes any difference.

CONTEMPORARY COUPLE RELATIONSHIPS: MYTH AND REALITY

As I have tried to trace the material and ideological changes which have contributed to contemporary social–therapeutic orthodoxies of marriage in the post-war period, I have implied at various points that it is important for social scientists and others to attempt to distinguish myth from reality. In her study of a group of parents with handicapped children, Voysey makes a vital distinction between her informants' beliefs about how their family lives *ought* to be conducted and their everyday experiences of family life (Voysey 1975). Such *public moralities*, generated by experts and moral guardians of various kinds (Rex 1974) and transmitted through encounters with members of therapeutic and welfare professions, are used as a means of evaluating their own and other people's performance of family and marital roles.

I would therefore wish to argue that contemporary public moralities of marriage, generated by the kinds of material and ideological changes already described, place considerable stress on marriage as a source of meaning, purpose and fulfilment. As David Morgan has argued, *Relationship*, in the strong sense, has become a key term in contemporary industrial societies. Marriage and its alternatives are seen as the context *par excellence* in which the achievements and stresses endemic to the pursuit of this ideal are experienced (Morgan 1985). Some of the specific elements of such public moralities, which are particularly relevant to a consideration of *unmarried* domestic partnership, include:

1 It is the Relationship, not its legal status which counts. Social–therapeutic experts would not therefore necessarily make any significant distinctions between married and unmarried couples.
2 Once a Relationship is defined as less than satisfactory by one or both partners it is threatened; if such Relationships 'die' they cannot be perpetuated by legal ties and should therefore be offered a 'decent burial'.
3 The Relationship of the conjugal pair is the foundation of their household/family unit. If the Relationship ends, this unit is broken.
4 Good Relationships are characterised by mutual sexual satisfaction and a high degree of intimacy and inter-personal communication.
5 The Relationship should be the couple's first priority and primary loyalty. Commitments and obligations arising from work, friendship or kinship, including children, should not be allowed to become so pressing as to threaten the Relationship.
6 The satisfactions and potential stresses attached to the pursuit of an ideal Relationship are common to both sexes and the essential symmetry of

their partnership is likely to be expressed in increasingly egalitarian sexual and domestic practices.

Although it would be quite possible to offer a detailed examination of the contribution made by social–therapeutic experts to the maintenance and transmission of orthodoxies and semi-official discourses stressing Relationships as a contemporary moral imperative (Morgan 1985, Chapter 2), it is much harder to locate systematic evidence of their incorporation into popular public moralities of marriage. Data which would allow us to compare 'theory' with 'practice' are even more limited. I would want to argue, however, that elements of each of these aspects of the ideal marital relationship are to be found in the, albeit patchy and insubstantial, ethnographic evidence where couples speak to us about their domestic partnerships – past, present and projected. My main reservations about the apparently universal appeal or relevance of such imperatives in a society such as our own, which is characterised by deep and continuing gender divisions, are illustrated in the discussion which forms the remainder of this chapter. This is based round a question which is frequently asked when marriage is discussed as a public issue, as well as in other settings when couples consider the 'private troubles' endemic to their Relationship. What, if anything, is there to be gained by a legal marriage?

THE CONTRADICTIONS OF UNMARRIED PARTNERSHIP

The following observations are drawn from a study of cohabiting couples which was conducted in Sheffield in 1983–4.[1] A total of twenty-nine couples participated, all of whom were interviewed on two occasions; a further subgroup was followed up for a third interview. Names and occupations have been changed to preserve the anonymity of those who took part. Full details of the research methodology can be found in Burgoyne (1985).

Those who live together outside of marriage as a matter of conscious choice frequently portray their decision to do so as a means of avoiding what they regard as the stereotyped roles and conventional scripts attached to being married. They regard their relationship as an essentially private matter which might be undermined by pressure to conform to the expectations of others. Stanley Brown, a 27-year-old builder who has lived with Penny Scott, a trainee beauty therapist for six years:

> I think the only difference it does make is that to be unmarried gives me an essential feeling of freedom . . . I think it would do more harm than good, getting married for me, because as I've said I think this reflects my attitude towards pressure on me, pressure from outside. . . . If you're

married it's like signing a lease that you can't assign, it's like taking on a commitment but if you're not married you're not in it. What you're doing is your own choice and to me that's a stronger bond.

After describing a sudden impulse to try to stop a close friend who was pregnant from getting married, Penny commented: 'I think if we got married it would destroy something.'

Other participants in this study who expressed similar sentiments spoke with some authority about the pitfalls of marriage, either their own or, more frequently among this particular group, their reactions to the break-up of their parents' marriages. For a minority this meant considered opposition to the whole institution of marriage. More commonly, respondents portrayed themselves as using the privacy of their present circumstances as a way of testing out their relationship before they committed themselves more publicly.

For most of the couples in this particular study their claims that the personal decisions they had made about their relationship did not affect others were substantiated by their descriptions of domestic circumstances and contacts with family and friends. An unusually large proportion of this sample had left their parental home rather earlier than might be expected given their particular family backgrounds; as a result they were making their own choices and decisions about where, and with whom, they lived at an earlier age and stage in the life course than the majority of their peers. Because of geographical moves, most frequently to take up a place in higher education, or because of family conflicts, or even in some instances moments of conscious choice in the face of competing claims of family ties and their commitment to their new relationship, most of the couples were not 'close' to either set of parents. With the exception of three working-class couples who, unusually, had begun to live together in what they described as a 'trial marriage' before marrying formally, the foundations of their domestic partnership – the habits and rituals of domestic life, the allocation of tasks, decisions made about housing and making a home – had not been subject to the scrutiny of close-knit networks of kin and friends of the kind described, for example, in Leonard's study of young couples in Swansea (Leonard 1980).

Within this particular sample the largest identifiable group were former students, nine couples in all, whose partnerships had grown out of earlier friendships and romantic attachments from their student days. Although these couples described being part of a network of shared friends – mainly other couples in similar circumstances to themselves – they were aware that they enjoyed a degree of privacy which made it relatively easy to avoid conforming to conventional norms. Doris McWilkie, a teacher, had recently moved with her partner into a terraced house in a former traditional working-class area. She contrasts this with the student-ghetto area where they used to live:

> You suddenly start noticing that it [living together] isn't always the norm. And I think a lot of that is the family pressure one . . . I mean had my parents lived in Sheffield I think I might have chickened out, but because there is that distance and I wasn't constantly having my mum round on the doorstep, then it was a lot easier, but looking at young people who live round here . . . they're not students, they're normal working people who are unemployed or whatever and to them we seem quite strange. I mean they take the mickey out of us, but it's quite obvious that they think we're different.

Several of the other couples in the study experienced an unwelcome degree of privacy, or social isolation as a result of poverty, domestic or personal conflicts. Whilst they were aware that this left them free of the kind of scrutiny which would draw attention to their 'deviant' marital status, these couples spoke, often obliquely, of the stresses of too much privacy and too great a degree of mutual dependency. It is also perhaps significant that the working and social lives of the three couples who had already married by the end of the study, meant that they formed part of social networks and communities which placed relatively high value on marriage as a source of conventional respectability. Two instances involved former students, who as qualified doctors now experienced some pressure to conform to the norms of their occupation; in the third instance a divorced woman and a single man who had lived together for over five years were persuaded to marry by members of a local church community which they had recently joined.

Most of these couples appeared to live relatively 'privatised' lives and spoke about their relationship in ways which emphasised the importance to them of this essentially private, individual character. However there is something here to do with creating that which is private out of that which is public: the analogy originally used by Goffman of laying down a towel on a crowded beach in order to create a private space for sunbathing springs to mind here. It offers instructive parallels with the creation and maintenance of the private domain which surrounds contemporary couple relationships. If access to 'real' privacy were to be unproblematic, then the need for ideological constructions of the private domain would not arise. Further, if its boundaries are themselves socially constructed, in what sense, if at all, can we regard those aspects of the Relationship of couples which are protected with the greatest privacy as being any more 'freely' chosen than their more public roles and obligations? As an extension of the kinds of therapeutic insights offered by marital therapists who uncover the sorts of personal and familial legacies which partners carry into their Relationship (see as an example, Clulow 1985), social scientists ought to develop more subtle ways of delineating and assessing the influences of, for example, class, educational and occupational experiences and ideologies.

Askham's study of a small sample of married couples in Aberdeen was designed as a way of exploring the potential tensions in contemporary marriage. She argues that the acquisition and maintenance of a sense of identity which confirms our standing as unique, valued individuals is made easier by the opportunities for intimate interaction which marriage provides. However, the requirements of identity maintenance – open and wide-ranging conversation, a certain amount of privacy, the possibility of new experiences for each individual – may also threaten the stability needs of couples (Askham 1984: 1–13). These are normally assuaged through a belief in home and family as the primary source of stability and continuity. Her discussion of the areas of married life which enhance couples' sense of stability helps to shed light on some of the tensions and contradictions experienced by *unmarried* couples. These include areas of marital behaviour which make 'the relationship seem more solid and real' and the 'discouragement of outsiders, who may interfere with the created stability of a relationship, from forming an intimate relationship with either of the partners' (Askham 1984: 12).

At first sight it might appear that unmarried partnerships offer fewer opportunities to confirm the stability of the relationship. For example, whether out of conscious choice *not* to marry or because they portray themselves as not yet ready to do so, they cannot refer to any publicly recognised transition point or rite of passage which would confirm their status as a co-resident couple of however many years standing. Similarly, ambiguities surrounding a partnership which does not have a 'proper', i.e. socially recognised, beginning inevitably affect the way significant others relate to them. On the one hand, uncertainty or even active disapproval seemed to have been a contributory factor in distancing many of the study couples from their families of origin so that they enjoyed a considerable measure of privacy or, in a small number of cases, social isolation. However, there was also evidence that friends and acquaintances of the opposite sex regarded their unmarried status as signalling their potential availability for new or additional romantic attachments. For the majority of the study couples such assumptions were unwelcome and were portrayed as potentially undermining of a relationship which they regarded, in this respect at least, as 'just like marriage'. There was little evidence from this sample of any enthusiasm for an 'open' relationship in which both partners were free to seek other sexual relationships, even amongst those most clearly committed to remaining outside the perceived constraints of marriage. This issue was discussed in some detail in follow-up interviews with six of the couples as part of a case study of gender and sexuality. Each of these couples had talked about infidelity quite explicitly and a conscious agreement to be faithful to one another had been an important means of signifying their mutual commitment.

Faced with problems generated by this lack of public recognition, how do unmarried couples create a sense of stability in their relationship? In the case of this particular group this was less of a problem than it might appear because, in their day-to-day activities and relationships they differed so little from their married peers that their 'deviant' status only surfaced as an issue in very specific circumstances.

As they described the details of their housekeeping arrangements, the way they divided their domestic tasks, the balance of work, home and leisure in their weekly timetables, frequent comments were made about being 'just like a married couple really'. For most of the couples, this sense of being 'like-a-married-couple-but . . . ' was also confirmed in the decisions they made about housing. Joint-ownership or tenancy was the norm even if co-residence had begun in rather different circumstances than those of a conventional marriage. When the couples in this study told their stories, recounting the way their relationship had developed, decisions about housing often had considerable emotional significance. For example, a gradual series of moves into 'better' accommodation often symbolised and underpinned a process of emotional engagement which was less easily described in interviews. Becoming more established as a couple in the domestic sense also made it easier for the families to 'understand' and respond to their relationship as a form of quasi-marriage. By the same token, they could also demonstrate to unwelcome potential third parties that, in their sexual as in their domestic lives, the norms and conventions of their partnership had been constructed in the shadow of marriage itself.

In other ways it is notable that some of these couples, especially but not exclusively the former-student, dual-career group, balanced conflicts between their identity and stability needs rather differently from couples – whether legally married or not – who enjoyed fewer occupational advantages. They were more likely to describe themselves and their relationship in studiedly unconventional terms and shared, as a result, a greater preoccupation with the maintenance and development of their identities as individuals. However, I would want to suggest, tentatively from this small sample, that such preoccupations do not inevitably result in an increase in instability. It appeared that the couples whose relationships were most likely to end in the foreseeable future were those where one partner was pressing hard for marriage in the face of the indifference or active opposition of the other. In such circumstances the 'insecure' partner regarded legal marriage as a source of public recognition which would strengthen their relationship. It is significant in this respect that many lawyers and counsellors can recount the case histories of couples who, having lived together for a considerable period, decide to part within months of their marriage.

CONCLUSION: PERMANENCE AND THE INTERRELATIONSHIP BETWEEN EMOTIONAL AND MATERIAL SECURITY

Although as I have already indicated, unmarried domestic partnerships have become more popular and widely accepted in recent decades, there is little evidence of the growth of any distinctive public moralities about how they should be conducted, beyond treating them as quasi-marriages. When in 1981 David Clark and I asked a representative sample of adults then living in Aberdeen and Sheffield about their attitudes to unmarried cohabitation, it was clear that there was a far greater measure of approval for cohabitation as a prelude to marriage than as a permanent alternative. Although over a fifth of the sample felt unable to give a definite answer by saying that 'it depended on the circumstances', 38 per cent thought that living together before marriage was a good idea, whilst only 15 per cent described in the same terms living together without intending to marry. When this sample were asked what they saw as the main disadvantages of living together, their answers focused on the potential insecurity of such arrangements. Particular emphasis was placed on the way cohabitation affected children. It was significant that, despite this sample's accurate awareness of current levels of divorce and their own contact with divorced people (over 65 per cent of them knew at least one or two divorced people personally) their answers to questions about unmarried cohabitation indicated that they saw such relationships as lacking the security of legal marriage.

Perhaps it was because the unmarried couples I have described here were anxious, as Voysey's parents had been, to render a satisfactory public account of their performance and standing as couples, that initially few obvious signs of insecurity were apparent. However, two or three couples were experiencing serious financial, personal and/or family problems and as a result did little to hide their difficulties and when at a later stage the attitudes and responses of each partner in this group were compared, it became clear that significant discrepancies existed in their commitments and plans for the future as well as in their characterisations of their relationship.

When they talked, most couples used imagery which indicated a realisation that domestic partnerships inevitably limit personal freedom and that 'living together' in whatever circumstances imposes certain constraints. This was true both in a general sense and was also particularised on the basis of the unique fads and foibles which they described as being attached to them as individuals. Most described the evolution of their relationship in a way which suggested that at first their willingness to adapt, change and accept constraints had been minimal, matching their uncertainty as to whether it was likely to be permanent. Most found that, as their relationship developed, an investment in the possibility of permanence involved accepting a greater loss of potential freedom. Independent accommodation was relinquished, joint purchases were made, and partners began to accept some measure of responsibility for each other's kin, for example, sending joint birthday cards or visiting together at Christmas.

For those who had not been married before and were now in their late twenties, the possibility of having a child was one of the strongest tests of their hope that their relationship was at least potentially permanent. For this group, legal marriage was only an issue because of a prior and more significant decision which was made about joint parenthood. For some of these couples this decision exposed their uncertainties and insecurities more starkly than any other issue. In one instance a woman teacher aged 30 ended her relationship whilst the study was in progress because she planned to have a baby 'before she was 35', in the face of her partner's continued resistance to the idea.

Unsurprisingly, it was the women in the study who talked more about having children. They were both more likely to mention the subject spontaneously and to discuss their feelings in greater detail when questioned specifically. The decisions, whether consciously and deliberately to delay having children or not to have them at all, were both described as highly significant. In each case they were reported in ways which illustrated many of the implicit connections made between permanence and security in both an emotional and material sense. For those women who did not have access to permanent jobs and who relied, wholly or partially, on being supported economically by their partner, having children was closely connected with their desire, and in some cases considerable anxiety, to be legally married. Where their partners shared the desire to start a family, marriage was a 'natural' next step; but other men resisted this, setting in train a spiral of uncertainty and insecurity which left these women in a very vulnerable position, both economically and emotionally. Although they were understandably reluctant to describe their lack of commitment very openly, some of these men referred to admiring comments made by their friends and family about their luck in acquiring the advantages of domestic partnership without enrolling for the responsibilities entailed in marriage.

The kinds of insecurities about their relationship experienced by some of the *men* in the study have parallel origins. Five men whose partners had satisfying careers, either currently or in prospect, seemed to suffer from a marked degree of personal insecurity, stemming from parental divorces, family conflicts and broken educational careers. To varying extents they portrayed themselves as living in the shadow of their partners and in each case their anxiety both to marry and have children had begun to undermine the established basis of their relationship. In this situation the fact that their partners were economically independent and highly committed to their own careers fed upon their own sense of insecurity.

We see in all this many of the hallmarks of recent debates about the nature of marriage, as both institution and relationship. Unmarried cohabitation, like marriage itself is a 'private' territory which is encroached on at numerous points by the structural elements of social-class and gender differences. Persisting inequalities in either married or unmarried heterosexual partnerships may in the long term depend far more on these structural factors than on elements of individual 'choice' within relationships. Perhaps especially in a period when *Relationships* have been constructed as the sites of ultimate satisfaction and meaning, it is important that social research should draw attention to their publicly scripted characteristics. To do this is not to imply a mechanistic view of the nature of contemporary partnership, but rather points to the need for an improved understanding of the interconnections, across the life course, between the public and the private elements of contemporary marriage and cohabitation.

NOTE

1   The study was conducted with Paul Wild and was assisted by a grant from the then Social Science Research Council.

REFERENCES

Askham, J. (1984) *Identity and Stability in Marriage*, Cambridge: Cambridge University Press.

Bell, C. (1968) *Middle Class Families*, London: Routledge & Kegan Paul.

Berger, P.L. and Kellner, H. (1964) 'Marriage and the construction of reality', *Diogenes* 1–23.

Busfield, J. and Paddon, M. (1977) *Thinking About Children*, London: Cambridge University Press.

Burgoyne, J. (1985) 'Cohabitation and contemporary family life', *End of Grant Report*, London: Economic and Social Research Council.

—— (1987) 'Change, gender and the life course', in G. Cohen (ed.) *Social Change and the Life Course*, London: Tavistock.

Burgoyne, J. and Clark, D. (1984) *Making a Go of It: A Study of Stepfamilies in Sheffield*, London: Routledge & Kegan Paul.

Burgoyne, J., Ormrod, R. and Richards, M. (1987) *Divorce Matters*, Harmondsworth: Penguin.

Chesser, E. (1956) *The Sexual, Marital and Family Relationships of the English Woman*, London: Hutchinson.

Clulow, C. (1985) *Marital Therapy: An Inside View*, Aberdeen: Aberdeen University Press.

Firth, R. (1956) *Two Studies of Kinship in London*, London: Athlone Press.

Fletcher, R. (1966) *The Family and Marriage in Britain*, Harmondsworth: Penguin.

Foucault, M. (1979) *The History of Sexuality: An Introduction*, London: Allen Lane.

Giddens, A. (1973) *The Class Structure of the Advanced Societies*, London: Hutchinson.

Goldthorpe, J., Lockwood, D., Bechhofer, F. and Platt, J. (1969) *The Affluent Worker in the Class Structure*, London: Cambridge University Press.

Green, M. (1984) *Marriage*, London: Fontana.

Haskey, J. (1982) 'The proportion of marriages ending in divorce', *Population Studies* 27: 2–11.

Ineichen, B. (1977) 'Youthful marriage: the vortex of disadvantage', in R. Chester and J. Peel (eds) *Equalities and Inequalities in Family Life*, London: Academic Press.

Kiernan, K. (1985) 'The departure of children: the timing of leaving home over the life cycles of parents and children', *Centre for Population Studies Research Paper* 85, 3. University of London.

Klein, M. (1965) *Samples from English Cultures*, London: Routledge & Kegan Paul.

Lasch, C. (1977) *Haven in a Heartless World. The Family Besieged*, New York: Basic Books.

Leonard, D. (1980) *Sex and Generation. A Study of Courtship and Weddings*, London: Tavistock.

Lockwood, D. (1966) 'Sources of variation in working class images of society', *Sociological Review* 14: 3.

Mace, D. (1948) *Marriage Counselling*, London: Churchill.

Macrae, S. (1986) *Cross-class Families: A Study of Wives' Occupational Superiority*, Oxford: Clarendon Press.

Martin, J. and Roberts, C. (1984) *Women and Employment: A Lifetime Perspective*, London: HMSO.

McGregor, O.R. (1957) *Divorce in England*, London: Heinemann.

Morgan, D.H.J. (1985) *The Family, Politics and Social Theory*, London: Routledge & Kegan Paul.

Oakley, A. (1974) *The Sociology of Housework*, Oxford: Martin Robertson.

Pollert, A. (1981) *Girls, Wives, Factory Lives*, London: Macmillan.

Platt, J. (1976) *Social Research in Bethnal Green*, London: Tavistock.

Rapoport, R. and Rapoport, R.N. (1976) *Dual Career Families Re-examined*, Oxford: Martin Robertson.

Reid, I. (1981) *Social Class Differences in Britain*, London: Grant McIntyre, second edition.

Rex, J. (1974) 'Capitalism, elites and the ruling class'. In P. Stanworth and A. Giddens (eds) *Elites and Power in British Society*, Cambridge: Cambridge University Press.

256 *Jacqueline Burgoyne*

Rimmer, L. (1981) *Families in Focus*, London: Study Commission on the Family.

Slater, E. and Woodside, M. (1951) *Patterns of Marriage*, London: Cassell and Co.

Townsend, P. (1957) *The Family Life of Old People*, London: Routledge & Kegan Paul.

Thornes, B. and Collard, J. (1979) *Who Divorces?* London: Routledge & Kegan Paul.

Voysey, M. (1975) *A Constant Burden: The Reconstitution of Family Life*, London: Routledge & Kegan Paul.

Weeks, J. (1981) *Sex, Politics and Society. The Regulation of Sexuality since 1800*, London: Longman.

Westwood, S. (1984) *All Day Every Day: Factory and Family in the Making of Women's Lives*, London: Pluto Press.

Willis, P. (1977) *Learning to Labour*, London: Saxon House.

Wright Mills, C. (1959) *The Sociological Imagination*, Oxford: Oxford University Press.

Young, M. and Willmott, P. (1957) *Family and Kinship in East London*, London: Routledge & Kegan Paul (reprinted by Penguin 1962).

—— (1973) *The Symmetrical Family*, Harmondsworth: Penguin.

Publications by Jacqueline Burgoyne
(in chronological order)

Mann, P. and Burgoyne, J. (1969) *Books and Reading*, London: Andre Deutsch.

Burgoyne, J. and Clark, D. (1980) 'Why get married again?' *New Society* 52, 913: 12–14.

—— (1981a) 'Starting again? Problems and expectations in remarriage', *Marriage Guidance* 19(7).

—— (1981b) 'Parenting in stepfamilies', in R. Chester *et al.* (eds) *Changing Patterns of Child-bearing and Child Rearing*, London: Academic Press.

Burgoyne, J. (1982a) 'Contemporary expectations of marriage and partnership', in S. Saunders (ed.) *Change in Marriage*, Rugby: National Marriage Guidance Council.

—— (1982b) *What Are We Doing to the Children?* London: BBC Publications.

Burgoyne, J. and Clark, D. (1982a) 'From father to stepfather', in M. O'Brien and L. McKee (eds) *The Father Figure*, London: Tavistock.

—— (1982b) 'Reconstituted families', in The Family Research Committee (eds) *Families in Britain*, London: Routledge & Kegan Paul.

—— (1983) 'You are what you eat: food and family reconstitution', in A. Murcott (ed.) *The Sociology of Food and Eating*, Aldershot: Gower.

—— (1984) *Making a Go of It: A Study of Step-families in Sheffield*, London: Routledge & Kegan Paul.

Burgoyne, J. (1984) *Breaking Even: Divorce, Your Children and You*, Harmondsworth: Penguin.

—— (1985a) 'Gender, work and marriage: change, conflict and inter-connections', *CMAC Bulletin* 25: 13–20 January.

—— (1985b) 'Marriage on the dole', The *Listener* 13 June, 113.2913, 12–13.

—— (1985c) 'Unemployment and married life', *Unemployment Unit Bulletin* 7–10 November.

—— (1985d) 'Gender, work and marriage: patterns of continuity and change', in C. Guy (ed.) *Relating to Marriage*, Rugby: National Marriage Guidance Council.

—— (1985e) 'Cohabitation and contemporary family life', *End of Grant Report*, London: Economic and Social Research Council.

Burgoyne, J. and Chester, C. (eds) (1985) *Employment, Unemployment and Marriage*, Special issue of *International Journal of Social Economics*, vol. 12, no 2.

Burgoyne, J. (1986) 'Stepfamilies and contemporary family values', *Concern* 61: 3–4.

—— (1987a) 'Material happiness', *New Society* 12–14, 10 April.

—— (1987b) 'Rethinking the family life cycle: sexual divisions, work and domestic life in the post-war period', in A. Bryman, B. Bytheway, P. Allatt and T. Keil (eds) *Rethinking the Life Cycle*, London: Macmillan.

—— (1987c) 'Change, gender and the life course', in G. Cohen (ed.) *Social Change and the Life Course*, London: Tavistock.

Burgoyne, J., Ormrod, R. and Richards, M. (1987) *Divorce Matters*, Harmondsworth: Penguin.

Ashworth, P., Burgoyne, J. and Stoddart, J. (1987) *Report of the Working Party on Demand as Perceived by Those Who Have Passed Through a Course of Management Education at either Undergraduate or Postgraduate Level*, BIM/CBI Study of Management and Business Education and Training in Great Britain: Sheffield City Polytechnic.

Burgoyne, J. (1989) *El Divorcio, Los Hijos Y Usted: para una ruptura equilibrada*, Barcelona: Medici.

—— (1991) 'Does the ring make any difference? Couples and the private face of a public relationship in post-war Britain', in D. Clark (ed.) *Marriage, Domestic Life and Social Change: Writings for Jacqueline Burgoyne*, (1944–88), London: Routledge.

Name index

Abercrombie, N. *et al.* 120, 121
Abrams, P. 222–4
Albemarle Report 15
Aldous, J. 124
Allen, S. 62
Ambrose, P. *et al.* 175
Anderson, D. 56
Anderson, M. 72
Ansell, V. *et al.* 224
Anthony, S. 95
Ashton, E.T. 190
Ashworth, P. xiii
Askham, J. 49, 57, 129, 141, 250
Atwell, F.C. 48

Backett, K.C. 67, 141
Bales, R. 20
Balfour, F. 177
Ball, R.R. 40
Bannister, K. 170
Barclay Committee Report 194, 199, 208
Barrett, M. 68, 140, 214
Becker, H.S. 196
Bell, C. 62, 65, 134, 239
Bentovim, A. 205
Berger, B. 225, 227, 230
Berger, P.L. xiii; *with* B. Berger family 225, 227, 230; *with* Kellner, marriage as construction of reality 35, 49, 52, 59, 139–40, 236, 239
Bernard, J. xiii, 50, 122, 140
Bernardes, J. 119
Beveridge Report 190, 207
Birch, K. 224
Blakeslee, S. 171, 175

Blumstein, P. 42, 48, 50, 51, 226
Booth, The Hon. Mrs Justice, Report 173
Bott, E. 22, 24, 34
Boulton, M.G. 66–7
Bowlby, J. 11–12, 175
Bozett, F.W. 226
Brannen, J. 58, 60, 66, 117, 141
Brown, A. 90
Bryant, M. *et al.* 209
Bryman, A. *et al.* 73
Burgoyne, J. ix–xv; continuities in family life 57; public face of private relationship 235–54; *with* Clark: cohabitation 252–4; stepfamilies 58, 73, 120, 141, 165, 184, 238; *with* Ormrod and Richards, divorce 201, 235
Burns, S. 171
Busfield, J. 238
Butler Sloss Report 200

Callan, V.S. 121
Campbell, B. 136, 219
Cancian, F.M. 37
Cant, C. 217
Chapman, R. 65
Charles, N. 61
Cherlin, A. 105–6
Chesser, E. 40, 45–6, 117, 119, 128, 243
Chester, R. 75, 219
Christensen, H.T. 47
Clark, D.: biography of Burgoyne ix–xv; life-course perspective 73; marriage, qualitative perspective

111–12, 139–65; remarriage 219;
   with Burgoyne: cohabitation 252–4;
   stepfamilies 58, 73, 120, 141, 165,
   184, 238; *with* Haldane, marital
   intervention 117, 141, 201
Clulow, C. 112, 167–85, 250
Coates, K. 19
Cohen, A.P. 230
Cohen, G. 73
Cohen, S. 207
Collard, J.: *with* Brannen 58, 117, 141;
   with Mansfield 142–3, 144;
      expectations of marriage 121, 124;
      ideology of marriage 123; marriage
      as Relationship 57–8, 59, 128, 129,
      132; pre-marital sex 41–2, 49;
      privacy 127, 129; stability 130
   with Thornes 245
Colvin, M. 196
Cook, T. 191
Cooper, D. 68, 222
Cornwell, J. 121
Coughey, K. 40
Crowther Report 14, 15
Cunningham-Burley, S. 141
Curtis Report 195

Daniell, D. 169
D'Antonio, W.V. 124
David, M. 56, 221
Davidoff, L. 33, 122
Davis, A. 195
Dawson, G. 56
Day, P.R. 209
Day, S. 195
Deakin, N. 220
Dearnley, B. 177
De'ath, E. 182
Delphy, C. 21
Demos, J. 219
Denning Report 202
Dennis, N. *et al.* 18, 19, 21, 25
Dicks, H.V. 118, 169
Dingwall, R. *et al.* 69, 198–9, 210–11
Dobash, R.C. and Dobash, R. 68, 69, 70
Donzelot, J. 199, 207
Douglas, J.D. 48
Dryden, W. 167
Du Maurier, D. 180–1
Dunnell, K. 40

Eagleton, T. 122
Edgell, S.R. 34, 134
Edwards, S. 69
Eekelaar, J. 172
Eitzen, D.S. 226, 229
Eldridge, S.M. 90
Elliott, B.J.: demographic trends 83–4,
   85–107; sex and marriage 1960s
   and 1970s 4, 33–52
Emery, R.E. 200
Ermisch, J. 103–4
Esterson, A. 222
Evans, W. 33

Feld, S. 50
Ferguson, A. 13
Finch, J.: community care 220;
   marriage 1945–59 3–4, 7–31;
   marriage 1980s 5, 55–78
Finer Report 85
Fink, A.E. 190, 191, 204
Firth, R. 239
Fischer, J. 206
Fitzgerald, F. 229
Fitzgerald, T. 56
Fletcher, R. 67; attacks on the family
   221–2, 227; change in family life
   18, 23–4, 219; divorce 241
Forster, N. xiii, 141
Foucault, M. 125, 243
Franks, H. 181
Friday, N. 45
Friedan, B. 222
Friedman, S. 63
Frykman, J. 124
Fyvel, T. 25

Gerstel, N. 49
Gibson, C. 93
Giddens, A. 240
Gilroy, P. 229
Gittins, D. 185–9, 194
Glick, P. 105
Goffman, E. 249
Goldthorpe, J.H. *et al.* 34, 240
Goode, W.J. 132
Gordon, S.L. 37
Gorer, G.: companionate marriage
   29–30, 35; expectations about
   marriage 121; sexuality 37, 39–40,

42–3, 46
Graham, H. 70
'Grant, Mary' (problem page) 35–7, 38–9, 40–1, 43–4
Green, M. 241
Gregg, C.F. 47

Haines, J. 209
Haldane, D. 117, 141, 201
Hall, C. 33, 122
Hall, P. 192
Hanmer, J. 69
Hardy, T. 182
Hargrove, B. 128
Harris, C.C. 34, 35, 62
Harris, R. 195
Harris Report 201
Hart, N. 141
Haskey, J. 92, 93–4, 96, 238
Hass, A. 40
Hearn, J. 65
Hebdige, D. 229
Hemmings, S. 217
Henwood, M. *et al.* 77
Hill, O. 190
Hite, S. 42, 48, 50
Hoggett, B. 173
Houseknecht, S.K. 219
Howe, D. 206, 207
Hubback, E. 12
Hulton, E. 11

Ineichen, B. 142, 245
Ingleby Report 195–6
Irvine, E. 224

Jacobs, B. 205
Johnson, V.E. 52n
Jones, M.M. 39
Jordan, B. 229
Joshi, H. 102
Jowell, R. *et al.* 42, 43, 48, 218

Kellner, H. 35, 49, 52, 59, 139–40, 236, 239
Kelly, J. 171, 175
Kelly, L. 69
Kerr, M. 61
Kiernan, K.E. 90, 239
Kilbrandon Committee Report 192

Kinsey, A.C. *et al.* 13, 40, 45, 46–7, 50–1, 52n
Kinston, W. 205
Klein, J. 20
Klein, M. 240
Komtar, A. 34

Laing, R.D. 68, 222
Land, H. 60
Lasch, C. 33, 140, 207, 227, 241–2
Lash, S. 227
Laslett, B. 220
Laslett, P. 225
Lavers, G.R. 13
Lawson, A. 42, 51, 58
Leach, E. 222
Leete, R. 95
Lemert, E. 196
Leonard, D. 48, 142, 239, 248
Lewis, C. 132, 141
Lewis, L. 66
Lewis, R.A. 134
Lidz, T. 204
Lockwood, D. 240
Löfgren, O. 124
Luckmann, T. 140
Lund, M. 171
Lyons, A. 169

Macauley, M. 132
McCulloch, A. 222–4
McGregor, O.R. 241
McIntosh, M. 68, 140, 214
McKee, L. 62, 65–6
Macklin, E. 42, 47, 48, 50, 51, 225–6
Maclean, M. 61, 70, 172
Macrae, S. 245
Mace, D. 243, 245
Mann, P. x
Mansfield, P., and Collard 142–3, 144; expectations of marriage 121, 124; ideology of marriage 123; marriage as Relationship 57–8, 59, 128, 129, 132; pre-marital sex 41–2, 49; privacy 127, 129; stability 130
Margolin, G. 205
Marris, P. 168
Marshall, J. 217
Martin, J. 64, 102–3, 245
Mason, J. 73, 141

Masters, W.H. 52n
Mattinson, J. 169, 176
Mayer, J.E. 206, 207
Merton, R.K. 116
Miller, J. 191
Millham, S. *et al.* 197, 199
Mills, C. Wright ix, xiii, 235–6
Mitchell, A. 171
Monckton Report 198
Montague, A. 132
Morgan, D.H.J.: critique of Berger and
    Kellner 140, 144; definition of
    family 189, 222, 226; ideologies
    111, 114–36; marriage 1980s 5,
    55–78; marriage as Relationship
    246–7; medical model 236, 237
Morris, L.D. 62
Moss, P. 66
Mount, F. 123, 228
Muller, A. 217
Muncy, R. 222

Nathan Report 191
Nava, M. 224
Newsom, J. 14–15
Ni Bhrolchain, M. 103
Noller, D. 121
Nordstrom, B. 129
Norwood Report 14
Nungesser, L.G. 230

Oakley, A. xii, 241
O'Brien, M. 65–6, 132
O'Neill, D. 198
O'Neill, N. and O'Neill, G. 42
Ormrod, Sir Roger xiii

Packman, J. 198, 199
Paddon, M. 238
Pahl, J.M. 34, 60, 70
Pahl, R.E. 34, 59, 61, 62
Pankhurst, J.G. 219
Parker, R. 191
Parkes, C.M. 168, 175
Parkinson, L. 203
Parsons, T. 20
Parton, N. 69
Pascall, G. 207
Patterson, S. 23
Peel, J. 98

Pengelley, P. 178
Phillips, A. 228
Phillips, M. 219, 220
Phillips, R. 52
Pincus, L. 169, 170
Pizzey, E. 68
Platt, J. 239
Plummer, K. 230
Plutarch 123
Pollert, A. 242
Pomeroy, W.B. 52n
Price, S. 207
Purcell, K. 131

Rapoport, R. and Rapoport, R.N. 34,
    225, 241
Rapp, R. 220
Raymond, J. 229
Raynor, P. 209
Reid, I. 245
Reiger, K. 117
Rex, J. 246
Richards, M.P.M. xiii, 4, 33–52
Rigby, A. 223
Riley, D. 9, 10–11, 12
Rimmer, L. 75, 238
Roberts, B. *et al.* 59
Roberts, C. 64, 102–3, 245
Roberts, S. 203
Robinson, G. 216
Romanyshyn, J. 192
Rose, J. 215
Rosser, K.C. 34
Rossman, P. 229
Rowntree, B.S. 13
Rutherford, J. 65

Sainsbury, E. 206
Salholz, E. 128
Salt, R.E. 134
Sandler, B. 125
Sarah, E. 63
Saunders, S. 69
Schutz, A. 140
Schwartz, P. 42, 48, 50, 51, 226
Seebohm Report 192, 194, 198
Segal, L. 222
Silburn, R. 19
Skynner, A.C.R. 169
Slater, E. 243

Smart, C. 56
Smith, J.H. 16
Smith, L.G. and Smith, J.R. 49
Sontag, S. 218
South, S.J. 92, 103, 107n
Spinley, B. 19, 24–5
Stanley, L. 69
Stoddart, J. xiii
Stone, L. 178
Strean, H.S. 50, 51
Summerfield, P. 3–4, 7–31
Summerskill, E. 11
Sutherland, J.D. 168
Sutton, A. 202

Taylor, B. 222
Taylor, L. *et al.* 197
Thane, P. 7
Thatcher, M. 51, 221
Thomas, G. 16, 17
Thompson, A.G. 169
Thompson, L. 34
Thornes, B. 245
Thornton, A. 40, 43
Thorpe, J. 197
Timms, N. 206, 207
Titmuss, R.M. 28–9, 190–1
Tolstoy, L. 240
Townsend, P. 19, 192–3, 239
Townsend, S. 183
Trent, K. 92, 103, 107n
Tutt, N. 197

Urry, J. 227

Veroff, J. 50
Vincent, C. 173, 178
Voeller, B. 229
Voysey, M. 120, 246, 252

Walczak, Y. 171

Walker, A.J. 34
Walker, J. 112–13, 188–211
Wallerstein, J. 171, 175, 183
Watney, S. 218
Weatherhead, L. 117–18
Webb, A. 193–4
Webb, D. 195
Weeks, J. 48, 113, 214–31, 242
Westwood, S. 242
Wicks, M. 220
Wild, P. xiii, 254n
Wilkes, R. 209
Williams, R. 115
Willis, A. 209
Willis, P. 242
Willmott, P.: family and friendship 229; 'subterranean social order' 228; *with* Young 17–18, 22; companionate marriage 20–1, 22, 34; housing 239; stability of marriage 24; 'symmetrical' family 241
Wilshire, D. 217
Wilson, E. 208
Wilson, G. 60
Wilson, P. 62
Winnicott, D.W. 11–12
Wise, S. 69
Wistow, G. 193–4
Wolkowitz, C. 62
Woodside, M. 243
Woodward, K.L. 128
Wootton, Lady Barbara 207
Wynne, L. 204

Yeandle, S. 64
Young, A.F. 190
Young, M. 18, 20–2, 24, 34, 239, 241
Younghusband, E. 188

Zinn, M.B. 226, 229

Subject index

Abortion Act (1967) 99, 106–7n
abortions 99–100
abuse, of children 68, 69, 136,
    197–200, 205, 219–20
adultery 42–4, 48–51, 58, 218
age, at marriage 87–9
AIDS 230
Ashton study 19, 21, 22, 25
Australian Institute of Family Studies
    225

bereavement 175–6, 177
Bethnal Green studies 18–19, 22
Birmingham Feminist History Group
    13
birth control 12–13
birth rate 8–10, 83, 96–9
breakdown of marriage 170–8; see
    also divorce
British Family Research Committee
    225
British Sociological Association 73

care, children in 196–7
Central Council for Education and
    Training in Social Work 193
charity 190
children: abuse of 68, 69, 136,
    197–200, 205, 219–20; in care
    196–7; delinquency 24–5, 195–7;
    and divorce 171–2, 176, 200, 202,
    207–8; parenthood 65–7; at risk
    197–200; and stepfamilies 182–5
Children Act (1948) 195–6
Children Act (1989) 113, 173, 210
Children and Young Persons Act

(1969) 193, 196
choice, marriage as 128; see also
    cohabitation
Chronically Sick and Disabled Persons
    Act (1970) 193
Church of England: and contraception
    12–13; and marriage breakdown
    118, 129, 241
class 240; and child abuse 199; and
    cohabitation 245; and divorce 83,
    93–4; and marriage 22
Cleveland 136, 200, 219
cohabitation 48, 89–90, 244, 245;
    study 247–54
communes 22–4
community 229–30
companionate marriage 7–31, 34,
    47–9; anxieties about 23–8; birth
    rate 8–10; dissent 28–30;
    employment of women 15–17;
    girls' education 14–15; models of
    marriage 10–12; motherhood 9–12;
    sexuality 12–14; sociological
    writings 17–23
Conciliation Project Unit, Newcastle
    University 203–4
conciliation services 173, 202–4
contraception 12–13
courtship 128, 142

delinquency, juvenile 24–5, 195–7
demographic trends 28, 83–4, 85–107,
    219; cohabitation 89–90; divorce
    91–4, 170, 235, 238, 241;
    employment of·women 101–4;
    fertility 96–9; household types

104–6; illegitimacy 83, 99–101; marriage rates and sex ratios 85–9; remarriage 94–6

divorce 24, 26–8, 200–4; and children 171–2, 176, 200, 202, 207–8; and class 83, 93–4; demographic trends 91–4, 170, 235, 238, 241; emotional aspects 173–6; and employment of women 103–4; grounds for 93, 173; and ideology of marriage 129; lengths of marriages 91–2; litigation 172–3, 236; marriage breakdown 170–8; rates 83, 91–4; and remarriage (*q.v.*) 94–6, 179

Divorce Reform Act (1969) 91, 95, 106n, 173, 201, 235

Domestic Violence Act (1976) 208

'drifting' marriages 144–9

economics of marriage 11, 60–2; divorce 172

education, of girls 14–15

employment of women: 1945–59 15–17; 1980s 64–5; demographic trends 84, 101–4; and divorce 103–4; homeworking 62; and motherhood 12, 84, 102–3; part-time 16, 84, 102–3, 241; pre-marriage 15

equality 62–3, 65; *see also* gender relations

'establishing' marriages 153–60

ethnicity 133–4, 211; and community 229, 230

Fabian Society 10

family 119; alternatives to 221–4; changes in 70–4, 104–6, 200–4, 220; conventional values 56–8; diversity 220–1, 225–7; eighteenth-and nineteenth-century 33; 1945–59 1921; ideologies of 114–36, 217–31; interventions in 188–211; 'network' 229; nuclear 19–21, 63, 76, 104–6; and the past 123–6; pretended relationships 214–31; and social welfare 204–9; sociological studies tradition 71–4; 'symmetrical' 241; therapy 204–6; values 219–21

Family Law Reform Act (1969) 88, 107n

Family Policy Study Centre 75, 77

fatherhood 65–7

feminism 59, 63, 140, 224

fertility 83, 96–9

gender relations 62–4, 131–3, 164–5; 1945–59 7–8, 10–12, 19–21, 27–30; division of labour 15, 34–5, 64–5; and employment 64–5; equality 62–3; and parenthood 65–7; and sexuality (*q.v.*) 243–4; and social welfare 207–8

General Household Survey 89–90

General Synod Marriage Commission 118

Getting Married booklets 39, 117–18, 125, 131, 132, 135

Girl Guides 15

girls, education of 14–15

Great Ormond Street Sexual Abuse Project 205

Greater London Council (GLC) 217

Guardianship of Minors Act (1971) 199

Health Services and Public Health Act (1968) 193

homeworking 62

homosexuality 215–18, 231; and families 226

households 104–6; research on 60–1; *see also* family

housework 14–15, 65

housing 7, 9, 61, 238–9, 251

identity, maintenance of 250

ideologies of marriage 111, 114–36; 1950s 28–9; concept of ideology 115–23; 'family talk' 114–15; gender and ethnicity 131–4; from institution to relationship 126–31; and the past 123–6

ideologies of the family 217–31

illegitimacy 9, 83, 99–101

incomes 11, 60–2

Institute of Community Studies 239, 241

institution, *vs.* relationship, marriage

as 7–8, 52, 58–9, 111, 126–31, 246–7
interventions in families 188–211; changing family life 200–4; children 195–200; future 209–11; history 189–90; partnership of social welfare and families 204–9; social welfare, post-war 190–5

kinship networks 20, 22, 239; and divorce 171–2

'labelling' 196
labour, sexual division of 15, 34–5, 64–5
Law Commission, Report on divorce 172, 173
Legal Aid and Advice Act (1949) 26
life-course analysis 6, 72–3
Local Authority Social Services Act (1970) 192
Local Government Bill (1987), Clause 28 113, 215–18, 231
love 128–9

marriage 235–54; age at 87–9; breakdown of 170–8 *see also* divorce; as choice 128; and commitment 48–9; 'commuter' 226; companionate 1945–59 7–31; counselling 201–2; demographic trends 28, 85–107; early, studies of 142–4; economics 11, 60–2; and housing 238–9; ideologies of 114–36; interventions in families 188–211; length of 91–2; making 168–70; medical models 237; as 'natural' 130; pretended family relationships 214–31; and privacy 242–4; psychodynamic image of 169–70, 174–5; as public issue 235–7; qualitative perspective 139–65; rates and sex ratios 85–9; realism, 1980s 55–78; relationship *vs.* institution 7–8, 52, 58–9, 111, 126–31, 140, 246–7; remaking *see* remarriage; as security 129–30; and sexuality 33–52; as stability 130; 'successful' 57–8; varieties of experience 21–3; *see also*

cohabitation; divorce; family
Marriage Guidance Council 13, 127, 201, 245
Marxism 60
Mass Observation 12
Matrimonial and Family Proceedings Act (1984) 91
methodology, research 5–6, 33
morality, public 246
motherhood: 1945–59 9–12; 1980s 65–7; and employment 12, 84, 102–3
mourning 175–6, 177, 179–80

National Health Service (NHS) 9
National Society for the Prevention of Cruelty to Children (NSPCC) 198
'natural', marriage as 130
'New Man', the 65, 77

parenthood 65–7; and divorce 171–2
part-time employment, women 16, 84, 102–3, 241
'patriarchalism' 63
politics 125–6; Local Government Bill, Clause 28 215–17, 231; marriage and family life 55–6, 75–7, 221
Poor Laws 189
population *see* demographic trends
poverty 19, 189–90
pretended family relationships 214–31; alternative families 225–7; alternatives to the family 221–4; family values 219–21; Local Government Bill, Clause 28 215–18, 231; 'subterranean social order' 227–31
privacy and privatisation 127, 240–4, 249
probation service 202, 208–9
'pronatalism' 9–11
psychodynamic image of marriage 169–70, 174–5
public *vs.* private dichotomy 121, 127, 140, 164, 235–7

qualitative perspective on marriage 139–65; 'drifting' 144–9; 'establishing' 153–60; 'struggling'

160–4; studies 142–4; 'surfacing' 149–53

realism in marriage, 1980s 55–78; change over time 70–4; conventional family values 56–8; gender relations 62–7; research agendas 74–7; violence 67–70
relationship, *vs.* institution, marriage as 7–8, 52, 58–9, 111, 126–31, 140, 246–7
remarriage 83, 94–6, 178–85; and divorce 94–6, 179; legacies of former relationships 165, 180–1; stepfamilies 182–5
Royal Commission on Marriage and Divorce (1956) 3, 26–9
Royal Commission on the Poor Laws (1909) 189–90
Royal Commission on the Population (1949) 9–10, 12

schizophrenia 204
security 18–19, 129–30, 251–2
Sexual Offences Act (1967) 217
sexuality 128–9; 1945–59 12–14; 1960s and 1970s 33–52; extra-marital 42–4, 48–51, 218; in marriage 37–9, 242–4; norms 244; pre-marriage 39–42, 47–8, 245, 252; problem pages study 35–44; research agendas 44–7; studies of 34–5; of women 243
Six Point Group 11
social welfare: and children 195–200; client groups 194–5; generic 192–4, 209; history 190–5; partnership with families 204–9; specialists

191, 194–5; stigma 196, 206
Social Work (Scotland) Act (1968) 192, 196
sociological writing on marriage 71–4; 1945–59 17–26; 1960s and 1970s 240–1
Solicitors Family Law Association 173
stability 130, 251
statistics *see* demographic trends
stepfamilies 182–5; *see also* remarriage
'struggling' marriages 160–4
Study Commission on the Family 63, 75
'subterranean social order' 227–31
'surfacing' marriages 149–53

teaching 16
teamwork *see* companionate marriage
theology, and marriage 123–4
therapy, family 204–6

unemployment 61–2

values, family 56–8, 219–21
violence 67–70; against children 68, 69, 136, 197, 200, 205; against women 68–70, 208

weddings 48–9, 89
welfare state, and family security 18–19; *see also* social welfare
Woman's Own 35–44
Women's Publicity Planning Association 11
work *see* housework
Working Party on Marriage Guidance 59, 127